Student Study Guide to Accompany

PSYCHOLOGY

Camille B. Wortman and **Elizabeth F. Loftus**

Prepared by

Wendy Dunn
Coe College

Alfred A. Knopf New York

First Edition

987654

Copyright © 1981 by Alfred A. Knopf.

ISBN: 0-394-32730-6

Manufactured in the United States of America

Table of Contents

INTRODUCTION

One of the strongest characteristics of Wortman and Loftus's *Psychology* is its purposeful integration of research, theory, and practical examples into a textbook that is both complete and readable. *The Study Guide to Accompany Psychology* has also been carefully organized to provide the best possible combination of activities to aid the student in two goals: to understand the relationships of concepts and their implications; and to help the student study effectively and prepare adequately for classroom evaluation. *The Study Guide to Accompany Psychology* has used four features to encourage students to accomplish their goals: Concepts, Behavioral Objectives, Chapter Summaries, and Student Self-Tests. Each of these features attempts to accomplish a different purpose, and the rationale for their use is discussed below.

☐ Concepts

One of the many innovative features in *Psychology* is its chapter previews, composed of roughly half a dozen basic concepts. These concepts introduce the student to the major ideas that will be presented in a chapter in a way that students unfamiliar with the chapter can understand.

The concepts are not intended as a complete survey of the chapter content; for that purpose a summary is included at the end of each chapter. The concepts provide conceptual anchors to which subsequent information can be tied. Consequently, all other ancillary materials are written to correspond to this most basic level of organization specified by the concepts.

☐ Behavioral Objectives

Whereas the Concepts are general summaries of basic ideas, the Behavioral Objectives in the *Study Guide* are specific cues to guide students in their study of chapter content. These objectives are stated unambiguously, informing students of what they should be able to *do* to demonstrate their understanding of the chapter concepts. If a student is able to satisfy the requirements of the Behavioral Objectives, he or she will have mastered the content of a chapter.

The Behavioral Objectives are useful both in guiding appropriate study as the student is learning a chapter's content and in serving as the basis for self-evaluation to test for content mastery. Sample examination questions presented in the Self-Test section of the Study Guide are keyed to the Behavioral Objective they test. This enables students to determine which objectives have been mastered and which need additional study.

The Behavioral Objectives are organized according to the Concepts discussed above, some concepts requiring more than one Behavioral Objective. The numbering system used for the objectives includes two digits: the first corresponds to the number of the concept; the second to the number of the objective keyed to that concept. For instance, objective 2.1 is the first objective written for the second concept.

☐ Chapter Summary

Brief chapter summaries appear in the text for immediate review at the end of each chapter. The Chapter Summaries presented in the *Study Guide* are quite different in both their format and their intended purpose. Most important, they are more inclusive and provide a good refresher or review for students who have read the chapter. They are especially useful to review for a test when time limitations preclude rereading the entire chapter. They are also keyed to the chapter concepts by number to help students relate the content to the organization of the chapter. (The chapter summaries provided in the text are intended for review immediately after reading the corresponding material and are therefore briefer and do not elaborate the logical connections between concepts.)

□ **Self-Test**

For several reasons, students may find the Self-Test to be the most useful section of the Study Guide. Students come from a variety of educational backgrounds, and some may be unfamiliar with testing methods used in college courses. Furthermore, many students suffer from test anxiety to an extent that adversely affects their grades. The questions in the *Study Guide* give students the opportunity to practice taking psychology tests, which should reduce their anxiety and prepare them for actual testing. This alone warrants the inclusion of sample exam questions in the *Study Guide*.

Undoubtedly, however, for most students, the major advantage of the Self-Test is the feedback it provides about the effectiveness of their study. Test questions are referenced to their respective objectives, and the answers, in an answer key at the end of the manual, are referenced to text pages. This helps the student to quickly identify and review the areas that require further study. It seems only reasonable to give each student the opportunity to discover what he or she needs to study further before that student is confronted with a classroom exam.

An important point must be made, however, about the correspondence between the questions in the *Study Guide* and those in the instructor's *Test Manual* provided with *Psychology*. There are no identical questions in these two volumes; the *Study Guide* does not give the student access to questions that will be included on the test if the test is drawn from the *Test Manual*. This element is essential if the integrity of the *Test Manual* is to be maintained.

Individual instructors may choose to use this Self-Test portion of the *Study Guide* in still other ways—perhaps as homework assignments or classroom discussion questions.

Because different instructors and students may prefer to test in different ways, the Self-Test has been subdivided into four sections, each including items of different format and purpose.

Matching Questions: Each Self-Test includes matching questions, designed primarily to test the students' grasp and comprehension of definitional information in the chapter. These items are not referenced to objectives, since they each tap a wide content area.

Multiple Choice Questions Testing Factual Knowledge: Because some students need practice answering multiple choice questions and because much of the content presented in *Psychology* is factual in nature, twenty multiple choice questions have been prepared for each chapter to test the students' ability to respond to factually oriented questions. These questions concentrate primarily on the knowledge and comprehension learning domains. They are keyed to Behavioral Objectives to provide evaluative feedback.

Multiple Choice Questions Testing Conceptual Knowledge: The study of psychology involves more than simply memorizing facts and learning about experiments presented in a text. Students must also learn to apply this factual knowledge to other situations and must understand the relationships among the elements presented in each chapter. Twelve multiple choice questions have been prepared for each chapter to sample the student's ability to apply factual knowledge in a variety of situations. Some questions also measure the student's ability to analyze, synthesize, and evaluate information, although those skills are more consistently tested with subjective Short Essay Questions. Again, each multiple choice question is objective-referenced for student feedback.

Short Essay Questions: The domain of possible short essay questions is nearly inexhaustible, and instructors will probably choose to write their own. A sample of five or six such questions for each chapter are included in the *Study Guide* to give the student practice in organizing and concisely presenting information. These questions are written to test the learning domains of application, analysis, synthesis, and evaluation; they are referenced to objectives for self-evaluation. Instructors may also assign these questions as homework or use them in class as discussion starters.

As you can see, the *Study Guide to Accompany Psychology* has been written and organized to present students with an opportunity to increase their understanding of text content and to give them formative feedback about their mastery of material. In all, it should prove a valuable tool for both students and instructors. Conscientiously used, it can help the student to acquire a strong, comprehensive understanding of psychology.

The Dimensions of Psychology

■ 1

1

5.2 Discuss the various types of academic preparation necessary for the different career opportunities in psychology.

5.3 Describe the benefits to the typical student of studying psychology.

□ **Chapter Summary**

I.   1. Psychology is a science, which means it relies on empirical data that is systematically observed, measured, and recorded.

2. Psychology as an academic discipline emerged from physiology and philosophy about one hundred years ago. It has grown rapidly—currently there are about 80,000 professional psychologists in the United States. Today psychology studies many aspects of human behavior. Psychological findings often contradict intuitive judgment.

II. 1. Psychologists believe that there are patterns underlying behavior and that by determining these patterns through experimentation, we can better explain and predict human behavior. Such experiments are difficult to devise. Basic research is conducted to gather knowledge for its own sake, but it often leads to applied research which attempts to use knowledge to improve the quality of human life. Both kinds of research are useful in building a sound base from which to generalize.

III. 1. Several branches of psychology have emerged over the last hundred years. Experimental psychologists (as well as most other psychologists) rely on experimentation. They focus on areas of behavior that are shared by man and other animals and that eventually are determined by the operation of the brain, such as sensations, perception, learning, memory, problem solving, communication, emotions, and motivation. Physiological psychologists study the underlying physical bases of behavior, primarily the nervous system and the endocrine glands. Psychopharmacologists study the effects of drugs.

2. Personality psychologists study individual differences in behavior. Social psychologists emphasize the role of environmental factors, especially the presence and actions of others, on our behavior.

3. Industrial and organizational psychologists focus on the relationship between individuals and their work. Subfields include personnel psychology, in which the psychologists match a person's qualifications to a job, and engineering psychology, which studies how humans interact with machines. The job-enrichment programs instituted by many industries to improve dull or routine jobs are an outgrowth of industrial psychology.

4. Developmental psychologists study how people change as they grow from conception to death. Educational psychologists are concerned with all aspects of the learning process, and school psychologists work in the applied area of solving specific or individual problems in the school situation.

5. Clinical psychologists specialize in the diagnosis and treatment of behavior disorders and have earned a Ph.D. Psychiatrists, on the other hand, first earn an M.D. and serve a residency in psychiatry. They work with psychologists and can prescribe drugs for treatment. Some psychiatrists pursue additional study to become psychoanalysts and practice therapy similar to that begun by Freud. Counseling psychologists typically help people who are experiencing milder or more common problems in social or emotional adjustment.

6. Several fields in psychology are just beginning to emerge. Environmental psychologists study the relationship between humans and all aspects of their environment. Forensic psychologists apply psychological principles to the problems of law enforcement and the courts. Psychologists are also more frequently in the health care field to help people remain physically healthy. Program evaluation is a field in which psychologists determine the effectiveness of government programs.

IV.   1. Wilhelm Wundt (1832–1920) established the first psychological laboratory in the late 1800s. He used the method of introspection (or controlled self-observation) to reveal the nature of human consciousness by attempting to analyze its constituent elements and the way they combined. His theories were too subjective, however, to be proven either right or wrong.

2. The behaviorists argued that psychology should study only observable, measurable events and studied how stimuli produced responses. Ivan Pavlov (1849–1936) documented the concept of the conditioned response, the learning of an association between a previously neutral stimulus and a reflex. John B. Watson (1878–1958) first delineated the behaviorist position and declared an organism's responses could be controlled by subsequent reward or punishment. B. F. Skinner (1904–) has refined and popularized this view and expanded it to apply to the function of society as a whole.

3. Sir Francis Galton (1822–1911), influenced by Charles Darwin's theory of evolution, advocated studying animal behavior in order to better understand human behavior. He also emphasized the genetic basis of human variability (or individual differences) as a result of his study of genius. In so doing, he pointed out the heredity–environment controversy we still examine today. Many of the statistical techniques we use today can be traced to Galton.

4. Sigmund Freud (1856–1939) emphasized the role of unconscious (or unobservable) conflicts in the demonstration of behavior. By using his approach of psychoanalysis in the study of neurotic patients and by using the techniques of free association (unguided talking), dream analysis, and hypnosis, he attempted to extract symbolic clues to the nature of the patient's unconscious conflict and to help the patient consciously recognize the psychological roots of his problem. Freud saw the mind as the constant interaction of the pleasure-seeking id, the realistic ego, and the idealistic superego; he believed that most neurosis stems from the conflict of sexual impulses and society's moral standards.

5. Present-day psychologists have built their current theories on past contributions from these influential psychologists.

V.   1. Although most Ph.D. graduates in psychology traditionally assumed college or university teaching or research positions, the increasing numbers of Ph.D. graduates and the declining undergraduate enrollments, coupled with increased job opportunity in private industry, are encouraging more Ph.D. graduates to seek employment outside academia. An applied degree, the Doctor of Psychology or Psy.D., which emphasizes practical experience rather than research methodology, is being offered in some schools to prepare graduates for nonacademic jobs.

2. Graduates with a master's or bachelor's degree in psychology can also find jobs in psychological fields. Furthermore, coursework in psychology can contribute to job success in related fields.

3. Even if a vocation in psychology is not planned, students in psychology can expect to learn more about themselves and other people by studying psychological

findings and principles. Furthermore, studying psychology will give the students a method for evaluating contemporary and widely publicized findings and conclusions of research and will make them more sophisticated consumers of information affecting their lives.

☐ **Self-Test**

A. Matching Questions

_____ 1. Father of psychological testing

_____ 2. Popularized the tenets of behaviorism

_____ 3. Believed that unconscious motives have a powerful effect on behavior

_____ 4. Defined psychology as the study of conscious experience

_____ 5. Studied stimulus–response associations, including the conditioned response

a. B. F. Skinner

b. Sigmund Freud

c. Ivan Pavlov

d. Sir Francis Galton

e. Wilhelm Wundt

f. John B. Watson

g. Charles Darwin

———————————————

_____ 6. Applies psychological principles to law enforcement and the courts

_____ 7. Involves treatment of people with mild and fairly common problems

_____ 8. Studies primarily the endocrine and nervous systems

_____ 9. Tries to improve the relationship between people and their jobs

_____10. Is interested in all aspects of the learning and educational process

a. Clinical psychology

b. Developmental psychology

c. Industrial psychology

d. Social psychology

e. Counseling psychology

f. Forensic psychology

g. Program evaluation

h. Environmental psychology

i. School psychology

j. Educational psychology

k. Physiological psychology

B. Multiple-Choice Questions Testing Factual Knowledge

1. According to your text, psychology is a(n):
   a. science
   b. academic discipline
   c. means of promoting human welfare
   d. all of the above   Objective 1.1

2. The major characteristic of a science is its reliance on:
   a. theory
   b. hypotheses
   c. objective rather than subjective methods
   d. empirical data   Objective 1.1

3. About how many professional psychologists are there in the United States?
   a. 10,000
   b. 50,000

    c. 80,000

    d. 125,000 Objective 1.1

4. According to research cited in the text, normally affectionate female monkeys can be made to throw their babies violently against the wall of their cage by:

    a. stimulating a region of their brain with a mild electric current

    b. giving them drugs

    c. using conditioning to change their behavior

    d. depriving them of social contact with other monkeys Objective 2.1

5. In 1939, LaPierre traveled across the United States with two Chinese friends. He later wrote to the establishments they visited to determine the strength of anti-Oriental prejudice. The major finding of his study was:

    a. in 1934 there was a great deal of anti-Oriental prejudice

    b. in 1934 there was almost no anti-Oriental prejudice; it developed after World War II

    c. people admitted they were prejudiced but did not show it in their behavior

    d. people behaved in a prejudiced way but would not admit to being prejudiced Objective 2.1

6. "A quest for knowledge purely for its own sake" is a definition of:

    a. science

    b. basic science

    c. applied science

    d. research Objective 2.2

7. For the behaviorists, the primary determinant of whether a particular phenomenon was fit for study by psychologists was if it:

    a. was uniquely human

    b. had applicability

    c. could be predicted on the basis of common sense

    d. was measurable Objective 3.1

8. Experimental psychologists generally believe their questions will ultimately be answered through a better understanding of:

    a. human behavior

    b. the methods of science

    c. the principles of conditioning

    d. the brain Objective 3.1

9. Psychologists involved in the field of health and health care are probably particularly interested in:

    a. what causes accidents

    b. the effect of stress on disease

    c. adjustment to a terminal illness

    d. all of the above Objective 3.1

10. Wundt concluded that conscious experience consisted of all of the following *except*:

    a. behaviors

    b. images

    c. feelings

    d. sensations Objective 4.1

11. The inclusion of the study of animals as well as humans in the discipline of psychology is primarily the result of the work of:

    a. Sigmund Freud

    b. Charles Darwin

    c. Josef Breuer

    d. Wilhelm Wundt Objective 4.1

12. Charles Darwin proposed in the theory of evolution that:

    a. all living organisms descended from simpler forms of life

b. human thought can be analyzed by observing animal behavior
c. intelligence is a genetically determined trait
d. all of the above   Objective 4.1

13. Sir Francis Galton emphasized the importance of heredity in his intensive study of:
a. eye color
b. genius
c. learning
d. development   Objective 4.1

14. Freud asked patients to talk about their dreams in order to:
a. give him symbolic clues to the nature of their unconscious conflicts
b. put them to sleep
c. relax them so they would talk about what was really bothering them
d. be able to observe their natural behavior   Objective 4.2

15. The goal of psychoanalysis is:
a. to make you forget the things that are troubling you
b. to make you conform to society's expectations
c. to produce a list of things you need to do to make your life happier
d. to help you consciously recognize the roots of your problems   Objective 4.2

16. Freud believed the human mind was composed of all of the following *except*:
a. ego
b. superego
c. psyche
d. id   Objective 4.2

17. Psychologists who use intelligence and personality tests in their work trace the origins of these tests back to:
a. Wilhelm Wundt
b. Sir Francis Galton
c. Sigmund Freud
d. B. F. Skinner   Objective 4.3

18. Which of the following people would be most likely to work in a hospital?
a. an experimental psychologist
b. a social psychologist
c. a clinical psychologist
d. a developmental psychologist   Objective 5.1

19. Which of the following would necessarily have undergone psychoanalysis?
a. a psychiatrist
b. a psychoanalyst
c. a mass murderer
d. none of the above   Objective 5.2

20. The major difference between a Ph.D. in psychology and a Psy.D. is:
a. more training is required for a Ph.D.
b. a Ph.D. emphasizes basic research; a Psy.D. emphasizes applied skills
c. a Ph.D. prepares you for academic work; a Psy.D. prepares you for a job as a psychiatrist
d. nonexistent; the two degrees are awarded for the same training   Objective 5.2

C.   Multiple-Choice Questions Testing Conceptual Knowledge

21. You meet a woman who tells you she is a psychologist. From this information, you infer that, professionally, she is probably most interested in:
a. what you do and the way you think
b. your personality

    c. your emotional stability

    d. animal (not human) behavior   Objective 1.1

22.   The *methods* of study used in psychology are most closely related to those used in:

    a. sociology

    b. religion

    c. physics

    d. philosophy   Objective 2.1

23.   The clearest example of applied research would be a study examining the relationship between:

    a. cigarette smoking and cancer

    b. colors of light and feelings of stress

    c. order of words on a list and the ability to remember the list

    d. age and problem-solving ability   Objective 2.2

24.   Which of the following research problems would probably *not* be explored by an experimental psychologist?

    a. What is the effect of electric shock on motivation?

    b. Does the display of emotion become less frequent when it is punished?

    c. Does Valium (a tranquilizer) help control hyperactivity in children?

    d. Do young infants prefer sweet foods over salty ones?   Objective 3.1

25.   Jake has received special training that allows him to ignore his own thoughts and instead attend to the actual process of how the elements of his mind fit together. He is using a technique similar to:

    a. mind control

    b. introspection

    c. psychoanalysis

    d. free association   Objective 4.2

26.   Behaviorists view learning as the development of:

    a. memory traces in the brain

    b. consciousness

    c. an association between events

    d. reflexes   Objective 4.2

27.   The issue of heredity versus environment as the major determinant of behavior would be most clearly represented by comparing the views of:

    a. Sigmund Freud and B. F. Skinner

    b. Wilhelm Wundt and Ivan Pavlov

    c. John B. Watson and B. F. Skinner

    d. Sir Francis Galton and John B. Watson   Objective 4.2

28.   Which of the following terms does not fit with the other three?

    a. stimulus

    b. response

    c. reinforcement

    d. free association   Objective 4.2

29.   The task of determining whether the off/on switch on a television should be designed to turn or to pull would probably be given to which type of psychologist?

    a. social psychologist

    b. developmental psychologist

    c. engineering psychologist

    d. experimental psychologist   Objective 5.1

30.   You are gravely concerned that you are losing your mind. You would probably go to see which kind of psychologist?

    a. an applied organizational psychologist

    b. a social psychologist

    c. a personality psychologist

    d. a clinical psychologist   Objective 5.1

31. An environmental psychologist's job would probably be most similar to that of a(n):

    a. developmental psychologist

    b. industrial psychologist

    c. school psychologist

    d. clinical psychologist   Objective 5.1

32. A person who has a Ph.D. and works with fairly common social problems such as drug addiction, marriage and divorce therapy, and family life therapy would typically be trained as a:

    a. psychoanalyst

    b. counseling psychologist

    c. psychiatrist

    d. clinical psychologist   Objective 5.2

D. *Short Essay Questions*

1. What does it mean to say that psychology is a science, an academic discipline, and a means of promoting human welfare? (Objective 1.1)

2. What is the distinction between applied science and basic science? Give an experimental example of each to demonstrate your understanding. (Objective 2.2)

3. What were the major differences between the purpose and methods used in Wilhelm Wundt's experimentation and those used by the behaviorists? (Objective 4.2)

4. Briefly describe Freud's contributions to present-day psychology. (Objective 4.2)

5. Describe each of the following subfields of psychology with regard to the type of problems studied and the focus of their research (basic, applied, or both). (Objective 3.1)

    a. Experimental psychology

    b. Personality psychology

    c. Industrial psychology

    d. Developmental psychology

    e. School psychology

    f. Clinical psychology

    g. Counseling psychology

    h. Psychiatrists psychology

    i. Forensic psychology

    j. Program evaluation psychology

6. What are the benefits to be derived from studying psychology? (Objective 5.3)

■2
The
Methods of
Psychology

□ **Preview of the Chapter**
Major Concepts and Behavioral Objectives

CONCEPT 1   Psychological research attempts to describe behavior, explain its causes, and predict the circumstances under which it might recur.

    1.1   Discuss the purpose of psychological research.

    1.2   Discriminate between adequate and inadequate methods of sampling.

CONCEPT 2   Examining the methods that psychologists use affords us a better and more critical understanding of the conclusions that can be drawn from their research.

    2.1   Describe and list the advantages and disadvantages of the research methods discussed in the text (experiment, correlation, survey, naturalistic observation, case study).

    2.2   Distinguish between a longitudinal study and a cross-sectional study and assess the strengths and weaknesses of each.

CONCEPT 3   Many research methods are available, but whatever the method used, the success of any research depends on careful and accurate measurement of the variables under study.

    3.1   Describe various techniques used in measuring variables and suggest when each is most appropriate.

    3.2   Describe how an experiment is conducted and distinguish between experimental and control groups and independent and dependent variables.

CONCEPT 4   After data is collected, descriptive statistics are used to communicate the results in abbreviated form; inferential statistics are used to ensure that the results are not simply due to chance.

    4.1   Compare and contrast the use of descriptive statistics and inferential statistics.

    4.2   Calculate each of the three measures of central tendency and determine when each is appropriately used.

    4.3   Describe two measures of variability and explain how each is used.

    4.4.   Define and discuss correlation coefficients.

    4.5   Describe how probability influences statistical significance and define what is meant by a significant result.

CONCEPT 5 Before they are fully accepted in the field, the findings of a scientific study must be replicated by other researchers.

     5.1 Define replication and explain why it is done.

CONCEPT 6 Psychologists must continually be aware of possible sources of error in their research. They must also consider the ethical implications of their work and conform to rules of conduct established by the American Psychological Association.

     6.1 Discuss each of the methodological and measurement problems presented in the text and indicate what steps can be taken to ensure that they do not occur.

     6.2 Restate the ethical guidelines of the American Psychological Association for conducting human research.

□ **Chapter Summary**

I.   1. Scientific research is intended to accomplish one or more of three basic goals: to describe behavior, to explain its causes, and to predict when it might occur again.

    2. Many research methods can be used, and most involve sampling, the technique of selecting a few individuals to represent the entire group. A sample must adequately and fairly represent its population, and this can be accomplished in two ways. In random sampling each member of a population has an equal chance of being selected in the sample. In representative sampling a chosen sample exactly matches the population on some characteristic(s) such as sex or age.

II.   1. The method called the experiment has the advantages of maintaining control over extraneous conditions and enabling inferences to be made about a cause-and-effect relationship between variables. Its major disadvantage is that so much control leads to an unnatural situation.

      The first step in conducting an experiment is to formulate a hypothesis, or a belief to be tested. The next step is to specify the variables. The independent variable is the condition directly manipulated by the experimenter. It affects the dependent variable, which is the variable the experimenter measures. Subjects are randomly divided into an experimental group, which experiences the experimental treatment, and a control group, which does not. The control group is needed so that comparisons can be made. If a change in the independent variable can be shown to produce a change in the dependent variable, a cause-and-effect relationship has been demonstrated.

    2. If, for practical or ethical reasons, an experimenter cannot conduct an experiment to test cause-and-effect, he or she may choose to study the degree of relationship between two variables by using correlational research. A positive correlation means that as one variable increases, so does the other. A negative correlation means that as one variable increases, the other decreases. Correlations can be represented numerically by a correlation coefficient.

    3. A survey is an attempt to estimate opinions, characteristics, or behaviors of a population by polling a representative or random sample. Surveys can be conducted through interviews, questionnaires, or public records. Problems with surveys often include use of inadequate sampling techniques or bias in questions and/or responses.

    4. Naturalistic observation involves watching and recording behavior as it naturally occurs. The major problem with this research method is that people behave

differently when they believe they're being observed. To avoid this difficulty a psychologist may instead use participant observation, in which he joins the group he wants to study.

5. A case study involves an intensive investigation of one person, rather than a representative sample.

III. 1. All of the above methods involve the measurement of variables, which can be done in different ways. Psychological tests measure all kinds of human attributes. Physiological measures detect changes in the body's functioning, and particular changes are known to be associated with particular psychological states. Rating scales are subjective estimates of a particular variable.

2. Another measurement decision involves change across time. A longitudinal study is a study in which one group of people is measured again and again over a number of years. Its major advantage is consistency in behavior. A cross-sectional study also measures change across time, but does so by comparing measures taken at the same time of subgroups of people of various ages. Although it is quicker and less expensive, it fails to consider time-related differences between groups. Often longitudinal and cross-sectional studies are used in combination.

IV. 1. Statistics are mathematical methods for assessing and presenting data in summary form. Psychologists use two general types of statistics: descriptive statistics and inferential statistics.

2. Descriptive statistics are a form of shorthand for representing a large amount of data. A histogram is a graph that depicts a frequency distribution. A frequency distribution shows the number of responses that occur in each category of events. Central tendency is an indication of the center, or middle, of a group of responses or scores. Three measures of central tendency are commonly used: the arithmetic mean (or average of the scores), the median (or middle score), and the mode (or most frequent score).

3. When a frequency distribution is symmetrical, the mean, median, and mode are identical. Such a symmetrical distribution is called a normal distribution, or normal curve. If a distribution is not normal but unbalanced, the median becomes the least biased indicator of central tendency.

4. In addition to knowing about the central tendency, psychologists also need to know the dispersion, or variability, of the scores. The range is one measure of variability, and it is simply the difference between the highest and lowest score. The standard deviation is generally the more preferred measure because it indicates the average extent to which all scores in a particular distribution vary from the mean.

5. Correlation coefficients express the degree of relationship between two variables. They range from -1 (a perfect negative correlation) to $+1$ (a perfect positive correlation). A 0 correlation indicates no relationship between the variables; thus, the closer a correlation coefficient aproaches either -1 or $+1$, the stronger the relationship between the two variables.

6. Inferential statistics are used to provide the rules for determining what conclusions can legitimately be drawn from data. They use probability estimates to determine the likelihood that a given set of scores would occur by chance factors alone. Since chance can never be entirely eliminated, psychologists use tests of statistical significance for this determination. Generally, results are deemed significant if the probability of the results occurring by chance is .05 (5 times in 100) or less.

V. 1. Measurement of variables can solve several problems. Sometimes the independent variable may remain the same for both the experimental and control groups, but the researcher is unable to detect this, causing the results to be misleading. Sometimes the dependent variable measure is not sensitive enough to pick up real differences between groups. Sometimes psychologists want to study phenomena that defy objective measurement, in which case they invent indirect methods of study. Because of these problems, studies are often duplicated or repeated by another researcher to make sure the results are consistent.

VI. 1. Many problems can occur that invalidate a study. Self-fulfilling prophecy refers to the notion that the expectations of investigators can influence their findings. One method used to alleviate this problem is a double-blind technique, in which neither experimenter nor subjects knows who is in the experimental or control groups. In a variation, the single-blind technique, the experimenter knows who is in which group, but the subjects do not.

2. Demand characteristics also operate, causing subjects to respond in ways they think will "please" the experimenter. These characteristics can be reduced by avoiding face-to-face encounters with the subjects and by interviewing the subjects after the experiment to detect any such demand response patterns.

3. In 1973 the American Psychological Association issued ten principles to guide researchers in the ethical conduct of experiments using human subjects. These principles state that harm to a subject should be avoided. If some possibility of harm exists, a subject should be informed prior to the experiment. Subjects should be allowed to withdraw anytime during an experiment, and if deception is used, the experimenter must later explain to subjects why this concealment was necessary.

☐ **Self-Test**

A. Matching Questions

_____ 1. Provides inferences about cause and effect.

_____ 2. Studies several groups of people of different ages at one time.

_____ 3. Uncovers the relationship between two variables.

_____ 4. The experimenter becomes a member of the group he is studying.

_____ 5. Study of one individual rather than a group.

a. Longitudinal study
b. Correlational research
c. Case study
d. Experiment
e. Cross-sectional study
f. Naturalistic observation
g. Survey
h. Participant observation

_____ 6. A graph of summary data.

_____ 7. The largest score minus the smallest score.

_____ 8. The degree of relationship between two variables.

_____ 9. The middle score of a distribution.

_____ 10. Accounts for chance results.

_____ 11. Identical mean, median, and mode.

_____ 12. The average score.

a. Mean
b. Mode
c. Median
d. Range
e. Standard deviations
f. Histogram
g. Statistical significance
h. Correlation coefficient
i. Statistical significance
j. Normal distribution

_____13. When subjects act as the investigator expects them to.

_____14. Used in control groups although it has no physiological effect.

_____15. The factor in an experiment that the researcher manipulates.

_____16. Repetition of an experiment.

_____17. Subjects who are not exposed to the experimental treatment.

_____18. Expectations of investigator influences his findings.

a. Independent variable
b. Demand characteristics
c. Replication
d. Self-fulfilling prophecy
e. Experimental group
f. Dependent variable
g. Control group
h. Placebo

B. Multiple-Choice Questions Testing Factual Knowledge

1. A sample is generally used when the group being studied is:
   a. all located in the same geographic area
   b. very large
   c. widely variant in the opinions they express
   d. predominantly male or female   Objective 1.2

2. The method that will allow cause-and-effect inferences to be made is the:
   a. correlational study
   b. survey
   c. experiment
   d. all of the above   Objective 2.1

3. The type of research that determines the strength of relationship between two variables is the:
   a. experiment
   b. correlational study
   c. survey
   d. all of the above   Objective 2.1

4. An attempt to estimate the opinions, characteristics, or behaviors of a particular population by investigating a representative sample is:
   a. a correlational study
   b. a correlational coefficient
   c. a case study
   d. a survey   Objective 2.1

5. Research conducted by watching other people's behavior as they go about their normal routine is called:
   a. naturalistic observation
   b. participant observation
   c. survey
   d. case study   Objective 2.1

6. An experimenter does an in-depth study of a particular individual. This is called a(n):
   a. experiment
   b. survey
   c. case study
   d. none of the above   Objective 2.1

7. Which of the following methods is the best?
   a. survey
   b. correlation
   c. experiment
   d. none of the above   Objective 2.1

8. A study that divides a group into subgroups according to certain criteria and then makes comparisons between the subgroups is a(n):
   a. experiment
   b. random sample
   c. longitudinal study
   d. cross-sectional study   Objective 2.1

9. Heart rate, respiration rate, and GSR are all used as:
   a. physiological measures
   b. psychological tests
   c. rating scales
   d. all of the above, at one time or another   Objective 3.1

10. The first step in conducting an experiment is to formulate the:
    a. hypothesis
    b. independent variable
    c. dependent variable
    d. control condition   Objective 3.2

11. The variable that the experimenter intentionally manipulates in a experiment is called the:
    a. placebo
    b. dependent variable
    c. experimental condition
    d. independent variable   Objective 3.2

12. Which of the following is used to determine whether a given set of conclusions can be arrived at from a particular set of data?
    a. descriptive statistics
    b. standard deviations
    c. inferential statistics
    d. correlations coefficient   Objective 4.1

13. In an unbalanced distribution, which measure of central tendency is least biased?
    a. mean
    b. median
    c. mode
    d. all are equally biased   Objective 4.2

14. The average extent to which all scores in a particular set vary from the mean is the:
    a. standard deviation
    b. central tendency
    c. probability statistic
    d. statistical significance   Objective 4.3

15. Suppose you are tossing a fair coin and it comes up heads on the first five tosses. The probability of it coming up heads again on the sixth toss is:
    a. 1:2
    b. 1:6
    c. 1:32
    d. 1:180   Objective 4.4

16. In order to replicate an experiment, you would:
    a. reanalyze the data using inferential rather than descriptive statistics
    b. substitute a new independent variable
    c. substitute a new dependent variable
    d. redo the experiment much as it was originally performed   Objective 5.1

17. When neither the experimenter nor the subjects knows who is assigned to the experimental and control groups, this is called:
    a. a placebo effect
    b. a single-blind technique

    c. a double-blind technique
    d. a self-fulfilling prophecy   Objective 6.1

18. Most experimental subjects try to help the researcher by doing their best to perform as they think they should, probably behaving differently than they normally would. This problem is called:
    a. the self-fulfilling prophecy
    b. demand characteristics
    c. the placebo effect
    d. measurement bias   Objective 6.1

19. Which of the following is *not* a way to reduce or control demand characteristics?
    a. videotape all instructions to subjects
    b. interview subjects about their participation after the experiment
    c. be particularly friendly to the subject
    d. use deception as to the real intent of the experiment   Objective 6.1

20. According to the American Psychological Association, a researcher cannot:
    a. subject a human to physical pain
    b. subject a human to psychological pain
    c. refuse to let a human subject quit in the middle of an experiment
    d. all of the above   Objective 6.2

C. *Multiple-Choice Questions Testing Conceptual Knowledge*

21. Suppose the population you are studying is 51 percent women and 49 percent men. Which of the following methods is used to get a sample which is also 51 percent women and 49 percent men?
    a. public opinion poll
    b. survey
    c. random sample
    d. representative sample   Objective 1.2

22. You decide the best way to study the Ku Klux Klan is to become a member yourself and observe what really happens from the inside. You are using a technique called:
    a. participant observation
    b. naturalistic observation
    c. representative sampling
    d. the self-fulfilling prophecy   Objective 2.1

23. A group of four-year-olds are given an IQ test, then are retested at ages eight, twelve, sixteen, twenty, thirty, and fifty. This is an example of:
    a. an experiment
    b. a longitudinal study
    c. a cross-sectional study
    d. a replication   Objective 2.2

24. Suppose you go into a laboratory and are asked to taste several different foods and indicate which you like most and least. You are being asked to perform:
    a. a psychological test
    b. a physiological measure
    c. a rating scale
    d. a self-fulfilling prophecy   Objective 3.1

25. Suppose you wish to study the effect of eating breakfast on test performance. You find a group of subjects who never eat breakfast and ask half of them to eat breakfast every morning for a week. This would be an example of establishing a(n):
    a. control group
    b. placebo
    c. dependent variable
    d. experimental group   Objective 3.2

26. Suppose you wish to study the effects of room temperature on job productivity on an assembly line. The independent variable in this study would be:
    a. the temperature in the room
    b. the number of people present
    c. the number of goods assembled
    d. how hot or cold people said they felt   Objective 3.3
27. Given the following set of scores—3, 4, 4, 4, 5, 7, 7, 8, 9—4 is the:
    a. mean
    b. median
    c. mode
    d. range   Objective 4.2
28. Given the following set of scores—3, 4, 5, 5, 6, 6, 6, 8, 10—what is the range?
    a. 5
    b. 5.9
    c. 6
    d. 7   Objective 4.3
29. Which of the following correlation coefficients expresses the strongest relationship between two variables?
    a. −.62
    b. +.46
    c. +4.23
    d. .03   Objective 4.4
30. Suppose I discover that as I eat more vegetables, my body weight decreases. I have demonstrated:
    a. a positive correlation
    b. a negative correlation
    c. a cause-and-effect relationship
    d. random sampling   Objective 4.4
31. Jack's parents have always expected him to be a lawyer, and now that he is 21, he is applying to law school. This may be an example of:
    a. demand characteristics
    b. the self-fulfilling prophecy
    c. experimenter bias
    d. a double-blind situation   Objective 6.1
32. Two researchers study the same problem. One finds a significant difference between the experimental and control groups; the other does not. A possible cause of this discrepancy is that:
    a. the placebo effect occurred in both experiments
    b. the second researcher's measures were not sensitive enough
    c. the variables probably defy measurement
    d. the self-fulfilling prophecy could not have been operating   Objective 6.1

D. Short Essay Questions

1. What is the purpose of science?   (Objective 1.1)

2. Why is sampling done? How is sampling done?   (Objective 1.2)

3. Suppose you wish to study the relationship between age and muscular strength. What research method would you use and how would you conduct this research?   (Objective 2.1)

4. Suppose you wanted to study the effect of jogging on memory. What research method would you use and how would you proceed with this research?   (Objective 3.2)

5. Why are there three measures of central tendency? What is each used for?   (Objective 4.2)

6. What does it mean to say that a particular research finding is statistically significant? (Objective 4.5)

7. What is a replication experiment? Why are research studies replicated? (Objective 5.1)

Biological Foundations of Behavior ■ 3

6.1 Compare the principles of mass action and multiple control and discuss their implications for future study of the brain.

☐ **Chapter Summary**

I.   1. By the early nineteenth century the idea that behavior was influenced by the brain was gaining popularity. Gall's theory of phrenology suggested that personality could be determined by studying the shape of the brain. Nowadays, physiological psychologists specialize in studying the brain.

2. The nervous system is composed of billions of interconnected nerve cells called neurons. Some neurons are highly specialized, such as the receptor cells that receive stimulation from the environment and the effector cells that contract muscles and cause glandular secretions.

3. The nervous system can be divided into the central nervous system (CNS), composed of the brain and spinal cord, and the peripheral nervous system (PNS), which extends to all parts of the body. The PNS is divided into the somatic division, which controls the skeletal muscles, and the autonomic division, which regulates the organism's internal environment. The autonomic division has two subdivisions: the sympathetic, which mobilizes the body's resources, and parasympathetic, which relaxes and conserves the body's energy. These two divisions work according to the principle of dual control, in which they have opposing effects on body functions.

II. 1. Most neurons have a cell body, or soma, which contains the nucleus, and two types of processes: the numerous and short dendrites and the long axon.

2. Neurons are categorized according to the structures between which they conduct messages. Sensory, or afferent, neurons carry information from the sense organs to the brain. Motor, or efferent, neurons carry signals from the CNS to the muscles and glands. Interneurons connect neurons. The simplest neuron connection, called a reflex arc, involves only two kinds of neurons: a sensory neuron coming into the spinal cord and a motor neuron going out.

III. 1. Neural impulses are conducted by an electrochemical process as follows: The nerve cell membrane selectively keeps sodium ions outside the cell and potassium and chloride ions inside during the normal resting state, when it is said to be polarized. If the cell is excited with enough stimulus energy, the cell membrane temporarily allows the ions to exchange places, causing an action potential to be conducted from the cell body down the length of the axon. The cell quickly reverts back to its resting potential, however, ready to be stimulated again.

2. The presence of a myelin sheath (a fatty whitish substance) around the axon enhances the neural conduction by as much as five times and is responsible for the white matter of the nervous system. (Gray matter is composed of nonmyelinated axons, dendrites, and cell bodies.)

3. The nature of a message is primarily determined by the particular pathway on which it is carried; the strength is conveyed by the neuron's rate of firing.

4. The axon of one cell comes close to but never touches the dendrites of the next cell. Conduction of the neural impulse across this space (called a synapse) is accomplished by the axon's release of neurotransmitters, which diffuse across the synapse and activate receptor cells on the adjacent cell. These messages may be excitatory or inhibitory; their relative combinations will determine the transmission of the impulse. Some neurotransmitters, such as acetylcholine, have been identified. They appear to be similar to certain poisons and drugs.

IV. 1. The endocrine system is a chemical communication system. Its messengers, called hormones, are secreted by the endocrine glands and are carried by the blood to the organs on which they have an effect.

2. The pituitary gland is the most influential gland in humans. It secretes the growth hormone and other hormones that regulate various glands such as the thyroid gland, the adrenal glands, and the gonads (sex glands).

3. The thyroid gland secretes thyroxin, which regulates metabolism. The adrenals secrete epinephrine and norepinephrine, which play a role in the body's reaction to stress, and many other hormones, including the sex hormones and especially male androgens. The gonads (ovaries in women, testes in men) also secrete sex hormones. The ovaries produce estrogen and progesterone; the testes secrete testosterone. It is important to note that the body's communication system is complex and intricately interconnected.

V. 1. The brain consists of three overlapping regions: the central core, the limbic system, and the cerebral hemispheres.

2. The central core includes several structures that together carry out survival functions. The brain stem is the top of the spinal cord and includes the medulla (which controls aspects of circulation, breathing, chewing, salivation, and facial movements), the pons (which integrates movements from the right and left body halves and transmits information to other brain parts), the midbrain (which contains important centers for visual and auditory reflexes and conveys information between the brain and spinal cord), and the reticular formation (which affects attention and the sleep-waking cycle).

3. Also included in the central core are the cerebellum, the thalamus, and the hypothalamus. The cerebellum coordinates voluntary movement and regulates balance. The thalamus acts as a relay station between sensory receptors and the higher brain and integrates various areas of the brain. The hypothalamus is an important structure that regulates much of the body's internal environment, such as temperature and metabolism.

4. The limbic system (or nose brain) lies above the central core and is probably involved with behaviors that satisfy certain motivational and emotional needs, such as feeding, fighting, fleeing, and mating. It also contains the pleasure center in the brain. It consists of structures such as the hippocampus, the amygdala, and the septal area.

5. The cerebral hemispheres are the large twin structures at the top of the brain; they are involved with the higher-level functions of learning, speech, reasoning, and memory. These hemispheres are covered by the cortex. They can be separated into four lobes: the frontal (front), parietal (top back), temporal (side), and occipital (lower back). The central fissure separates the frontal from the parietal lobe; the lateral fissure marks the top boundary of the temporal lobe.

6. The area of the frontal lobe next to the central fissure is called the motor cortex and is responsible for regulation of voluntary movements. The same area in the parietal lobe is the somatosensory cortex, and it registers body sensations. Hearing is located in the temporal lobe of each hemisphere. Visual information is primarily processed in the occipital lobe. Such areas show localization of function—that is, certain locations correspond to particular functions. However, many functions, especially the abstract mental processes, occur not in a single location but in generally defined association areas.

7. The two hemispheres appear to have somewhat different functions, according to studies of patients who had the connecting fibers (or corpus callosum) cut to relieve epilepsy. First, control is contralateral—that is, the left half of the brain

seems to control the right half of the body and vice versa. Language, mathe matics, and analytical thinking are generally left-brain activities; perception of spatial relationships and artistic abilities are generally attributes of the right hemisphere. Split-brain subjects (those whose corpus callosum is severed) act as if they have two separate brains in their head, each independently responsible for its own tasks.

8. Several techniques have been developed to study the functioning of the brain. The oldest method, clinical observation, involves careful observation of behav ioral deficits in people with localized brain damage due to injury, tumors, or strokes.

9. In brain stimulation, a technique used by Penfield, a mild electric current is ap plied to an exposed area of the brain. Subjective reports indicate that such stim ulation evokes the functions associated with the particular region of the cortex stimulated. This technique is often used with animals. Chemicals can be substi tuted for the electric current since neural conduction is electrochemical.

10. Lesioning, or destroying small portions of brain tissue, is often used in conjunc tion with electrical stimulation since the two techniques appear to have opposite effects.

11. The evoked potential, or pattern of electrical activity in the brain, can also be recorded and studied. An electroencephalograph, or EEG, is taken to show the pattern. In an EEG, electrodes are placed on the scalp. However, it has recently become possible to measure the electrical activity of a single neuron. It can be recorded by inserting a microelectrode into the brain until it contacts a neuron.

VI. 1. Karl Lashley formulated the principle of mass action, which indicates that most of the brain is probably involved in most of the things we do. Furthermore, the principle of multiple control suggests that any single part of the brain is prob ably involved in many different behaviors. Thus, although the brain is composed of billions of cells, it appears to function as a complete unit.

□ **Self-Test**

A. Matching Questions

_____ 1. Indirectly controls physical growth and many other body functions

_____ 2. Produce estrogen, progesterone, and testosterone

_____ 3. Plays a central role in autonomic activities such as circulation and breathing

_____ 4. Closely related to control of attention and the sleep–waking cycle

_____ 5. Coordinates voluntary movement of the skeletal muscles

_____ 6. Regulates the body's internal environ ment

a. Adrenal glands
b. Gonads
c. Pons
d. Reticular formation
e. Thalamus
f. Pituitary gland
g. Cerebellum
h. Medulla
i. Hypothalamus
j. Limbic system

_____ 7. Region in the frontal lobe next to the central fissure

_____ 8. Region linked to speech and audition

_____ 9. Region that participates in higher-level mental processes

_____10. Link between the left and right hemi-spheres

_____11. Brain damage to this portion of the cortex can produce blind spot in the visual field.

a. Parietal lobe

b. Association cortex

c. Lateral fissure

d. Occipital lobe

e. Frontal lobe

f. Motor cortex

g. Corpus callosum

h. Temporal lobe

i. Somatosensory cortex

B. Multiple-Choice Questions Testing Factual Knowledge

1. Specialized cells for receiving various types of stimulation are:
   a. neurons
   b. receptors
   c. effectors
   d. afferent neurons   Objective 1.1

2. Which of the following terms does not fit with the other three?
   a. parasympathetic
   b. autonomic
   c. sympathetic
   d. somatic   Objective 1.1

3. The sympathetic and parasympathetic divisions work by dual control. This means they:
   a. augment (help) one another
   b. work antagonistically
   c. take turns
   d. are located in different areas of the body   Objective 1.1

4. What kind of neurons carry information from the brain to the muscles and glands?
   a. sensory neurons
   b. afferent neurons
   c. motor neurons
   d. interneurons   Objective 2.1

5. The major function of the glial cells is to:
   a. manufacture RNA
   b. stimulate hormones
   c. speed neural conduction
   d. nourish and support neurons   Objective 2.1

6. Your pupils will dilate in which of the following situations?
   a. You see something you want to buy.
   b. You are looking at a pleasantly erotic picture.
   c. You are in dim light.
   d. All of the above will cause dilation.   Objective 2.1

7. When the interior of a neuron is positive and the exterior negative, the neuron is in a state known as:
   a. polarization
   b. resting potential

c. action potential
d. none of the above   Objective 3.1

8. Which of the following is most clearly responsible for speeding the conduction of a neural impulse?
   a. myelin
   b. glial cells
   c. interneurons
   d. hormones   Objective 3.1

9. A synapse is a:
   a. gap between two neurons
   b. kind of neurotransmitter
   c. neural insulator
   d. particular division of the nervous system   Objective 3.1

10. Whether or not neural conduction from one neuron to the next occurs depends primarily on:
    a. excitatory neurotransmitters
    b. inhibitory neurotransmitters
    c. both a and b
    d. none of the above   Objective 3.1

11. The messages conducted in the nervous system are _____; in the endocrine system they are _____.
    a. electrochemical; chemical
    b. chemical; electrochemical
    c. physical; chemical
    d. electrical; physical   Objective 4.1

12. Which part of the human brain would be most similar to the brain of a snake?
    a. the limbic system
    b. the central core
    c. the corpus callosum
    d. the cerebral hemisphere   Objective 5.1

13. Which of the following brain areas has the least involvement with vision?
    a. midbrain
    b. occipital cortex
    c. thalamus
    d. cerebellum   Objective 5.1

14. The major function of the hypothalamus is to:
    a. control attention
    b. coordinate body movements
    c. maintain a steady internal environment for the body
    d. transfer information from one part of the brain to another   Objective 5.1

15. The pleasure center discovered by Olds and Milner is located in the:
    a. limbic system
    b. medulla
    c. right cerebral hemisphere
    d. thalamus   Objective 5.1

16. The somatosensory cortex is located in the:
    a. limbic system
    b. parietal lobe
    c. right cerebral hemisphere
    d. occipital cortex   Objective 5.1

17. Severing a person's corpus callosum causes the person to:
    a. die

b. be unable to speak or understand language
c. have two brains in one head
d. become blind   Objective 5.2

18. Which of the following would most typically be controlled primarily by the right cerebral hemisphere?
   a. language
   b. the right half of the body
   c. analytical thinking
   d. spatial relationships   Objective 5.2

19. The practice of studying people or animals who have suffered from brain damage is called the technique of:
   a. lesioning
   b. clinical observation
   c. electrical stimulation
   d. evoked potential   Objective 5.3

20. Wilder Penfield engaged in research in which he applied tiny amounts of electric current to the surface of the brain. His research seems to support the notion of:
   a. localization of function
   b. mass action
   c. multiple control
   d. evoked potentials   Objective 6.1

C. Multiple-Choice Questions Testing Conceptual Knowledge

21. If you went to a phrenologist, you would expect him to tell you about your personality by:
   a. giving you an EEG
   b. giving you a series of personality tests
   c. doing a brain scan
   d. feeling the bumps on your head   Objective 1.1

22. You are walking home at night from the library and a person jumps out of the bushes in front of you and acts like he is going to hurt you. Your body mobilizes for action and in so doing, calls into play the:
   a. sympathetic division
   b. parasympathetic division
   c. hypothalamus
   d. somatic system   Objective 1.1

23. Compare your neural conduction mechanism to the U.S. Post Office. The nature of the message sent in the neural system would be analogous to what in the postal system?
   a. the route by which you sent the letter
   b. the amount of money you paid for the stamp
   c. the number of letters you sent
   d. the weight of the letter   Objective 2.1

24. A tumor growing in John's head has stopped his growth at a height of only four feet, nine inches. This tumor is probably located near his:
   a. thyroid
   b. limbic system
   c. pituitary
   d. reticular formation   Objective 4.1

25. Mary is having problems with regulation of estrogen and progesterone production. If the doctor suspects an endocrine disorder, he would probably first examine Mary's:
    a. adrenal glands
    b. ovaries
    c. thyroid gland
    d. pons   Objective 4.1

26. Blaine is suffering from a head injury that is causing him difficulty in regulating his breathing and blood flow. Also, his face is contorting, he is salivating heavily and making chewing movements. You conclude the accident caused injury to his:
    a. amygdala
    b. cerebellum
    c. medulla
    d. hypothalamus   Objective 5.1

27. A boy is brought into a hospital suffering from head injuries. The most noticeable symptom is his inability to sleep regularly for eight hours. You suspect brain damage to the:
    a. cerebellum
    b. reticular formation
    c. thalamus
    d. hypothalamus   Objective 5.1

28. Suppose you lesion a portion of a male rat's brain. The rat now exhibits inappropriate mating behaviors, has difficulty feeding, and engages in inappropriate fight and flight responses. You conclude you have damaged the rat's:
    a. right cerebral hemisphere
    b. limbic system
    c. hypothalamus
    d. pons   Objective 5.1

29. A man's brain is damaged in such a way that he has no control over his body movements. The damage is probably in which lobe of his brain?
    a. parietal
    b. occipital
    c. temporal
    d. frontal   Objective 5.1

30. You volunteer for an experiment in which electrodes are attached to your scalp and you are asked to think about certain memories. This researcher is probably using the technique of:
    a. evoked potential
    b. lesioning
    c. brain stimulation
    d. clinical observation   Objective 5.3

31. Suppose I believe that any particular part of the brain has many different functions. This belief is essentially that expressed by:
    a. Olds and Milner in their work with pleasure center
    b. Lashley's principle of mass action
    c. the principle of multiple control
    d. the principle of localization of function   Objective 6.1

32. According to Lashley's principle of mass action, to destroy the problem-solving behavior of a cat, you would lesion:
    a. the left frontal lobe
    b. the left and right frontal lobes
    c. the left parietal lobe
    d. any part of the brain, since loss depends on amount, not location, of destruction
                                                               Objective 6.1

D. Short Essay Questions

1. Describe how neural conduction occurs, both within a particular neuron and from one neuron to the next.   (Objective 3.1)

2. How does the endocrine system work? How does its operation differ from that of the nervous system?   (Objective 4.1)

3. What are the general functions of the central core of the brain, the limbic system, and the cerebral hemispheres?   (Objective 5.1)

4. What kinds of information are derived from each of the following methods of studying the brain: clinical observation, brain stimulation, brain lesions, evoked potentials? (Objective 5.3)

5. Compare and contrast the principles of mass action and multiple control. What do they imply about the course of further research into the relationship between the brain and behavior?   (Objective 6.1)

Sensation and Perception ■ 4

☐ **Chapter Summary**

I.   1. A stimulus is any form of energy to which an organism can respond. The organism's response is called a *sensation* and can be affected by both the quality, or kind, of sensation it produces and the quantity, or amount, of stimulation. There are individual as well as cross-species differences in our ability to sense physical stimuli.

2. The absolute threshold is generally defined as the lowest intensity stimulus to which a person will respond 50 percent of the time under ideal conditions. Sensory capacity can be limited by several factors, including background noise, lack of prior information about the stimulus, and motivation to ignore weak stimuli. Signal detection theory attempts to separate out these various influences.

3. Weber's Law postulates that a "just noticeable difference" in sensation (the smallest detectable change in stimulation) is always a constant proportion of the initial stimulus intensity. It does not hold under all circumstances, but is a useful approximation. Stevens's Power Law states that the relationship between stimulus magnitude and magnitude of sensation is quite constant, but like Weber's Law, varies from one sense to another.

4. All sensory systems display adaptation, the reduction of sensitivity due to constant stimulation, although the degree of adaptation varies from one sense to another. Thus, sensory systems are maximally sensitive to change.

II.   1. Humans possess more senses than the basic five of sight, sound, smell, taste, and touch. Each sense depends on a particular sense organ (or receptor) to change (or transduce) stimulation into sensation.

2. Electromagnetic energy, or light, is transduced in the eye. The wavelength of light determines color; the intensity determines brightness.

3. Light enters the eye through the transparent cornea, goes through a hole in the iris called the pupil and through the lens, which focuses the image on the retina. The outermost layer of the retina contains two types of receptor cells, rods and cones. These receptors channel their impulses through the bipolar cells, then the ganglion cells to the optic nerve, which carries visual information to the brain for interpretation. The blind spot is the area of the retina through which the optic nerve exits the eye. The optic nerves cross over at the optic chiasma so that fibers from the left half of each eye go to the left hemisphere of the cerebral cortex and vice versa. Glaucoma is caused by pressure on the optic nerve.

4. Cones, cells that function in bright light and are responsible for color vision, are highly concentrated in the fovea, a depression at the center back of the eye. Foveal vision provides the sharpest detail. Rods are denser in an area about 20 degrees away from the center of the fovea, sense black and white, and work in dim light. Both rods and cones transduce light by means of chemical reactions in which a pigment, such as rhodopsin in the rods, is bleached out. Consequently, when coming from a light to a dark area, vision is diminished until the pigment is replenished.

5. The trichromatic theory of color vision suggests that there are three types of cones, each maximally sensitive to a different wavelength (color) of light. The opponent-process theory explains that the three types of cones are linked to form three opponent systems in the brain, red-green, yellow-blue, and light-dark. It explains the occurrence of afterimages and color blindness. People who see all colors are called trichromats. The most common color blindness affects people called red-green dichromats, who have difficulty distinguishing red from green. Less common are the blue-yellow dichromats. Monochromatic people see no color, since their visual information is transmitted only by rods.

6. Sound waves are produced by vibrating molecules and are transduced in the ear. Their frequency determines pitch; their intensity, or amplitude (measured in decibels), determines loudness. Normal conversation occurs at about 60 decibels; sounds above 120 decibels are painful and can cause hearing loss.

7. The pinna, or outer ear, funnels sound into the auditory canal, which amplifies the sound. A thin membrane called the eardrum, or tympanic membrane, seals off the end of this passage and moves in harmony with the sound waves. Three small bones, or ossicles—the hammer, anvil, and stirrup—amplify and conduct this information from the eardrum to the oval window, by which time the original message is amplified up to ninety times. The oval window transmits the message to the cochlea, in which is embedded the Organ of Corti, the organ of hearing. The Organ of Corti consists of hair cells (receptors) positioned between the basilar membrane and the tectorial membrane. These membranes rub against the hair cells, triggering a neural impulse that travels via the auditory nerve to the brain.

8. The place theory argues that the pitch we perceive depends on which part of the basilar membrane is most displaced; however, it cannot explain all phenomena. The valley principle suggests that loudness is perceived according to how often the fibers of the auditory nerve fire.

9. Olfaction (smell) and taste are closely related in that both respond to the chemical composition of stimuli. Olfaction requires that vaporized molecules of a substance enter the nasal passages, which are lined with the olfactory membranes containing the receptor cells. These receptor cells transduce the chemical stimuli, sending nerve impulses along the olfactory nerves to the brain. Our sense of taste is restricted to four basic categories: sweet and salty, which are sensed on the front of the tongue; sour, sensed on the sides; and bitter, sensed on the back. Transduction takes place in the taste buds, the papillae (or bumps) of the tongue. Each of the four basic taste categories seems to operate independently of the others.

III. 1. Sensations are interpreted by the brain in a process called perception. This interpretation does not always exactly match the original sensation; for example, we sometimes perceive a subjective contour, in which we see details of shapes that do not actually exist.

2. Gestalt psychologists believe we are constantly organizing pieces of information into meaningful patterns called Gestalts. Two of the major Gestalt concepts are grouping and figure-ground. Grouping is the forming of associations among sensory data and includes our tendency to group together things that are close (proximity), that form a continuous pattern (continuity), and that resemble one another (similarity). Some psychologists believe all these grouping principles can be integrated by the single concept of simplicity: Simple patterns are more easily perceived than complex ones. Figure-group refers to our tendency to separate a visual scene into regions that represent objects (the figure) and regions that represent space between objects (the ground). This tendency seems to be inborn and occurs in vision, audition, olfaction, and possibly other senses.

3. Perceptual constancy is our ability to perceive objects as having certain constant properties, even though the sensations they produce vary.

4. Depth perception, which arises from several sources, is the ability to tell how far away an object is. Binocular disparity aids in depth perception, since each eye sees an object at a slightly different angle. Motion parallax refers to the fact that as we move, movement of objects in our field of vision is relative to their distance from us. Monocular (or single-eye) cues to depth include interposition (where one object blocks the view of an object behind it), linear perspective

(produced by the apparent convergence of lines), and texture gradient (in which near objects appear larger and coarser).

5. An illusion is a perception not in accord with the true characteristics of an object or event. Some illusions, such as mirages, are caused by the physical distortion of stimuli; others, such as the Ames room illusion, Müller-Lyer illusions, and the Ponzo illusion, are caused by our processing of information.

IV. 1. We are programmed by prior knowledge, expectations, and psychological states to perceive the world in certain ways: This is called a perceptual set. This learning plays an important role in perception. If, for instance, an organism is deprived of certain kinds of sensory experience, it may never develop the ability to perceive related stimuli. Thus, perception probably arises from early life experience, genetic predisposition, and variations in learning, memory, and motivation.

V. 1. Some illusions are not universal—that is, not all people see them as illusions. Such individual differences may be hereditary or may depend on previous experience. Some cultures that have not experienced the world in ways similar to ours do not see the same illusions we see.

☐ Self-Test

A. Matching Questions

_____ 1. The process of interpretation of the world around us

_____ 2. The smallest detectable change in stimulus

_____ 3. Irrelevant, competing stimuli

_____ 4. The notion that the just noticeable difference is a constant proportion of the original stimulus intensity

_____ 5. The notion that our sensory systems are most sensitive to change in stimulation

_____ 6. Process of changing a stimulus to a sensation

a. Perception

b. Signal detection theory

c. Just noticeable differences

d. Adaptation

e. Weber's Law

f. Sensation

g. Absolute threshold

h. Noise

i. Stevens's Power Law

j. Transduction

_____ 7. Affected by cataracts

_____ 8. Stimulus characteristic responsible for color

_____ 9. Transducer for black and white

_____10. Center back depression in the eye

_____11. Place where the optic nerve exits the eye

_____12. Crossover point of the optic nerves in the brain

a. Rods

b. Wavelength

c. Rhodopsin

d. Optic chiasma

e. Fovea

f. Intensity

g. Lens

h. Blind spot

i. Cones

j. Cornea

_____13. Hammer, anvil, and stirrup

_____14. Tissue at the inner end of the auditory canal

_____15. Receptors in the ear

_____16. Part of the ear that contains the Organ of Corti

_____17. States that pitch is related to the area stimulated

a. Place theory

b. Eardrum

c. Basilar membrane

d. Cochlea

e. Organ of Corti

f. Hair cells

g. Volley principle

h. Tectorial membrane

i. Ossicles

_____18. A sense that relies on the chemical configuration of the stimulus

_____19. Location of receptor cells for the sense of smell

_____20. Sensations detected by the back of the tongue

_____21. Location of the taste buds

_____22. Patterns of organization

_____23. A readiness to ignore certain types of stimuli

a. Sour

b. Olfactory membranes

c. Papillae

d. Salty

e. Perceptual set

f. Olfaction

g. Gestalts

h. Bitter

B. Multiple-Choice Questions Testing Factual Knowledge

1. Sound waves, light waves, heat, and pressure are examples of:
   a. transducers
   b. sensations
   c. stimuli
   d. perceptions   Objective 1.1

2. Which of the following is a function of the quality of a stimulus?
   a. pitch
   b. loudness
   c. brightness
   d. saltiness   Objective 1.1

3. According to the principle of sensory adaptation, our sensory systems are particularly well-designed to detect:
   a. duration
   b. intensity
   c. quality
   d. change   Objective 1.1

4. The translation of the energy in environmental stimuli into neural activity is called:
   a. interpretation
   b. transduction
   c. sensation
   d. perception   Objective 1.1

5. Signal detection theory is unique in that it accounts for the effects of:
   a. the just noticeable difference
   b. noise
   c. Weber's Law
   d. Stevens's Power Law   Objective 1.2

6. Stevens's Power Law describes the relationship between stimulus magnitude and:
   a. the just noticeable difference
   b. stimulus duration
   c. magnitude of sensation
   d. the absolute threshold   Objective 1.2

7. Which of the following cells is closest to the back of the retina?
   a. cones
   b. ganglion cells
   c. bipolar cells
   d. all equally close   Objective 2.1

8. After passing through the optic chiasma, which fibers go to the right hemisphere of the brain?
   a. left half of the right eye and right half of the left eye
   b. right half of the right eye and left half of the left eye
   c. left half of both eyes
   d. right half of both eyes   Objective 2.1

9. Which of the following statements regarding the rods and cones is *false*?
   a. They both transduce light.
   b. There are more types of cones than rods.
   c. Rods are concentrated in the fovea.
   d. None of the above are false.   Objective 2.1

10. Jeff can tell red from green but confuses yellow and blue; he is a:
    a. blue-yellow dichromat
    b. red-green dichromat
    c. monochromatic
    d. trichromatic   Objective 2.1

11. In a study discussed in depth in the text, researchers discovered that young children were more likely than older children to be deficient in their ability to see the color blue. On further study, this was discovered to be due to:
    a. later development of cones than rods
    b. metabolic changes
    c. differential developmental of the visual cortex
    d. an error in the research design   Objective 2.1

12. Decibels are used to measure:
    a. loudness
    b. pitch
    c. brightness
    d. frequency   Objective 2.2

13. The actual organ of transduction in the ear is the:
    a. Organ of Corti
    b. cochlea
    c. hair cells
    d. basilar membrane   Objective 2.2

14. Which of the following is *not* one of our senses?
    a. olfaction

b. balance and equilibrium
c. touch
d. none of the above (all are senses)   Objective 2.3

15. Which of the following is *not* one of the basic skin senses discussed in the text?
a. warmth
b. sharpness
c. cold
d. pressure   Objective 2.3

16. Which of the following is *not* one of the basic categories of taste?
a. sour
b. salty
c. bland
d. bitter   Objective 2.4

17. The phenomenon of perceiving connecting lines even though they do not exist is called:
a. grouping
b. Gestalt psychology
c. subjective contour
d. the principle of simplicity   Objective 3.2

18. Perceptual capabilities vary:
a. between species
b. among members of the same species
c. according to certain kinds of hereditary endowments
d. all of the above   Objective 4.1

19. The fact that identical twins tend to see illusions in the same way more frequently than best friends do indicates the impact on perception of:
a. heredity
b. experience
c. motivation
d. age of the subject   Objective 4.1

20. The fact that some cultures do not see the same illusions as Americans tend to demonstrates the impact on perception of:
a. motivation
b. experience
c. genetics
d. deformity   Objective 5.1

C. Multiple-Choice Questions Testing Conceptual Knowledge

21. You suspect you have a hearing loss, so you go to a specialist who fits you with earphones and tells you to raise your right hand whenever you hear a tone. She is testing your:
a. just noticeable difference
b. absolute threshold
c. Weber's ratio
d. adaptation   Objective 1.2

22. Suppose you find that when lifting a fifty-pound barbell, you can just notice the difference when two pounds are added. According to Weber's Law, if you were lifting a twenty-five-pound barbell, the just noticeable difference would be:
a. one-half pound
b. one pound
c. two pounds
d. four pounds   Objective 1.2

23. Some people compare the human eye to a camera. Using this analogy, the aperture (the hole that lets light in) corresponds to the:
    a. retina
    b. lens
    c. iris
    d. cornea
    Objective 2.1

24. You go to an optometrist who tells you that you have abnormally high pressure inside your eyes. You suspect you might be suffering from:
    a. glaucoma
    b. cataracts
    c. presbyopia
    d. a blind spot
    Objective 2.1

25. Suppose I believe that vision is best described by a series of on-off switches and that the pattern of ons and offs determines the colors I see. I would subscribe to:
    a. place theory
    b. trichromatic theory
    c. volley theory
    d. opponent-process theory
    Objective 2.1

26. The phenomenon of color blindness is _____ trichromatic theory and _____ volley theory.
    a. not supportive of; unrelated to
    b. supportive of; contradictory to
    c. contradictory to; supportive of
    d. contradictory to; not supportive of
    Objective 2.1

27. According to the text, which of the following people would be most likely to suffer a hearing loss?
    a. a radio disc jockey
    b. a telephone repairman
    c. an airplane ground crew worker
    d. a medical doctor
    Objective 2.2

28. Which of the following has a function that differs from the rest?
    a. auditory canal
    b. ear ossicles
    c. eardrum
    d. Organ of Corti
    Objective 2.2

29. Which of the following is technically *not* a transducer?
    a. Meissner's corpuscles
    b. taste buds
    c. nasal passage
    d. rods and cones
    Objective 2.3

30. Suppose you believe that hearing is set up the same way as a harmonica: The note you hear depends on the place you blow. You would probably subscribe to which theory?
    a. trichromatic theory
    b. volley theory
    c. opponent-process theory
    d. place theory
    Objective 2.2

31. You look at the following picture and say you see a white triangle against a red backdrop. This illustrates the principle of:
    a. simplicity
    b. figure and ground
    c. monocular depth cues
    d. perceptual constancy
    Objective 3.1

32. Most people see the following display as three groups, one of 3 A's, one of 3 B's, and one of 3 C's. This is consistent with the Gestalt principle of:

AAABBBCCC

    a. similarity
    b. proximity
    c. continuity
    d. subjective contour   Objective 3.2

D. Short Essay Questions

1. What is the difference between Weber's Law and Stevens's Power Law? (Objective 1.2)

2. How do the rods and cones differ? (Objective 2.1)

3. Describe the process of auditory transduction. (Objective 2.2)

4. How are smell and taste related? (Objective 2.4)

5. What is the major difference between sensation and perception? (Objective 3.1)

6. What is an illusion? Why do we see illusions? (Objective 3.2)

7. What are the factors that influence perception? How does each influence the perceptual process? (Objective 5.1)

Basic Principles of Learning

□ **Preview of the Chapter**
Major Concepts and Behavioral Objectives

CONCEPT 1   An understanding of learning is necessary in order to explain human behavior. Learning is inferred from changes in performance.

    1.1   Define performance and contrast it with learning.

CONCEPT 2   Awareness of external stimuli is the simplest kind of learning. Classical and operant conditioning—learning that certain events interrelate—are more complex.

    2.1   Describe and compare the orienting reflex and habituation, and analyze the learning process that underlies them.

    2.2   Describe what is meant by association learning, and give examples to demonstrate your understanding.

CONCEPT 3   In classical conditioning, the onset of one stimulus predicts a second one. For example, if a warning light repeatedly precedes a shock, you learn to move in response to the light. In operant conditioning, the probability of a response is affected by its consequences. For example, if kindness were always financially rewarded, you would be kinder.

    3.1   Describe the process of classical conditioning both in terms of definitions and examples.

    3.2   Describe the process of operant conditioning both in terms of definitions and examples.

    3.3   Distinguish between the various kinds of reinforcements and punishment, and describe the various reinforcement schedules.

    3.4   Discuss the application of operant conditioning to programmed instruction and behavior modification.

    3.5   Compare and contrast classical and operant conditioning.

    3.6   Describe generalization and discrimination, and compare them to each other.

CONCEPT 4   Extinction, or the gradual disappearance of learned responses, occurs when stimuli are no longer associated with or contingent on each other.

    4.1   Define extinction and explain what circumstances in classical and operant conditioning produce it.

CONCEPT 5   Cognitive psychologists maintain that important thought processes intervene between stimulus and response and that learning can occur without reinforcement.

    5.1   Define cognitive psychology and describe the research that supports its premises.

☐ **Chapter Summary**

I. 1. Learning is defined as a relatively permanent change in performance potential resulting from experience.

2. Learning is involved in almost every phenomenon psychologists study; however, it is neither observable nor measurable. Consequently, psychologists measure performance and infer that changes in performance reflect learning, although factors such as physical maturation, emotion, motivation, health, and fatigue can affect performance without affecting learning.

II. 1. Two of the simplest kinds of learning are the orienting reflex and habituation. Both give us knowledge about stimuli in the environment. The orienting reflex is a response designed to focus our attention on a new stimulus and may include turning toward it, looking at it, and generally ascertaining what it is. Habituation involves learning to ignore familiar stimuli in the environment.

2. Another kind of learning involves knowledge that certain events are associated with one another. Associative learning includes classical conditioning and operant conditioning. Some psychologists argue that a third type of learning, cognitive learning, is necessary to explain complex learning situations.

III. 1. Classical conditioning involves reflex behavior in which a stimulus naturally produces (or elicits) an involuntary response. In classical conditioning, an originally neutral stimulus (one that elicits no response) is repeatedly presented just before the reflex stimulus (or unconditioned stimulus, UCS). The neutral stimulus eventually becomes associated with the unconditioned stimulus–unconditioned response (the reflex response) pattern and soon comes to elicit that unconditioned response (UCR) even in the absence of the unconditioned stimulus. This previously neutral stimulus becomes a conditioned stimulus (CS), and the reflex response it produces is called the conditioned response (CR). This tendency to react to a previously neutral stimulus, or CS, as though it were the UCS was called stimulus substitution by Ivan Pavlov, one of the first scientists to systematically study the phenomenon of classical conditioning.

2. One of the necessary conditions for classical conditioning is a contingency, or relationship, between the CS and UCS. Generally, the CS must precede the UCS by only a short time for maximal conditioning to occur. Backward conditioning involves presenting the UCS before the CS and is much less effective in establishing a conditioned response. Random presentation of the CS and UCS also is ineffective in producing a CR.

3. A series of experiments conducted by Garcia demonstrates that some stimulus response associations are learned much more easily than others. Rats, for instance, associated the taste of a substance with physical illness and the visual cues in a situation with electric shock, but they did not make the reverse associations. Garcia explained this tendency as a function of the evolutionary history of the species: Natural selection has favored a nervous system that allows easy learning of contingencies crucial to survival. This same tendency has also been demonstrated in humans.

4. John B. Watson found that classically conditioned fear responses could be diminished by a technique now called systematic desensitization: A person is taught to relax and then is gradually introduced to anxiety-producing situations, starting with mildly fear-arousing ones and eventually working up to situations that before desensitization would have produced excessive anxiety.

5. Using cats and puzzle boxes, Edward L. Thorndike examined another form of

association learning, which we now call operant conditioning. His law of effect stated that responses that led to satisfying consequences would be strengthened; those that led to unsatisfying consequences would be weakened.

6. B. F. Skinner has refined Thorndike's law of effect and renamed it the principle of reinforcement. According to this principle, a consequence that increases the probability of the behavior that caused it is called a reinforcement (or reward). A consequence that results in suppression of the causal behavior is called a punishment. Skinner argues that operant conditioning is the basic mechanism for controlling human behavior.

7. Positive reinforcement increases the frequency of response because that response is followed by a pleasant stimulus. Negative reinforcement also increases the frequency of a response, but it does so by removing a painful or unpleasant stimulus. Punishment decreases the frequency of response by following it with an unpleasant stimulus. When an organism mistakenly assumes a contingency between a response and some consequences when in fact none exists, the resulting behavior is called superstitious behavior.

8. Operant conditioning experiments are usually conducted with animals in a maze, a Skinner box (cage with a lever that delivers a food reward when pressed), or a jump stand (a stand from which an animal can jump in two or more directions).

9. When a subject does not typically make the response a psychologist wants to condition, a technique called shaping is used. Shaping involves reinforcement for closer and closer approximations of the desired behavior.

10. Reinforcement can be applied in many patterns or schedules. Continuous reinforcement, in which every response is followed by a reward, is usually most effective for establishing a new behavior. Partial reinforcement schedules, in which only some instances of the desired behaviors are rewarded, are usually the best way to maintain a behavior. There are four types of partial schedules: A fixed-ratio schedule provides reward each time the subject makes a specified number of responses. A fixed-interval schedule rewards the first response made after a specified period of time has elapsed. Variable-ratio and variable-interval schedules are like their fixed counterparts, except the number of responses or amount of elapsed time varies randomly from trial to trial.

11. Stimulus control refers to the situation in which the reinforcement schedule only operates in the presences of a particular stimulus—for example, when a red light is lit. Consequently, the subject learns to respond only when the stimulus is present.

12. Operant conditioning techniques have been applied to humans in the form of programmed instruction and behavior modification. Programmed instruction involves active repetition, frequent testing, and immediate feedback for every response. Behavior modification is the selective use of operant conditioning principles to change human behavior. Reward programs often consist of token economies in which tokens (such as poker chips that can later be exchanged for other reinforcers) are earned by demonstrating appropriate behavior.

13. There are several similarities between classical and operant conditioning. Reinforcement, for instance, plays an important role in both. Stimulus control is also present in both: In classical conditioning, behavior is controlled by the conditioned stimulus; in operant conditioning, environmental cues associated with the learning situation control when the behavior will be exhibited.

14. Both kinds of conditioning are also subject to generalization (the expression of a learned response in a new but similar situation) and discrimination (learning to make a particular response only to a particular stimulus). Generalization can be limited through the technique of discrimination training, in which only cer-

tain stimuli (the discriminative stimuli)) are associated with reinforcement. A generalization gradient depicts response strength to both the original stimulus and similar stimuli (which typically elicit a smaller proportion of responses than the original stimulus). The effect of discrimination training is to make the generalization gradient steeper.

15. Primary reinforcers, such as food or water, satisfy a basic need. Secondary or conditioned reinforcers, such as praise or money, signal that a primary reinforcer is forthcoming. Similarly, first-order conditioning involves the delivery of a primary reinforcer. Second-order conditioning signals the expected delivery of a primary reinforcer. Learning a sequence of behaviors that eventually ends with primary reinforcement is called chaining.

16. Punishment is generally successful in helping to suppress maladaptive behaviors, but does have some limitations. It is fairly temporary; when it is no longer present, or in conditions of high motivation, the behavior can reappear; it can cause emotional disturbances; and it can come to be an aversive stimulus to be escaped from or avoided. Furthermore, it does not indicate what a desirable behavior would be. Consequently, it is usually best used in conjunction with reinforcement of appropriate behavior.

17. Perhaps the major difference between classical and operant conditioning is that classical conditioning applies to reflexes or respondent behavior, whereas operant conditioning applies to spontaneously emitted or operant behavior.

IV. 1. In classical conditioning, extinction is the slow weakening and eventual disappearance of the conditioned response. It is accomplished by no longer pairing the CS with the UCS.

2. Extinction occurs in operant conditioning when the reinforcement or punishment no longer follows the response. If an animal is removed from an experimental chamber for a while after its response has been extinguished and is then put back in, the extinguished response will recur. This is called spontaneous recovery.

V. 1. The cognitive approach to learning, fathered by Edward Tolman, objects to classical and operant conditioning's exclusion of the mental activity that goes on inside the organism during the learning process.

2. Cognitive psychologists stress that association learning involves learning an expectation that two events will be associated with one another.

3. Support for the cognitive view comes from experiments demonstrating that learning can occur without reinforcement. Latent learning experiments, for example, show that an organism can learn a new behavior but not demonstrate it until an incentive to do so arises. Social learning through observation experiments demonstrates that organisms can learn without direct reinforcement. Such learning is called observational learning, imitative learning, or modeling. Modeling appears to be a very common form of human learning, although it can also be demonstrated in animals.

□ **Self-Test**

A. Matching Questions

_____ 1. Response designed to learn about a new stimulus

_____ 2. Learning of an association between a particular action and a desirable consequence

a. Reflex

b. Habituation

c. Unconditioned response

_____ 3. Behavior produced involuntarily by a specific stimulus

_____ 4. Response elicited by conditioned stimulus

_____ 5. Reaction to a conditioned stimulus as though it were an unconditioned stimulus

d. Classical conditioning

e. Orienting reflex

f. Stimulus substitution

g. Conditioned response

h. Operant conditioning

_____ 6. Weakening of a learned association

_____ 7. Technique for treating phobias

_____ 8. Thorndike's account of reinforcement

_____ 9. Removal of an unpleasant consequence

_____10. Technique used to condition seldom-exhibited behaviors

a. Stimulus control

b. Extinction

c. Negative reinforcement

d. Punishment

e. Systematic desensitization

f. Shaping

g. Law of effect

h. Spontaneous recovery

_____11. One reinforcement for every response

_____12. Descriptive of a slot machine in a gambling casino

_____13. Use of secondary reinforcers in behavior modification

_____14. Learning to make a particular response only to a particular stimulus

_____15. An example of learning in the absence of reinforcement

a. Modeling

b. Token economy

c. Variable-ratio schedule

d. Generalization

e. Variable-interval schedule

f. Chaining

g. Continuous reinforcement schedule

h. Discrimination

B. Multiple-Choice Questions Testing Factual Knowledge

1. Which of the following is a characteristic of learning but not of performance?
   a. observable
   b. measurable
   c. a mental activity
   d. all of the above are characteristics of learning   Objective 1.1

2. All instances of classical conditioning are based on:
   a. the orienting reflex
   b. reflex behavior
   c. habituation
   d. operant conditioning   Objective 2.2

3. In Pavlov's example, the unconditioned stimulus (UCS) was:
   a. a tone or bell
   b. salivation
   c. hunger
   d. food placed in the mouth   Objective 3.1

4. According to Pavlov, the tendency to react to a previously neutral stimulus as though it were an unconditioned stimulus is called:
   a. stimulus substitution
   b. reflex behavior
   c. refining of the operant
   d. backward conditioning   Objective 3.1

5. In most cases of classical conditioning, the:
   a. CS occurs just before the UCS
   b. CS occurs just after the UCS
   c. CR occurs before the CS
   d. CS and UCS occur randomly   Objective 3.1

6. According to Garcia's studies, rats are especially likely to attribute the occurrence of food shock to:
   a. the taste of the food they were eating when they were shocked
   b. the taste of the food they were eating about two hours before they were shocked
   c. the auditory and visual characteristics of the food
   d. none of the above   Objective 3.1

7. As a psychologist, Edward Thorndike had the most in common with:
   a. Ivan Pavlov
   b. Edward Tolman
   c. John B. Watson
   d. B. F. Skinner   Objective 3.2

8. The device in which a hungry animal learns to find its way along a complex path that leads to food is called a:
   a. jump stand
   b. Skinner box
   c. Pavlovian apparatus
   d. maze   Objective 3.2

9. A light flashes, a bell sounds, then a dog is given food. If the dog begins salivating as soon as the light flashes, this is called:
   a. primary reinforcement
   b. secondary reinforcement
   c. first-order conditioning
   d. second-order conditioning   Objective 3.2

10. Decreasing the frequency of a response by following the response with a negative consequence is:
    a. systematic desensitization
    b. punishment
    c. negative reinforcement
    d. behavior modification   Objective 3.3

11. When an individual mistakenly assumes a contingency between a response and reinforcement when no such contingency exists, the behavior that is produced is called:
    a. superstitious behavior
    b. sporadic behavior
    c. partial behavior
    d. noncontingent behavior   Objective 3.3

12. New operant behavior is usually best established by using which of the following reinforcement schedules?
    a. fixed interval
    b. variable interval
    c. continuous
    d. variable ratio   Objective 3.3

13. Which of the following is most likely a primary reinforcer?
    a. praise
    b. money
    c. attention
    d. a candy bar   Objective 3.3

14. Which of the following is *not* a side effect of punishment?
    a. It may create an emotional disturbance.
    b. It gives long-term control of behavior.
    c. It does not indicate what appropriate behavior would be.
    d. It can become an aversive stimulus to be escaped.   Objective 3.3

15. The effect of discrimination training on a generalization gradient is to:
    a. make it steeper
    b. flatten it out
    c. leave it as is
    d. any of the above, depending on the situation   Objective 3.6

16. A rat learns that he will only be reinforced when a red light in his cage is on. This is
    an example of:
    a. generalization
    b. stimulus control
    c. continuous reinforcement
    d. the Garcia effect   Objective 3.6

17. How would you extinguish an operantly conditioned response?
    a. stop reinforcement
    b. prevent the response
    c. punish the response
    d. any of the above   Objective 4.1

18. The tendency for an extinguished response to recur after a rest from the experimental
    procedure is called:
    a. time out
    b. discrimination
    c. spontaneous recovery
    d. behavior modification   Objective 4.1

19. According to cognitive psychologists, what an organism learns during classical condi-
    tioning is a(n):
    a. cognition
    b. cognitive map
    c. expectation
    d. stimulus–response association   Objective 5.1

20. Modeling refers to a process of learning through:
    a. reinforcement
    b. observation
    c. operant conditioning
    d. classical conditioning   Objective 5.1

C. Multiple-Choice Questions Testing Conceptual Knowledge

21. You are walking down the street when an explosion occurs off to your left. You im-
    mediately turn to the left and devote your attention to trying to figure out what hap-
    pened. This is an example of:
    a. the orienting reflex
    b. habituation
    c. classical conditioning
    d. operant conditioning   Objective 2.1

22. Watson's experiment with little Albert served to demonstrate:
    a. habituation
    b. the orienting reflex
    c. association learning
    d. the cognitive point of view   Objective 2.2

23. You teach your dog to sit by giving him a doggie biscuit every time he sits on command. This is an example of:
    a. the orienting reflex
    b. habituation
    c. classical conditioning
    d. operant conditioning   Objective 3.2

24. Teaching a tiger to jump through a flaming hoop (something it would never do on its own) almost certainly involves the process of:
    a. shaping
    b. systematic desensitization
    c. discrimination training
    d. classical conditioning   Objective 3.2

25. You work on an assembly line and you know that every day your work output is checked by a computer. You do not, however, know when it is checked, since the time changes from day to day. You are on which of the following reinforcement schedules?
    a. fixed ratio
    b. fixed interval
    c. variable ratio
    d. variable interval   Objective 3.3

26. A fourth-grade teacher promises that if Billy does well on the spelling test, he will not have to stay in from recess. She is using the technique of:
    a. positive reinforcement
    b. negative reinforcement
    c. punishment
    d. token economies   Objective 3.3

27. You are teaching a mentally retarded child to dress herself. When she does something correctly, you give her a poker chip, which she can later exchange for food or privileges. This is an example of:
    a. programmed instruction
    b. discrimination training
    c. a token economy
    d. systematic desensitization   Objective 3.4

28. Marty is terrified of spiders, so he goes to a therapist who teaches him relaxation techniques and gradually introduces mildly arousing "spider" situations. Marty's therapist is using the technique of:
    a. classical conditioning
    b. operant conditioning
    c. behavior modification
    d. systematic desensitization   Objective 3.5

29. You teach a child to be afraid of the dog next door (who bites little children), but now the child becomes afraid of all dogs. This is an example of:
    a. discrimination
    b. generalization
    c. stimulus control
    d. a discriminative stimulus   Objective 3.6

30. You have conditioned your dog to bark every time you say the word *Friday*. Now, however, you are no longer reinforcing the dog for barking. This second circumstance should produce:
    a. spontaneous recovery
    b. extinction
    c. the Garcia effect
    d. a phobia
    Objective 4.1

31. Recent research has indicated that different people have different "cognitive styles," or ways of thinking about problems. This research would be most consistent with the beliefs of:
    a. Edward Thorndike
    b. B. F. Skinner
    c. Edward Tolman
    d. John B. Watson
    Objective 5.1

32. You drive around all day in a strange city looking for a particular building. You finally find it. Now your friend wants you to go to another building and, even though you weren't looking for it, you can drive directly to it since you remember it from earlier in the day. This example is similar to:
    a. latent learning
    b. stimulus control
    c. modeling
    d. discrimination training
    Objective 5.1

D. Short Essay Questions

1. Is there a hereditary base for tendencies to learn certain kinds of associations more easily than others? Cite experimental evidence to support your answer. (Objective 2.2)

2. When should punishment be used? What are the negative side effects of punishment? (Objective 3.3)

3. What is the role of reinforcement in operant conditioning? In classical conditioning? (Objective 3.5)

4. What is meant by stimulus control? How does it operate in classical conditioning? in operant conditioning? (Objective 3.5)

5. What is the cognitive view of learning? What evidence is there to support this approach? (Objective 5.1)

Memory and Forgetting ■6

□ **Chapter Summary**

I.   1. Psychologists usually distinguish three types of memory: sensory memory, short-term memory, and long-term memory.

       2. Sensory memory is a very brief (perhaps only a second or two) and temporary store for information coming in through our sensory channels. We have a sensory memory to correspond to each of our five senses. George Sperling's experiments demonstrated that sensory memory may be able to process more information than was previously thought. It is during this brief period of sensory memory that we select what information will warrant further processing in short-term memory.

       3. Sensory gating acts to help us focus our attention on the most important sensory channel at any given time, although we continue to monitor our other senses. Selective attention allows us to select and attend to only certain information from any single sensory channel. It has been examined by using a dichotic listening technique in which subjects hear two different messages at the same time, one in each ear. If one of the messages is "shadowed" (repeated aloud by the subject), only the most general characteristics of the messages that are not shadowed are remembered, thus demonstrating selective attention.

       4. Short-term memory also has a limited duration (about twenty seconds), but information can be maintained in short-term memory through rehearsal, or repetition. Short-term memory rehearsal is believed to be acoustical—that is, the sounds of the words are repeated and stored. Our short-term memory probably holds "seven plus or minus two" (that is, five to nine) pieces of information at any one time, according to George Miller and most other psychologists. Consequently, if we can "chunk" information—that is, organize it into a smaller number of units—we can increase the capacity of short-term memory.

       5. Long-term memory is the permanent, unlimited-capacity part of our memory; it is the repository of all our accumulated information. Transfer of information from short-term to long-term memory involves elaborative rehearsal, a deeper form of processing than maintenance rehearsal, the process used to maintain information in short-term memory.

II.   1. Retrieval from memory can be in the form of recognition (you are presented with a stimulus and asked if you've encountered it before) or recall (you are asked to remember an event). Recognition may explain the *déjà vu* phenomenon, which is a feeling of having experienced something before although you know you could not have. Recognition is generally easier than recall since it involves only a matching rather than a memory search process. Retrieval cues (hints) are helpful in recall.

       2. Memory can be improved by using mnemonic devices. One such technique is the method of loci, in which items are visually associated with a series of well-known places. A key-word system involves memorizing a list of simple words or sentences and then visually associating each item of a sequential list with the ordered key words. Recall in both cases involves going back through the place or key words and stating the visually associated objects. Both techniques also make use of organization and imagery. Some people, especially children, can form eidetic images, commonly called photographic memories. All of us can improve our memory through reconstruction—that is, breaking down of a complex memory task into its simpler components.

       3. Reconstruction, however, may lead to memory distortion if gaps in memory are filled in with what seems to be true rather than what actually occurred. Distortions often are consistent with our expectations or stereotypes, and inconsistent

information may simply be forgotten. Also, when we are set to perceive a situation in a particular way, we tend to recall the event as we were ready to perceive it rather than as it actually occurred. Memory distortions have obvious impact on eyewitness testimony. Indeed, Elizabeth Loftus has demonstrated that eyewitnesses' recall can be influenced by the kinds of questions the eyewitness is asked at the scene of the crime.

III. 1. Many psychologists believe that short-term and long-term memory are two separate systems. Evidence for this dual memory includes experiments testing free recall. If free recall of word lists are graphed, a serial position curve emerges, showing that words from the middle of the list are least well remembered. This is explained by an end-of-list advantage due to short-term memory recall and a start-of-list advantage due to greater rehearsal and likelihood of long-term memory storage. Also, when asked to remember a word list after performing a distracting task such as counting backwards, only the end of the list (the part held in short-term memory) suffers from interference. Anterograde amnesia appears to affect transfer from short-term to long-term memory, but it does not affect items already stored in long-term memory.

2. Other psychologists criticize the dual memory view and instead tend to see differences between short-term and long-term memory as due to the way information is processed. Shallow processing leaves an easily forgotten memory; deep processing would correspond to long-term memory. Research indicates that shallow processing (based on visual or auditory rehearsal) led to more forgetting than deep processing (based on semantic rehearsal). Although the depth of processing view is not necessarily incompatible with the dual memory view, it seems likely that physiological examination of the brain will ultimately answer the dual versus unitary question.

IV. 1. Many neurophysiologists believe memory is transferred from short- to long-term memory by a temporary circulation of electrical impulses through interconnected neurons. This view is consistent with retrograde amnesia, in which the victim cannot remember events that occurred just prior to a head injury. Apparently, this transfer or consolidation takes time, as demonstrated by an experiment in which rats shocked up to an hour after a learning trial appeared to have no memory of their learning.

2. Many scientists also believe that long-term memory involves some sort of permanent synaptic change, either structural, chemical, or both. Research has demonstrated that rats placed in enriched environments developed thicker and heavier cerebral cortices with more blood vessels, more dendritic spines, and more neurotransmitter-related enzymes than did rats raised in an impoverished environment. Research such as this clearly indicates that neural change does accompany learning.

3. Learning may also change the structure of RNA, thereby changing the genetic code, which is the basic mechanism of heredity. However, it is generally agreed that a "memory molecule" would not act to transfer specific memories from one animal to another.

V. 1. Psychologists have suggested three causes of forgetting: decay, interference, and motivated forgetting. Decay theory states that as time passes, memories that are not rehearsed simply fade away. Interference theory postulates that forgetting occurs because new events get confused with old memories. Two examples are retroactive interference, in which a new event prevents us from remembering an old one, and proactive interference, in which an already learned event interferes with our ability to learn a new one. Motivated forgetting, or repression, involves intentional forgetting of anxiety-arousing or unpleasant events.

2. For the most part, research contradicts decay theory and supports interference theory and motivated forgetting.

3. Most psychologists believe that memories are never really forgotten; they are just inaccessible at times, a notion that is consistent with theories of interference and motivated forgetting. It is demonstrated by brain stimulation in which subjects report long-forgotten memories and by improved recall under hypnosis and psychoanalysis. One problem in this research involves the possibility of confabulation, creating new information to fill in the lost details.

4. Other research, however, indicates that memories may be entirely dismissed. Loftus, for instance, demonstrated that once subjects have incorporated false information into a memory, they cling to that misinformation and appear to forget what actually happened. In fact, forgetting is a valuable process; if we never forgot anything (like Luria's famous subject), our memories would be very confusing and unmanageable.

☐ Self-Test

A. Matching Questions

_____ 1. Selective tuning to only one sensory channel, such as vision

_____ 2. Experiment in which two different messages are presented simultaneously

_____ 3. Renewal of information through repetition

_____ 4. Reduction of the amount of information through organization

_____ 5. Type of rehearsal used in transfer of information from short-term to long-term memory

a. Shadowing
b. Chunking
c. Sensory gating
d. Elaborative rehearsal
e. Dichotic listening
f. Maintenance rehearsal
g. Selective attention
h. Rehearsal

_____ 6. Retrieval process that is primarily a matching process

_____ 7. Technique for improving memory

_____ 8. Similar to photographic memory

_____ 9. Shows the recall percentages for word lists according to word position on the list

_____10. Time it takes for material to become firmly fixed in long-term memory

_____11. The problem when the first list learned interferes with one's ability to learn a second list

a. Serial position curve
b. Eidetic images
c. Retroactive interference
d. Recall
e. Proactive interference
f. Mnemonic device
g. Consolidation
h. Confabulation
i. Recognition
j. Repression

B. Multiple-Choice Questions Testing Factual Knowledge

1. Memories are permanently stored in the:
   a. long-term memory
   b. sensory memory
   c. short-term memory
   d. all of the above

2. Humans have a sensory memory that corresponds to their sense of:
   a. taste
   b. smell
   c. vision
   d. all of the above   Objective 1.1

3. The memory that lasts about twenty seconds and is maintained by acoustic rehearsal is:
   a. sensory memory
   b. long-term memory
   c. short-term memory
   d. acoustic memory   Objective 1.1

4. If you were asked to "shadow" a message, you would:
   a. ignore it
   b. repeat it aloud
   c. focus your attention on it
   d. try to remember it for later recall   Objective 1.2

5. In his research on sensory memory, Sperling flashed a twelve-item pattern on a screen. He found that subjects could report:
   a. only the top row of four items
   b. only the bottom row of four items
   c. any one of the rows
   d. all three rows   Objective 1.2

6. One way to interfere with information held in short-term memory is:
   a. to engage in elaborative rehearsal
   b. to engage in maintenance rehearsal
   c. to count backwards from one hundred by threes
   d. all of the above   Objective 1.3

7. The type of rehearsal that is especially effective in transferring information from short- to long-term memory is:
   a. effective rehearsal
   b. elaborative rehearsal
   c. maintenance rehearsal
   d. recombinatory rehearsal   Objective 1.3

8. Essay tests require _____; multiple-choice tests require _____.
   a. recall; recognition
   b. recognition; recall
   c. recall; recall
   d. recognition; recognition   Objective 2.1

9. The feeling that what you're presently experiencing has happened before, even though you know it has not is called:
   a. déjà vu
   b. key word system
   c. repression
   d. eidetic imagery   Objective 2.2

10. Techniques we can use to improve our memories are called:
    a. eidetic techniques
    b. confabulation techniques
    c. consolidation techniques
    d. mnemonic devices   Objective 2.2

11. Most of the people who have the ability to form eidetic images are:
    a. women
    b. men

    c. blind
    d. children   Objective 2.2

12. Distortion in memory can be produced by:
     a. expectations about the outcome
     b. stereotypes
     c. suggestions from other people
     d. all of the above   Objective 2.2

13. Loftus's research on eyewitness testimony indicates:
     a. eyewitnesses often lie to protect themselves
     b. eyewitnesses can distort the truth without realizing it
     c. eyewitnesses are typically accurate in their recall
     d. none of the above   Objective 2.2

14. The serial position curve indicates that the most trouble in recall comes when trying to
     remember items from:
     a. the first part of a list
     b. the middle of the list
     c. the last part of the list
     d. all parts of the list are equally hard to remember   Objective 2.2

15. The dual memory view states that there are two separate memory systems:
     a. sensory memory and short-term memory
     b. sensory memory and long-term memory
     c. short-term memory and long-term memory
     d. recognition and recall   Objective 3.1

16. Which of the following supports a depth of processing view?
     a. anterograde amnesia
     b. serial position curve
     c. the fact that semantic rehearsal is better than visual or auditory rehearsal
     d. all of the above   Objective 3.1

17. Neurophysiologists believe that temporary circulation of electrical impulses around
     complex loops of interconnected neurons is responsible for:
     a. confabulation
     b. retrograde amnesia
     c. long-term memory
     d. short-term memory   Objective 4.1

18. The notion that storage into long-term memory requires time is called:
     a. consolidation
     b. synaptic rehearsal
     c. enrichment
     d. confabulation   Objective 5.1

19. Which of the following theories is *least* well supported by empirical data?
     a. motivated forgetting
     b. decay
     c. interference
     d. repression   Objective 5.2

20. Which of the following pieces of experimental evidence indicates that memories are
     not permanent and unchangeable?
     a. Penfield's brain stimulation studies
     b. improved recall under hypnosis
     c. improved recall in psychoanalysis
     d. Loftus's studies of eyewitness testimony   Objective 5.3

C. Multiple-Choice Questions Testing Conceptual Knowledge

21. Which of the following groups of letters most likely exceeds the limits of short-term memory?
    a. I-O-U
    b. P-B-G-Q-X-R
    c. Q-X-L-T-M-A-R-C-F-P
    d. D-O-G-C-A-T-C-O-W-H-O-R-S-E   Objective 1.1

22. Suppose you are asked to remember a list of thirty words. Your short-term memory would facilitate your recall of:
    a. the first words on the list
    b. the middle words on the list
    c. the last words on the list
    d. both the first and last words but not the middle words   Objective 1.1

23. You notice that when you are watching a television show with no sound, it is difficult to listen to a radio broadcast that does not correspond to the television program. This demonstrates:
    a. confabulation
    b. selective attention
    c. proactive interference
    d. sensory gating   Objective 1.2

24. You are talking to a friend at a large party when you hear someone else mention your name. You immediately start paying attention to the other conversation. This is called:
    a. dichotic listening
    b. selective attention
    c. sensory gating
    d. shadowing   Objective 1.2

25. You are taking part in an experiment in which each eye sees a different slide projected for a fraction of a second. This experiment is similar to experiments in:
    a. dichotic listening
    b. selective attention
    c. sensory gating
    d. retroactive interference   Objective 1.2

26. A memory expert remembers long lists of words by imagining that he is walking down a familiar street and at each step placing an object on the sidewalk. To remember the list, he simply walks down the street and picks up the objects. This technique is an example of:
    a. déjà vu
    b. method of loci
    c. key word system
    d. eidetic imagery   Objective 2.1

27. You participate in three word-recall experiments. In the first you rehearse by looking at the word lists. In the second, you concentrate on words that rhyme with the list words. In the third, you study the meaning of the words. You will probably recall which list best?
    a. first
    b. second
    c. third
    d. all of them equally well   Objective 2.1

28. Jack is eighty-seven years old and has good recall of events before his sixty-fifth birthday. However, he remembers virtually nothing since then. He probably suffers from:
    a. anterograde amnesia
    b. retrograde amnesia

    c. repression
    d. consolidation   Objective 2.2

29. Retrograde amnesia is supportive of the existence of:
    a. confabulation
    b. consolidation
    c. elaborative rehearsal
    d. genetic influences in human memory   Objective 4.1

30. Suppose you conceptualize learning as building a complex system of roads in your brain. Consequently, forgetting involves taking the wrong road. This theory is similar to:
    a. repression
    b. decay
    c. motivated forgetting
    d. interference   Objective 5.1

31. Marlene is raped as a child but has no memory of this traumatic event. The theory that best accounts for this is:
    a. motivated forgetting
    b. interference
    c. consolidation
    d. decay   Objective 5.1

32. If you delivered electroconvulsive shock to a depressed patient, you would expect the resulting memory loss to be for that period of time:
    a. in the long distant past
    b. just after the patient woke up after the shock treatment
    c. about one to three days after the shock
    d. just before the shock was given   Objective 5.2

D.   Short Essay Questions

1. How does sensory memory differ from short-term memory? How does information transfer from sensory memory to short-term memory?   (Objectives 1.1, 1.2)

2. How does short-term memory differ from long-term memory? How does information transfer from short-term memory to long-term memory?   (Objectives 1.1, 1.3)

3. What is the difference between the dual memory view and the depth of processing view? Which is correct?   (Objective 3.1)

4. What is the neurophysiological explanation for memory transfer and storage? (Objective 4.1)

5. Do we ever forget things? Why do we sometimes have trouble remembering past events?   (Objective 5.1)

6. Are memories permanent? Cite research presented in the text to support your answer. (Objective 5.3)

Cognition and Problem Solving

7

□ **Chapter Summary**

I.   1. Thought is the process of organizing information in our minds to help accomplish some desired end. Humans excel in their ability for complex thinking.

      2. One of the first methods used to study thought was introspection: A subject was asked to describe in detail the thought process he or she used in problem

solving. Early behaviorists objected to the subjective nature of introspection and decreed that the study of thought processes had no place in the scientific investigation of behavior. Contemporary psychologists compromise these positions and believe cognitive (thought) processes should be studied in as objective a way as possible, although such study is very difficult.

II. 1. The mental constructs that enable us to classify objects and events are called concepts. Concepts are the building blocks of thought, allowing us to generalize from one situation to another.

2. Several theories have been formulated to explain how we develop concepts. In using a *global hypothesis* you assume that the characteristics of a particular member of a concept category are the defining characteristics of all members of the category, at least until further experience indicates you are wrong. In using a *focusing strategy* you start with a set of characteristics you believe to characterize a concept and, as you gain more experience with varied category members, begin eliminating those characteristics not shared by all members. In using a *scanning strategy* you begin with a limited group of defining characteristics and then systematically compare category members to nonmembers to determine the relevant features that define the concept.

3. Young children tend to be scanners and to overextend categories; adults are more likely to adopt a global focusing strategy, which makes errors of underextension more common. People are likely to build new concepts by using a "win–stay, lose–shift" strategy—that is, they stay with a concept usage that appears correct but change their concept if they receive feedback indicating they have used the concept incorrectly.

4. Natural concepts are categories we use every day. Because arbitrary categories are much easier to define and study, natural concepts are seldom examined in laboratory experiments. Rosch criticizes this practice because she thinks we use different strategies to encode natural concepts. She believes that natural concepts (such as *birds*) are encoded in terms of a prototype and an understanding of the allowable degree of variation in stimuli regarded as members of the category.

III. 1. Problem solving requires a knowledge of concepts and the relationships among them. Reproductive thinking involves the direct application of previous knowledge to a new situation, whereas in creative thinking previously learned rules cannot be directly applied, and a novel solution must be generated.

2. Problem solving can be conceptualized as a three-step process. First, the problem must be interpreted. For a difficult problem, often the best strategy is to try to examine the problem from several perspectives; however, we have a tendency to cling to a commonplace interpretation of a problem, despite the fact it is not helpful in a particular situation. This is called fixation, and it can be influenced by situational factors. A particular type of fixation, called functional fixedness, is the tendency to view an object as being used only for its customary function.

3. Next, we must search for possible solutions. An algorithmic strategy is a precisely stated set of rules that generally solves all problems of a particular type. A heuristic strategy does not guarantee success, but it has the advantage of usually being faster than an algorithmic method. People use several general heuristics, such as subgoal analysis (dividing a complex problem into smaller component problems) and means–end analysis (comparing present to desired end positions and trying to find a way to reduce the difference). Heuristics are useful in overcoming the limits imposed by our short-term memories; however, we often fall into a mental set in which we tend to repeat heuristic solutions that have worked in the past even when they are not appropriate. One way to reduce the effect of

mental set is to seek a period of incubation (a time to stop actively thinking about the problem).

4. The final step in problem solving is deciding when a satisfactory solution is reached. Reaching a solution often involves insight, a sudden perception of the correct solution. Kohler's work with chimpanzees provided evidence that animals as well as humans do not always solve problems by trial and error, as the behaviorists maintained. At times, however, deciding on the best solution is difficult, and pressures of time and cognitive capacity may determine when the problem solving ends.

5. Exceptionally creative people solve problems much as the rest of us do, except their experiences appear to be more intense in some respects. Creative thought is characterized by sudden insight, often after a period of incubation. In addition, creative people tend to show independence in judgment and preference for the asymmetrical and complex.

IV. 1. In making decisions, two sets of variables are considered: the value one places on the potential outcomes (called utility); and the likelihood that each outcome will actually take place (called probability). Although we seldom formally calculate utility and probability in making a decision, research demonstrates that we generally follow this model in decision making. Research also shows that if we formalize this process by filling out a balance sheet, we tend to have fewer regrets about the decisions we make.

V. 1. We do not, however, always make logical decisions. When we must make decisions under unusual stress, our decision-making abilities may be impaired by rationalization (making up excuses), procrastination (putting off action until a later time), and buck passing (blaming someone else).

2. Also, when decisions are complex and exceed our limited cognitive capabilities, we reduce our possible choices, often ignoring pertinent information. This sometimes leads to choices that are less than optimal.

3. People often rely on heuristics to solve problems. If the limitations of these heuristics are ignored, these strategies can lead to serious errors. The representativeness heuristic involves stereotyping people and attributing to them stereotyped characteristics. Although this is a useful method of reducing information, people using it sometimes overlook objective information and base their judgments on inaccurate data. The availability heuristic specifies that easy-to-remember events are more frequent than events that are difficult to remember. Although this information is generally useful, factors other than frequency of occurrence affect our ability to recall events. Even when we are rewarded for correct judgments, heuristics may override the rewards, and judgments may be biased, causing misperceptions regarding risk and reinforcing erroneous stereotypes. Perhaps by learning about common biases we can learn to make better decisions.

☐ **Self-Test**

A. Matching Questions

_____ 1. Method in which the subject attempts to describe his or her thought process

a. Concept

_____ 2. The process of organizing information in our minds to accomplish a desired end

b. Global hypothesis

c. Creative thinking

d. Scanning strategy

_____ 3. Assumption of all features of an object as defining characteristics of its category

_____ 4. Systematic search of category items to define category characteristics

_____ 5. Direct application of previous knowledge to a new situation

e. Introspection

f. Reproductive thinking

g. Focusing strategy

h. Thought

_____ 6. General tendency to retain a common interpretation of a problem, even though it is useless

_____ 7. A set of rules that usually leads to a correct solution

_____ 8. Strategy of reducing a complex problem into simpler component problems

_____ 9. Tendency to repeat a solution that has worked in the past

_____10. Probabilistic matching of an event to a stereotyped category

_____11. A sudden perception of the correct solution

a. Fixation

b. Representativeness heuristic

c. Subgoal analysis

d. Algorithm

e. Mental set

f. Functional fixedness

g. Heuristic

h. Means–end analysis

i. Incubation

j. Insight

k. Availability heuristic

B. Multiple-Choice Questions Testing Factual Knowledge

1. The major problem with using the method of introspection to study thought is that:
   a. people have no insight into their own thoughts
   b. it is not objectively measurable
   c. it can only be used to study algorithmic thought
   d. it can only be used to study heuristic thought   Objective 1.1

2. A major difficulty we encounter in problem solving is the cognitive limitations imposed by:
   a. short-term memory
   b. long-term memory
   c. both short-term and long-term memory
   d. our perceptual systems   Objective 1.1

3. According to the text, the building blocks of thought are:
   a. heuristics
   b. insights
   c. algorithms
   d. concepts   Objective 2.1

4. The categories that we use every day, such as _furniture, dogs,_ etc., are called:
   a. constructs
   b. arranged constructs
   c. predetermined concepts
   d. natural concepts   Objective 2.1

5. The concept formation strategy in which you begin with a general composite hypothesis and gradually narrow in on the relevant characteristics is:
   a. win–stay, lose–shift
   b. scanning strategy
   c. focusing strategy
   d. global hypothesis   Objective 2.2

6. The person most likely to use a scanning strategy is:
   a. an adult male
   b. an adult female
   c. a child
   d. a psychologist   Objective 2.2

7. If a person has adopted a global focusing strategy, the errors he or she will most likely commit will be errors of:
   a. overextension
   b. underextension
   c. mental set
   d. functional fixedness   Objective 2.2

8. Rosch proposes that in everyday usage, concepts are encoded according to:
   a. a prototype
   b. an understanding of the degree to which stimuli can vary
   c. both a and b
   d. none of the above   Objective 2.2

9. A sudden perception of the solution for a problem is called:
   a. insight
   b. incubation
   c. satisfactory solution
   d. revealed solution   Objective 3.1

10. Kohler demonstrated that insight learning is available to:
    a. babies
    b. small children
    c. mentally retarded adults
    d. chimpanzees   Objective 3.1

11. Which of the following characteristics is most frequently associated with highly creative problem solvers?
    a. exceptionally high IQ
    b. lack of patience
    c. independence in judgment
    d. preference for simple and symmetrical relationships   Objective 3.1

12. The first step in solving a problem is:
    a. interpreting the problem
    b. deciding when a satisfactory answer has been found
    c. searching for solutions
    d. establishing a mental set   Objective 3.2

13. The tendency to view an object as being usable only for its customary use is called:
    a. mental set
    b. natural construct
    c. an algorithm
    d. functional fixedness   Objective 3.2

14. The inclination to repeat a solution that has worked in the past, even though it is not helpful, is called:
    a. mental set
    b. functional fixedness
    c. fixation
    d. incubation   Objective 3.2

15. Another name for a rule-of-thumb problem-solving strategy is:
    a. algorithm
    b. heuristic

    c. mental set
    d. subgoal analysis   Objective 3.3

16. The two factors that affect a rational decision-making process are the probability of each potential outcome and each outcome's:
    a. length
    b. utility
    c. certainty
    d. consequences   Objective 4.1

17. Some decision-making processes involve listing possibilities and consequences. This is generally referred to as:
    a. a balance sheet
    b. a mnemonic device
    c. a curriculum vitae
    d. a guidance session   Objective 4.1

18. Compared to normal decision-making processes, decisions made under stress are _____ likely to be effective.
    a. more
    b. less
    c. about equally
    d. for men more and for women less   Objective 5.1

19. One way to deal with making a difficult decision is to put it off to a later date. This is called:
    a. rationalization
    b. buck-passing
    c. subgoal analysis
    d. procrastination   Objective 5.1

20. Frequent events are generally better recalled than infrequent events. This is the assumption we make when using:
    a. means–end analysis
    b. subgoal analysis
    c. the availability heuristic
    d. the representativeness heuristic   Objective 5.2

C. *Multiple-Choice Questions Testing Conceptual Knowledge*

21. Suppose you volunteer for a psychology experiment in which you are asked to describe your thought processes. This experimental method would be similar to:
    a. an algorithm
    b. a heuristic
    c. introspection
    d. subgoal analysis   Objective 1.1

22. You see a birch tree and declare that the defining characteristics of all trees are: white bark; drops leaves in fall; seeds are catkins. The concept-formation strategy you are using is:
    a. global hypothesis
    b. scanning strategy
    c. focusing strategy
    d. win–stay, lose–shift   Objective 2.1

23. Gene goes to Las Vegas and keeps putting his money on red at the roulette wheel as long as red comes up, but moves his money to black as soon as black is a winner. His strategy is:
    a. global hypothesis
    b. algorithm

c. scanning hypothesis
d. win-stay, lose-shift   Objective 2.2

24. Which of the following would most likely be a characteristic feature rather than a defining feature of the category "sheep"?
    a. has hair
    b. bears live young
    c. feeds its young with milk
    d. is white   Objective 2.2

25. Suppose someone asks you to list all the possible uses of a brick you can think of. This would most likely be a test of your:
    a. prototype knowledge
    b. creative thinking
    c. ability to use algorithms
    d. reproductive thinking   Objective 3.1

26. Suppose you are working a word puzzle in which you are to arrange the following letters into a word: S E V O A R I. You repeatedly try to solve the problem by starting the word with an R, although you know that this response will not produce a correct answer. Your tendency is called: (note: the word is *ovaries*).
    a. global hypothesis
    b. fixation
    c. functional fixedness
    d. win-stay, lose-shift   Objective 3.2

27. Suppose you are constructing a suit for an astronaut to use when on the moon. You tackle the problem by dividing it into smaller problems, such as fabric, life-support, elimination, etc. This is an example of:
    a. subgoal analysis
    b. means-end analysis
    c. utility analysis
    d. reproductive thinking   Objective 3.2

28. You have been working hard on a problem without much luck. Your professor tells you to go for a walk and relax. She is prescribing:
    a. an algorithm
    b. a period of incubation
    c. a period of insight
    d. a mental set   Objective 3.2

29. Suppose I tell you that to calculate the mean of a distribution, you must always add the scores and divide the total by the number of scores. This is an example of:
    a. a subgoal analysis
    b. a heuristic strategy
    c. an algorithmic strategy
    d. a means-end analysis   Objective 3.3

30. Suppose you are receiving some help in making a difficult decision. Your consultant first has you specify all possible outcomes and then asks you to evaluate how desirable each outcome would be. This second step is called establishing:
    a. probability
    b. a rationalization
    c. utility
    d. a means-end analysis   Objective 4.1

31. Marcia does not study and fails a test. She explains that she failed because the test was much too difficult and the teacher was unfair. This is an example of:
    a. rationalization
    b. buck-passing

     c. means–end analysis

     d. procrastination   Objective 5.1

32. You meet John, who is forty-five years old, intelligent, dedicated, verbal, concerned about other people's welfare, and wealthy. You conclude that he is more likely to be a doctor than a truck driver. You are using the heuristic called:

     a. probabilistic inference

     b. utility analysis

     c. availability

     d. representativeness   Objective 5.2

D. *Short Essay Questions*

1. What is a concept? How are concepts formed? (Objective 2.1)

2. How do creative problem solvers differ from common people? (Objective 3.1)

3. What are some tendencies that interfere with problem solving? (Objective 3.2)

4. Which is better, an algorithmic or a heuristic problem-solving strategy? (Objective 3.3)

5. How rational or logical is human decision making? What factors produce nonrational decisions? (Objective 4.1)

Life-span Development ■ 8

☐ **Chapter Summary**

I. 1. Developmental psychology is the branch of psychology that attempts to explain the regular patterns of growth and change that occur during the human life cycle. Developmental psychologists generally ask two closely related questions: How do people change as they grow older, and why do these changes occur in the ways they do?

II. 1. Development is sequential; present change builds on previous development. However, individuals vary widely in the age at which certain behaviors develop. The concept of sequence emphasizes that development is not random and that it is predictable.

2. Any developmental event is the product of heredity (inherited factors) and environment (learned factors).

3. Hereditary traits are established at conception when a male germ cell (or sperm) penetrates the female germ cell (the egg or ovum). The germ cells, both male and female, are produced by a cell division process called *meiosis*. Each germ cell contains twenty-three chromosomes. At conception, the two sets of twenty-three chromosomes pair up to the normal human complement of forty-six chromosomes.

4. These chromosomes carry the genes, which are the basic units of the hereditary mechanism. A gene is a small portion of a DNA (deoxyribonucleic acid) molecule containing a code for the development and maintenance of a living organism. Genetic instructions can be modified by inadequate nutrition, various drugs such as thalidomide, and emotional deprivation. Some kinds of genetic defects such as PKU (phenylketonuria) can be compensated for by environmental intervention. Almost all genetic traits, at least to some extent, are susceptible to environmental influences. Even the retardation produced by Down's syndrome can be reduced by environmental enrichment.

III. 1. Newborns come equipped with a set of motor reflexes that help them survive. The rooting reflex is a tendency to turn the head in the direction of an object stimulating the cheek. The grasping reflex is the tendency to firmly grasp an object placed in the hand.

2. Human infants also have sophisticated perceptual capabilities. Young babies can discriminate the sound of a familiar voice and may have the ability to determine the source of a sound. Through experiments with the "visual cliff," psychologists have demonstrated that newborns can also see depth, although 20/20 vision does not develop until a child is six to twelve months old.

IV. 1. Development of thinking (called cognitive development) can be viewed as a series of qualitative changes (changes from one discrete form to another). Jean Piaget has proposed the most influential stage (qualitative) theory of cognitive development. He believes that intellectual development progresses through four major stages: the sensorimotor stage (birth to two years), the preoperational stage (two to six years), the concrete-operational stage (six to twelve years), and the formal-operational years (age twelve to adulthood). Other psychologists maintain that development is quantitative, each new development growing from previous behaviors. Both perspectives have merit.

2. Newborns are capable of learning from birth and perhaps even prenatally. Experimental observation leads one to believe, as did John S. Watson, that infants derive pleasure from solving problems. Research indicates that infants can remember over fairly long periods of time.

3. During the sensorimotor period infants learn to act in the world, but they do not appear to be able to think about their behavior until they develop the object concept (also called the concept of object permanence). Early in this period infants do not understand that objects and people have a permanent existence. Instead they act as if objects cease to exist when the objects are removed from their presence. The development of object permanence is gradual: At four months a baby will reach for a partially hidden object; between four and eight months, it will visually track an object being placed behind a screen; between eight and twelve months, it will search for a hidden object. Only in the last period of this stage will a baby follow the placement of an object from one location to another to another.

4. When the child learns that objects can be represented by symbols, it can begin to acquire language. These preschool years (the preoperational period) are most importantly characterized by representational thought, the ability to think about objects not immediately present. A preschooler's thought differs from an older child's in that it is egocentric (the child is unable to understand a situation from another person's perspective).

5. Older children (concrete-operational stage) can think in logical ways that preschoolers cannot. During this stage they learn conservation, the ability to attend to more than one dimension of an object. Piaget suggests that this learning reflects a qualitative change in cognition, but recent work by Gelman suggests that conservation may be the result of the development of several cognitive capabilities. During the concrete operation stage, children also can remember better, perhaps due to a more sophisticated understanding of retrieval strategies or more experience with objects they are remembering. Metacognition (our knowledge of what things we know and can do) also develops during later childhood.

6. Formal-operational intelligence expands the child's cognitive abilities to include systematic (scientific) testing of hypotheses, and hypothetical and abstract thinking.

7. Cognitive development does not stop with the formal operations stage at adolescence. Early adulthood (age twenty to forty) is a time of peak intellectual accomplishment, especially on tasks involving memory, speed, or intellectual flexibility. Middle adulthood (age forty to sixty) is accompanied by even better verbal skills and reasoning ability as well as increases in IQ, provided the individual remains healthy. Only on tasks involving hand-eye coordination do middle adults perform less well than when they were younger. (Recent research, however, indicates that some slight decline can generally be detected in laboratory experiments.) Like younger adults, older adults have most difficulty in remembering events from the distant past. Of course, the effects of aging vary a great deal from person to person and result from both biological (hereditary) and environmental factors. It appears that the active use of one's mind throughout adulthood contributes to good cognitive functioning in old age.

V. 1. Interaction with other humans begins at birth, and early in development a baby will form an attachment (or bond) to its principal caregivers. Social learning theorists specify that attachment is a learned response to need satisfaction (food, warmth, comfort, etc.). Harlow used newborn monkeys separated at birth from their mothers to demonstrate that need satisfaction alone was not enough to cause the development of attachment. Indeed, when placed in a cage with a wire milk-giving surrogate (mother substitute) and a terrycloth nonmilk-giving surrogate, the baby monkeys showed attachment preferences for the terrycloth surrogate. Factors that added to attachment were: tactile sensation, food, warmth, and rocking motions. Disrupting the attachment in monkeys by separating babies from their mothers produced profound behavioral abnormalities, perhaps caused by abnormal development in the cerebellum and the limbic system.

2. Although similar research with human infants would certainly be unethical, infants who have been deprived of cognitive sensory and emotional stimulation exhibit apathetic behavior. In comparing attachment behaviors of infants raised at home to those attending day-care centers, no real differences appear. The quality of the day-care center may have some impact on attachment, but more research must be conducted to determine the relationship between quality of care and attachment.

3. By the time a child is two years old, he or she has begun to develop a sense of self. Consequently, the parents' role changes from caregiver to teacher and disciplinarian. Parents typically attempt to teach their child society's rules and values in a process called socialization. The basic goal of socialization is internalization, the incorporation of society's values into the self-concept so that violation produces feelings of guilt.

4. Gender roles are patterns of behavior that are either masculine or feminine. Some gender role differences are present at a very early age, indicating a possible biological basis. For example, newborn boys are more active than girls, and male toddlers tend to cry more and sleep less than girls of the same age. Also, sex hormone differences may predispose males to behave more aggressively than females in certain situations. Biological differences probably interact with environmental factors. The importance of environment is clearly seen in cross-cultural comparisons, which show widely varying gender roles.

5. According to Freud, gender roles develop as a result of the oedipal conflict between the ages of three and five or six. At this age, children see themselves as rivals of their same-sex parent for the affection of their opposite-sex parent. Anxiety develops from the ensuing conflict and eventually the child identifies with (assumes the gender role of) the same-sex parent. Even though the oedipal conflict may not be present in all cultures, identification is an important part of gender-role acquisition.

6. Social learning theorists reject the notion of the oedipal conflict and believe the gender role acquisition is a gradual learning process shaped by parents and society. This theory rests on the assumption that parents treat their male and female children differently, an assumption that is supported by research. It is also quite possible that parents interpret the same behavior differently, depending on whether it is displayed by a son or a daughter.

7. Cognitive development theorists believe that once a child recognizes himself as male or herself as female, the child will be automatically motivated to imitate behaviors observed in members of the same sex. The cognitive development view differs from others in that it specifies that children must know their gender identity *before* they learn the appropriate gender role behaviors.

8. Many psychologists argue that a full understanding of sex role acquisition probably will incorporate aspects of more than one theoretical approach.

9. Moral development involves learning rules of proper conduct. Freudian psychologists believe a child's moral code is established during the resolution of the oedipal conflict. Research, however, has indicated that moral development is more gradual than would be specified by this approach.

10. Social learning theorists view moral development as a product of reinforcement and punishment patterns. Research shows that power-assertive techniques of punishment tend to be associated with low levels of moral development and that reasoning with children appears to be associated with high levels of moral development.

11. The cognitive development view proposes that a child goes through stages of moral development. Kohlberg has formulated a theory based on subjects' responses when faced with a moral dilemma. His theory specifies three general levels of moral development: the preconventional stage (motivated by winning the approval of others); the conventional stage (motivated by fear of punishment); and the postconventional stage (motivated by the recognition of universal ethical principles). Adults tend to be more advanced in their moral reasoning than children, but few adults function at the postconventional level. Cross-cultural studies have supported Kohlberg's theory, and many psychologists believe it to be the best presently available.

12. The period of adolescence is marked by the onset of puberty, the period of sexual maturation. The major concern of this period is to establish an independent identity. Erikson states that adolescents must establish a sense of personal continuity by trying out different roles before they can resolve the adolescent "identity crisis." Some—but not all—adolescents have a difficult time achieving this goal.

13. Some psychologists, such as Freud, believe that personality development ceases in adulthood. However, recent research has indicated that an individual's outlook changes as he or she matures through adulthood. Early adulthood is typically a period of action, in which commitments are made and responsibilities assumed. This period today poses special challenges to women, since their roles in our society are undergoing marked change. Around age thirty a crisis often develops in which the person questions the future direction of his or her life. After the turmoil of this crisis has subsided, the next stage of adulthood is characterized as an extremely productive period. At about age forty, the mid-life transition begins. In this crisis, people question their past accomplishments and outline their future goals. Upon resolution of this crisis, middle adulthood emerges and is characterized by increased importance of personal relationships and awareness that life is finite. Stress is especially acute when a traumatic event (such as retirement or death of a spouse) occurs at an unexpected time in the life cycle; however, most adults cope successfully with life, including its final stages.

☐ Self-Test

A. Matching Questions

_____ 1. What every normal human has twenty-three pair of

_____ 2. Baby's tendency to turn its head in the direction of an object stimulating its cheek

_____ 3. Experimental apparatus for testing infant depth perception

_____ 4. The general category in which behavioral and learning theories would fit

_____ 5. Knowledge that things have a permanent existence

a. Genes
b. Rooting reflex
c. Qualitative theory
d. Quantitative theory
e. DNA
f. Grasping reflex
g. Object concept
h. Chromosomes
i. Visual cliff

_____ 6. Piaget's stage during which conservation develops

a. Formal operations
b. Cognitive development

_____ 7. One's ability to monitor his or her own thoughts

_____ 8. Piaget's stage in which children learn to think systematically and hypothetically

_____ 9. A psychological term for a strong emotional bond between baby and caregiver

_____10. Substitute mother

c. Metacognition
d. Preoperational stage
e. Surrogate
f. Concrete operations
g. Attachment
h. Love

_____11. The process of instilling society's values in an individual

_____12. Results in the child's recognition that the opposite-sex parent is unattainable

_____13. Knowing one's own sex

_____14. Kohlberg's stage in which moral reasoning depends on conforming to society's standards

_____15. Marked by the onset of puberty

a. Oedipal conflict
b. Identification
c. Gender role
d. Preconventional
e. Socialization
f. Gender identification
g. Adolescence
h. Internalization
i. Conventional

B. Multiple-Choice Questions Testing Factual Knowledge

1. Developmental psychologists believe that human development progresses:
   a. sequentially
   b. unpredictably
   c. with little individual variation
   d. all of the above   Objective 1.1

2. Which of the following can affect an unborn fetus?
   a. drugs
   b. malnutrition
   c. thalidomide
   d. all of the above   Objective 2.1

3. If a human cell undergoes meiosis, how many single chromosomes normally remain?
   a. twelve
   b. twenty-three
   c. thirty-six
   d. forty-six   Objective 2.2

4. The advantage of the rooting reflex is that it helps the infant:
   a. cling to its mother
   b. not swallow air, only milk
   c. find a food source
   d. none of the above; it has no advantage in humans   Objective 3.1

5. Of which of the following is a newborn _not_ capable?
   a. 20/20 vision
   b. depth perception
   c. locating the direction from which a sound comes
   d. discriminating different sounds   Objective 3.1

6. Which of the following is _not_ one of Piaget's stages of development?
   a. concrete operations
   b. preoperational period

c. sensorimotor period
d. hypothetical period   Objective 4.2

7. According to an experiment reported in the text, if you tied a string from a baby's arm to a mobile hanging above her crib, what outcome could you expect?
   a. she would cry and be frightened
   b. she would go to sleep
   c. she would exhibit pleasurable response when she learned she could control the mobile
   d. she would not learn the relationship between her movement and that of the mobile   Objective 4.2

8. Sensorimotor intelligence is best characterized by:
   a. action
   b. concept construction
   c. thought
   d. conservation   Objective 4.2

9. A young infant often acts as if objects stop existing when they are moved out of the infant's perceptual range. This tendency is called:
   a. attachment
   b. concept formation
   c. sensorimotor intelligence
   d. an object concept   Objective 4.2

10. The increased memory capacity that older children have is probably related to all of the following except:
    a. greater familiarity with commonly used items
    b. more highly developed short-term memories
    c. better learning strategies
    d. increased use of memory cues   Objective 4.2

11. According to the text, people are intellectually most flexible during which decade of their life?
    a. thirty to forty
    b. forty to fifty
    c. fifty to sixty
    d. sixty to seventy   Objective 4.3

12. At least some decline in old age is typically associated with which of the following memory systems?
    a. short-term memory
    b. long-term memory
    c. both a and b
    d. none of the above   Objective 4.3

13. When Harlow's monkeys were deprived of attachment, they eventually:
    a. grew out of the attachment stage into normal adults
    b. died
    c. became withdrawn and apathetic
    d. became more dependent on friendships in their peer group   Objective 5.1

14. Generally, studies of attachment deprivation have not been conducted with humans because:
    a. humans are extremely resistant to attachment deprivation
    b. humans do not form strong attachments
    c. such research is unethical
    d. the consequences of such deprivation on humans are not particularly interesting   Objective 5.1

15. Which of the following appears to be a major difference between infants in day care and infants raised at home?
    a. day-care infants formed attachments to their teachers rather than their mothers
    b. day-care infants formed weaker attachments
    c. day-care infants formed attachments later in their development
    d. none of the above   Objective 5.1

16. Some critics distrust the results of studies comparing day care to home care because the studies have been typically conducted in day-care centers that predominantly:
    a. offer high-quality care
    b. are very large
    c. serve low-income families
    d. are minority oriented   Objective 5.1

17. Research has shown that there appear to be differences between the sexes in their:
    a. aggressiveness
    b. intelligence
    c. creativity
    d. dominance   Objective 5.2

18. According to Erikson, the crisis encountered in adolescence centers around:
    a. sexual frustrations
    b. establishing an identity
    c. achieving one's goals
    d. evaluating one's contribution to society   Objective 5.4

19. Many adults encounter a time of crisis in which they ask "what is life all about now that I have done what I am supposed to do?" This crisis typically occurs around age:
    a. thirty
    b. forty
    c. fifty-five
    d. sixty-five   Objective 5.4

20. According to research and theory presented in the text, in the typical person's life the period of greatest stability is from:
    a. twenty to thirty
    b. thirty to forty
    c. fifty to sixty
    d. seventy to eighty   Objective 5.4

C. Multiple-Choice Questions Testing Conceptual Knowledge

21. Suppose your friend has a baby who is diagnosed as having the genetic defect called PKU (phenylketonuria). You would assume that treatment will consist of:
    a. genetic engineering
    b. drug therapy (chemotherapy)
    c. eating a special diet
    d. none of the above since there is no treatment for this disorder   Objective 2.1

22. Suppose you believe that human development is sequential, each new aspect of development stemming directly from previously developed abilities. Your theory would qualify as:
    a. quantitative
    b. qualitative
    c. both a and b
    d. none of the above   Objective 4.1

23. Jackie is shown a rattle she wants. Her mother partially hides it behind a book. Jackie now acts as if the rattle has ceased to exist. Jackie is probably about how old?
    a. two months

b. six months
c. ten months
d. fourteen months

Objective 4.2

24. Bobby is shown two balls of clay that he believes are the same size. As he watches, one ball is flattened. He now claims the flatter ball has more clay in it than the un-touched ball. He is in which of Piaget's stages?
    a. formal operations
    b. preoperational
    c. concrete operations
    d. sensorimotor

Objective 4.2

25. Gelman's research in which she tested children's conservation skills using toy mice is _____ Piaget's theory.
    a. supportive of
    b. contradictory to
    c. unrelated to
    d. essentially the same as research conducted according to

Objective 4.2

26. Jack is given an experiment to conduct. He approaches it by first specifying all possi-ble solutions and then systematically testing each until he arrives at the correct answer. He is probably in which of Piaget's stages?
    a. preoperational
    b. concrete operations
    c. hypothetical
    d. formal operations

Objective 4.2

27. Typing is primarily a speed-related skill. Which age group could generally be expected to be the best typists?
    a. ten- to sixteen-year-olds
    b. twenty- to thirty-year-olds
    c. thirty-five- to forty-five-year-olds
    d. fifty- to sixty-five-year-olds

Objective 4.3

28. Generalizing from Harlow's monkey studies, if a baby was routinely cuddled only by one woman and routinely fed only by another, the baby would most likely develop an attachment to:
    a. the cuddler
    b. the feeder
    c. both a and b
    d. neither a nor b

Objective 5.1

29. Jerry believes that children acquire their gender roles through a process of coping with a deep affection for the opposite-sex parent, a relationship that ultimately cannot be realized. To compensate, a child identifies with this parent and internalizes his or her gender role. Jerry's theory would be most like that of:
    a. social learning theorists
    b. biological theorists
    c. cognitive development theorists
    d. Freudian theorists

Objective 5.2

30. Louise's parents are attempting to teach her to accept their values and incorporate them into her own moral code. A psychologist would say the parents' goal is:
    a. attachment
    b. resolution of the oedipal conflict
    c. socialization
    d. moral development

Objective 5.3

31. Doris believes that moral reasoning is acquired through reinforcement of sex-appropriate behavior and punishment of sex-inappropriate behavior. She would best be classified as a:
    a. Freudian theorist
    b. biological theorist
    c. cognitive development theorist
    d. social learning theorist   Objective 5.3

32. John refuses to jaywalk because he is afraid he will get stopped by a policeman and ticketed. According to Kohlberg's theory of moral development, John is functioning at which of the following levels?
    a. conventional
    b. agreed
    c. preconventional
    d. authority   Objective 5.3

D. Short Essay Questions

1. What topics do developmental psychologists explore?   (Objective 1.1)

2. How does the hereditary mechanism work? How do heredity and environment influence development?   (Objectives 2.2, 2.3)

3. Describe the research techniques used in the study of perceptual and motor development in infants.   (Objective 3.2)

4. Describe Piaget's theory of cognitive development, and cite one major developmental change that occurs in each of his four stages.   (Objective 4.2)

5. Describe Harlow's research and generalize his results to account for human attachment behavior.   (Objective 5.1)

6. Restate the Freudian, social learning, and cognitive development perspectives that attempt to explain the acquisition of gender roles and moral development. (Objective 5.2)

7. What cognitive and personality changes take place in adulthood? Does one period of adulthood differ from other periods?   (Objectives 4.3, 5.4)

Language and Its Development

□ **Preview of the Chapter**
Major Concepts and Behavioral Objectives

CONCEPT 1   Language functions as our principal means of communication, facilitating most of the activities we consider uniquely human.

     1.1   Describe language and relate its function.

     1.2   Discuss how language can be structurally studied according to its phonology, morphology, and syntax.

CONCEPT 2   Chimps can learn sign language, an accomplishment that reflects an ability to communicate symbolically, conditioning, or a combination of both.

     2.1   Describe the procedures used in the chimpanzee studies, and discuss the results of these attempts to teach chimps to talk.

CONCEPT 3   A region in the human brain may be specialized for the acquisition of language, and there may be an optimal time in our development for learning language.

     3.1   Describe how the human brain is especially adapted for language learning.

     3.2   Define a *critical period* and cite evidence relating to the existence of a critical period for language learning.

CONCEPT 4   Language develops rapidly and sequentially. In early stages, this development is characterized by primitive grammatical rules, not simply imitation and reinforcement.

     4.1   Describe the sequence of stages in human language development.

     4.2   Discuss the factors that influence language acquisition.

CONCEPT 5   Some psychologists believe language determines the form of thought; others, that thought processes determine language use.

     5.1   Discuss the relationship between language and thought.

CONCEPT 6   Nonverbal communication—intonation, posture, gesture, and body movement—is subtle and harder to control than language.

     6.1   Define nonverbal communication and discuss individual differences in human sensitivity to nonverbal information.

CONCEPT 7   Nonverbal behavior, which is somewhat consistent and somewhat varied among cultures, is probably in part inherited and in part learned.

     7.1   Discuss the roles of heredity and environment in nonverbal communication.

□ **Chapter Summary**

I. 1. Language is complex and central to human existence. It functions as our primary means of communication. It is extremely flexible and rich in the meanings it can convey.

2. Because it is symbolic (using symbols to represent other objects and events), it allows us to communicate beyond the concrete and the present. Furthermore, the symbolism is arbitrary, being agreed on only by convention. Language is based on a principle of combination in which components are arranged in many different ways. This makes exact repetition of any sentence unlikely, unless it is a cliché.

3. To a large extent the structure of language determines its function. It can be structurally analyzed at three basic levels: phonology, morphology, and syntax.

4. A phoneme is a class of slightly varying sounds that speakers of a language perceive as linguistically similar. Different languages use somewhat different phoneme classes. Similarly, most languages exclude some phonemes that may be included in other languages. English uses about forty-five phonemes; other languages may have as few as fifteen to as many as eighty-five phonemes.

5. Every language has its own morphological rules for combining phonemes into meaningful units. A morpheme is the smallest unit of language that has meaning.

6. Syntax rules specify how words should be combined into phrases or sentences. Such rules are numerous and complex and, like other language structures, are arbitarily determined.

7. Linguistic competence refers to a person's grasp of the rules of grammar (morphology plus syntax). The application of this linguistic competence to interpreting or producing speech is called linguistic performance. Linguistic performance is a complex mental process, but it can be somewhat understood by examining a sentence's surface structure (the words themselves and their organization) and its deep structure (its meaning). The deep structure of a sentence can further be reduced to the basic propositions (or single ideas) expressed in the sentence.

8. Speaking and listening both involve the same structures but in different sequence: In speaking, the underlying representation is transformed into appropriate surface structure, whereas in listening surface structure is transformed into the propositions represented. The process involved in listening is probably performed by dividing the structure of a sentence into its subphrases (called constituents). Meaning is probably extracted from each constituent, and it is this shorthand representation of the original sentence that is remembered. According to this syntactic approach, constituents are probably identified by cues (such as prefixes, conjunctions, or pauses) imbedded in the syntax of the sentence.

9. The semantic approach, on the other hand, suggests that we infer meaning from listening to the key words in a sentence. Both the syntactic and semantic approaches are used in actual conversations.

II. 1. In the 1940s, Keith and Cathy Hayes unsuccessfully attempted to teach a chimpanzee named Vicki to talk. Their failure was attributed to chimpanzees' lack of the physiological development necessary for speech production. Beatrice and Allen Gardner repeated the Hayes's experiment with a chimp named Washoe, this time using Ameslan, the sign language used by deaf humans. After four years of training, Washoe had learned 160 signs, had learned to generalize a sign to unique situations, and had learned to use several signs in combination. The Gardners felt Washoe's "language" was roughly equivalent to that of a three-year-old child. David Premack has had similar results with a chimp named

Sarah, whom he taught a language based on plastic symbols that represented words. Another chimp, Lana, learned a computer language called Yerkish. She was able to create names for previously unnamed objects. From such research, some psychologists conclude that chimps have at least some capacity for understanding syntax.

2. Other psychologists (such as Herbert Terrace, who taught sign language to a chimp named Nim Chimpsky) question whether this capacity has been adequately demonstrated. They believe that chimps simply create sentences by word substitution. Also, chimps' language growth is extremely limited when compared to that of children. Further research will probably be directed at establishing the limits of a chimp's ability to communicate, rather than simply determining whether or not chimps can talk.

III. 1. Humans seem particularly well adapted for language learning. Compared to the brain of a chimpanzee, the human brain is larger, heavier, and more convoluted (wrinkled); it has a greater area devoted to sensorimotor activities; and most important, it is lateralized (different functions are controlled by different halves of the brain). The left hemisphere is specialized for analytical thought, and that specialization makes language learning possible. Noam Chomsky believes that all languages are similar and that the human brain has built-in underlying mechanisms for language learning.

2. Studies of people with anterior aphasia (a language disorder produced by brain damage) contribute to psychologists' understanding of language.

3. There is evidence for the existence of a "critical period" in human development during which a person has a special facility for learning language. Such critical periods for attachment (called "imprinting") have been demonstrated in lower animals. The critical-period theory in language learning is supported by research showing that brain injury resulting in speech loss becomes less correctable with increased age. Also, deaf people have great difficulty learning language after, but not before, puberty; and all people typically experience greater difficulty in learning a second language after puberty than before. Lenneburg argues that a critical period of language learning may be related to progressive lateralization of the brain. Other researchers doubt Lenneburg's suggestions, pointing out that experimentation has indicated that lateralization occurs very early in life.

IV. 1. All normal children go through a series of stages in the development of language, regardless of their culture. There are, however, individual variations in the rate of progress through the stages.

2. From the earliest weeks of life, newborns develop three distinguishable patterns of crying: the basic rhythmical cry, the anger cry, and the pain cry. By age three months they can coo; by six or seven months they can babble. Babbling does not seem to be directly related to adult speech. It contains sounds from all languages. Intonation (pitch pattern) and gesturing are also important in prespeech communication.

3. Children speak their first words at about the end of their first year. These words all focus on present objects and events. Meaning is changed according to context and by using different intonations.

4. Around age two, children begin putting words together in sentences, the first being two-word combinations. This telegraphic speech is characterized by elimination of descriptors and connectors; it focuses on nouns and action verbs. Even this early speech is highly structured.

5. Between age two and five, complex grammatical rules are mastered, and the child's ability to communicate moves beyond the immediate situation. These rules are acquired in sequential steps. Occasionally, young children interpret complex sentences correctly, only to develop incorrect interpretations as they get older. This is probably the result of a temporary grammatical advancement that in some cases results in incorrect formations. Young children often commit errors of overregularization in which they extend rules to instances in which the rules do not apply.

6. Although most parents feel that their children learn language through imitation and reinforcement, research indicates that parents reinforce meaning rather than grammar. Consequently, most psychologists believe that language acquisition is highly creative, although reinforcement and imitation probably have some effect.

V. 1. Benjamin Whorf argued that language shapes thought. Through forced observation dictated by a particular language, a person perceives the world in a way consistent with the confines of his or her language. This notion is called the linguistic relativity hypothesis.

2. Recent research on cultural differences in the perception of color reveals that different cultures perceive the same colors, regardless of the number of basic color terms in their language. This evidence is contradictory to the linguistic relativity hypothesis, which states that language determines thought.

3. Other theorists believe that thought processes determine language characteristics. These psychologists attempt to reveal language universals, those features found in all languages. Our long-term memories and our ability to fit a message into an appropriate context also determine our ability to understand language.

VI. 1. Messages can be communicated nonverbally through facial expressions, body movements, and voice intonation.

2. By administering a test called PONS (Profile of Nonverbal Sensitivity) to hundreds of subjects, Rosenthal found evidence for individual differences in receptiveness to nonverbal messages. Most women and those men in jobs demanding nonverbal sensitivity scored higher than most other men on PONS. Also, adults are more sensitive than children, indicating the influence of learning on nonverbal sensitivity.

3. Apparently nonverbal channels of communication are more difficult to control than verbal channels. Consequently, people tend to trust them more than verbal messages as indicators of true feeling. A double-bind situation is created when verbal and nonverbal messages contradict one another. A double-bind situation may be a cause of schizophrenia. Research has shown that people oftentimes send unintentional nonverbal messages that do not reflect the message they are trying to convey.

VII. 1. Heredity and environment are both important in the development of nonverbal communication. Charles Darwin suggested that man's nonverbal behaviors evolved because at one time they had survival value. Support of a biological basis in nonverbal communication comes from studies of blind and disabled children who show appropriate nonverbal behavior without having observed it. Also, nonverbal expressions of several basic emotions can be correctly identified by people from diverse cultures.

2. Nonverbal communication is also influenced by environment, as evidenced by individual and cultural differences in nonverbal expressions. Different cultures score differently on the PONS, highest scores going to people from cultures

similar to the United States. In addition, adult women are more expressive than men, although this gender difference is absent in children. Finally, monkeys raised in isolation were retarded in nonverbal skills compared to those raised by adults, indicating the importance of learning in nonverbal communication.

☐ **Self-Test**

A. Matching Questions

_____ 1. Involves the use of sounds to represent objects, events, and ideas

_____ 2. Sounds of a language

_____ 3. Words that can stand alone

_____ 4. Morphology plus syntax

_____ 5. Meaningful units of the underlying representation of a sentence

a. Symbolic
b. Grammar
c. Morphology
d. Free morphemes
e. Linguistic performance
f. Propositions
g. Syntax
h. Phonemes
i. Phonology

_____ 6. A group of words that has a conceptual unity

_____ 7. Analysis of language according to pauses, prefixes, suffixes, connectors, etc.

_____ 8. Division of the brain into left and right hemispheres

_____ 9. "Baby do!" for example

_____10. "I have two hands and two *foots,* for example

a. Anterior aphasia
b. Syntactic approach
c. Overregularization
d. Linguistic relativity hypothesis
e. Constituent
f. Telegraphic speech
g. Lateralization
h. Double bind
i. Semantic approach
j. Critical period

B. Multiple-Choice Questions Testing Factual Knowledge

1. Which of the following is *not* a characteristic of language?
   a. It is symbolic.
   b. It is tied to concrete representations.
   c. It can be used to express past, present, and future.
   d. All of the above are characteristics of language. Objective 1.1

2. Which of the following is *not* one of the basic levels of structural analysis for language?
   a. morphology
   b. syntax
   c. linguistic relativity
   d. phonology Objective 1.2

3. Morphology plus syntax equals:
   a. phonology
   b. semantics
   c. deep structure
   d. grammar Objective 1.2

4. The application of our knowledge of grammar during speaking or listening is called:
   a. linguistic performance
   b. linguistic competence
   c. semantics
   d. morphology   Objective 1.2

5. The transformation of a sentence's surface structure into its underlying representation is the process involved in:
   a. talking
   b. writing
   c. listening
   d. translating foreign languages   Objective 1.2

6. When a person remembers a sentence, he or she generally remembers:
   a. the entire sentence verbatim
   b. the constituents
   c. the nouns but not the adjectives
   d. the propositions   Objective 1.2

7. Why was the chimpanzee Vicki unable to learn more than four words?
   a. She was retarded.
   b. She lacked the necessary vocal apparatus.
   c. She was culturally deprived.
   d. English is too difficult a language.   Objective 2.1

8. Which of the following human languages would a chimp be best able to learn?
   a. Ameslan
   b. English
   c. Spanish
   d. Chinese   Objective 2.1

9. Chimps are capable of:
   a. learning the names of objects
   b. combining words into sentences
   c. creating names for novel objects
   d. all of the above   Objective 2.1

10. According to the text, the major distinction between the human and chimpanzee brains as they are adapted for language learning probably is that the human brain is:
    a. larger
    b. heavier
    c. lateralized
    d. more convoluted   Objective 3.1

11. The theorist who proposes that humans' brains are especially well suited for language development and that all human languages are very similar is:
    a. Herbert Terrace
    b. Noam Chomsky
    c. David Premack
    d. Robert Yerkes   Objective 3.1

12. Brain damage can cause difficulty in producing and comprehending speech. A general term for this condition is:
    a. regression
    b. amnesia
    c. stammering
    d. aphasia   Objective 3.1

13. Which of the following pieces of evidence does *not* support the notion of a critical period in language learning?
    a. Deaf people have greater difficulty learning language after puberty.

    b. Once you've learned two languages, others are much easier to learn.

    c. A second language is more easily learned before puberty.

    d. Children are more likely to recover speech lost due to brain injury than are adults.

                                                             Objective 3.2

14. Which of the following develop first?

    a. babbling phonemes of foreign languages

    b. intonation patterns

    c. simple words for objects

    d. simple words for commands   Objective 4.1

15. Two-year-olds did better than four-year-olds in their ability to understand which of the following sentences?

    a. It's the horse that the cow kisses.

    b. The cow kisses the horse.

    c. The horse is kissed by the cow.

    d. It's the cow that kisses the horse.   Objective 4.1

16. According to studies reported in the text, parents generally reinforce their children for correct:

    a. grammar

    b. pronunciation

    c. meaning

    d. phrasing   Objective 4.2

17. Benjamin Whorf felt that the way people perceive the world is largely determined by their:

    a. intelligence

    b. native language

    c. hemispheric dominance

    d. early experience   Objective 5.1

18. The linguistic relativity hypothesis holds that:

    a. language determines thought

    b. thought determines language

    c. intelligence determines thought

    d. culture determines language   Objective 5.1

19. Features found in all languages as a result of shared characteristics of thought are called:

    a. cultural similarities

    b. semantic differentials

    c. linguistic universals

    d. Whorfian units   Objective 5.1

20. Suppose you want to measure how sensitive a group of subjects is to nonverbal cues. A test you could give would be the:

    a. PONS

    b. ITBS

    c. IQ

    d. Rorschach Inkblots   Objective 6.1

C. Multiple-Choice Questions Testing Conceptual Knowledge

21. Which of the following represents more than one English phoneme?

    a. i

    b. th

    c. tr

    d. do   Objective 1.2

22. You analyze the word *dog* by breaking it into *d* plus *o* plus *g*. You are analyzing this word according to its:
    a. phonology
    b. semantic
    c. morphology
    d. syntax   Objective 1.2

23. You analyze *anticommunism* by breaking it into *anti* plus *commun* plus *ism*. You are analyzing this word according to its:
    a. syntax
    b. grammar
    c. morphology
    d. phonology   Objective 1.2

24. Which of the following consists of a single bound morpheme?
    a. th
    b. re
    c. dog
    d. undone   Objective 1.2

25. Which of the following sentences has surface structure but no underlying representation?
    a. I must go.
    b. Ran stop go.
    c. Monkeys borrow justice.
    d. I can't go.   Objective 1.2

26. David believes that he analyzes sentences according to the meanings of the major words. His would be considered which kind of approach?
    a. semantic
    b. syntactic
    c. grammatical
    d. verbatim   Objective 1.2

27. Jack believes that if a child has not learned to talk by age six, the child will never acquire normal language. Jack's notion is that of a(n):
    a. aphasia
    b. imprinting
    c. syntactic approach
    d. critical period   Objective 3.2

28. Which of the following is an example of telegraphic speech?
    a. I must have it now! (accompanied by a gesture)
    b. I'd like that.
    c. Doggy bye-bye.
    d. Please give me my dolly.   Objective 4.1

29. Which of the following is an obvious example of an error of overregularization?
    a. Me, too.
    b. I goed, too.
    c. Mommy likes me.
    d. Daddy bye-bye.   Objective 4.1

30. Suppose you stumble onto a culture that has only three basic color terms. According to research, which of the following will *not* be one of them?
    a. black
    b. purple
    c. red
    d. white   Objective 5.1

31. Which of the following people would typically be the most receptive to nonverbal cues?
    a. a four-year-old girl

  b. a four-year-old boy

  c. a male truck driver

  d. a female housewife   Objective 6.1

32. Jackie's mother is verbally approving of her attempts to learn to play the violin, but every time Jackie makes a mistake, her mother has a horrible, pained expression on her face. This situation is an example of:

  a. evolutionary influences

  b. the linguistic relativity hypothesis

  c. linguistic universals

  d. a double-bind situation   Objective 6.1

D. *Short Essay Questions*

1. How does the structure of language relate to its function? (Objective 1.1)

2. Can chimpanzees talk? Cite research evidence to support your answer. (Objective 2.1)

3. Is there a critical period for learning language? Cite research evidence to support your answer. (Objective 3.2)

4. How is thought related to language? (Objective 5.1)

5. How does heredity contribute to nonverbal communication? What role does environment play? (Objective 7.1)

Perspectives on Emotion

☐ **Chapter Summary**

I.   1.   Although difficult to define, emotions can be thought of as states of feeling that can affect behavior. They often arise in response to social relationships and are frequently accompanied by physiological changes and cognitive components.

2. Emotions can be measured by noting the subject's physiological changes, his or her verbal report, or his or her behavior. Because each of these measures is imperfect, research studying emotion has been somewhat limited.

3. Strong emotion is associated with the autonomic nervous system. This system works quite automatically and regulates the body's internal environment. It is composed of the sympathetic division, which generally functions in emergency situations, and the parasympathetic division, which dominates during periods of relaxation.

4. If you were placed in an emotion-arousing situation you would expect to experience physical changes such as these:
   a. Digestion stops.
   b. Blood flows away from internal organs to carry nutrients and oxygen to the skeletal muscles.
   c. Endocrine glands stimulate liver to release sugar (energy) into the bloodstream.
   d. Breathing becomes deeper and faster, and bronchioles expand.
   e. Heart rate increases.
   f. Eye pupils dilate and visual sensitivity increases.
   g. Salivary glands stop working, and sweat glands increase their activity.
   h. Hair on the body stands up.

   Although these preparations can increase the amount of work your body can do, human capacity is limited by structural factors.

5. Emotions are coordinated in the brain primarily by the hypothalamus and the limbic system. Stimulation of the hypothalamus has been shown to elicit an emotional response; lesions in the amygdala (part of the limbic system) inhibit emotionality. Damage to the amygdala can also produce violent behavior. Psychosurgery involves the destruction of brain tissue in order to control behavior. It is sometimes performed on humans, in which case part of the amygdala is removed in order to control extremely violent behavior.

II. 1. Two phenomena are associated with emotion: physiological arousal, and a subjective feeling of the appropriate emotion. Several theories have been offered to explain the relationship between these two characteristics.

2. The James-Lange theory of emotion proposes that emotion-arousing situations give rise to specific physiological changes. These changes prompt the subjective feeling of emotion. The particular emotion we feel (such as hate, fear, joy) is determined by the specific pattern of physiological change.

3. The Cannon-Bard theory was a critical reaction to the James-Lange theory on several grounds. First, contrary to James-Lange predictions, researchers were unable to find physiological differences in the various emotions. Second, Cannon and Bard believed that we feel emotions more quickly than the underlying physiological changes could take place. Third, injection of a drug that produced physiological arousal (such as epinephrine) was not sufficient to produce emotions.

4. The Cannon-Bard theory suggests that the thalamus serves an important function in emotion in this way: An emotionally arousing stimulus activates the thalamus, which sends out two consecutive signals, one to the cerebral cortex where feeling is produced, and one to the sympathetic nervous system, which physiologically activates the body. Thus, subjective feelings and physiological change are produced simultaneously. Even though we now know that the hypothalamus and limbic system (not the thalamus) mediate emotional events, the Cannon-Bard theory has had a major impact on current research.

5. Recent research has indicated that the Cannon-Bard theory may be too strong.

For instance, there does appear to be some difference in physiological response (stomach movement, gastric secretions, dilation of vessels in the stomach lining, sweating, and breathing rate) to stimuli producing different emotions. It also appears that there are differences between those emotions related to stimulation of the sympathetic nervous system and its release of norepinephrine (excitement, aggression, anger) and those related to stimulation of the parasympathetic system and its release of epinephrine (anxiety, sadness, depression). This research, however, is very speculative at present, and more research will be needed for greater clarification.

6. From a study of army veterans with severed spinal cords, Hohmann concluded that lack of a fully functioning physical system interferes with a full emotional expression.

7. Research by Maranon and Schachter demonstrates, however, that physiological arousal alone is not enough to produce feelings of emotion. Schachter and Singer conducted an experiment that supported their contention that people label physiological arousal so that the emotion they feel is consistent with their situation. In this experiment subjects were injected with epinephrine and placed in one of three conditions: informed (they were warned of the appropriate physiological changes); misinformed (they were warned of side effects unrelated to those produced by epinephrine); ignorant (they were told the injection would have no side effects). A fourth group received a placebo (an injection of saline solution rather than epinephrine). All subjects then waited with either a happy or an angry confederate. Those subjects in the misinformed and ignorant groups were more likely to feel aroused in this situation. Thus, Schachter's theory states that physiological arousal signals to a person that an explanation for that arousal is needed. To label the arousal, a person looks to environmental cues that can indicate what emotion is appropriate in the particular situation.

8. Schachter's theory has been supported by additional evidence. Valins gave male subjects false feedback about their heart rate changes as they viewed *Playboy* centerfolds. Subjects rated most favorable those women they saw when they were told their heart rate was fast. This indicates that it is not real arousal, but merely perceived arousal, that influences the labeling of emotions. Nisbett and Schachter gave subjects a placebo pill but told them they would experience side effects. Later, the subjects were given electric shocks. Those subjects told that the pill would produce arousal attributed such symptoms to the pill; those who were not so informed attributed the arousal to the shocks. Consequently, the former group tolerated four times stronger shocks than did the latter group.

9. Perhaps research such as this will help patients suffering from emotional disorders misattribute anxiety away from their anxiety-arousing object onto alternative stimuli that are easier to control.

10. Some researchers criticize the Schachter and Singer experiment on methodological grounds. Indeed, not all researchers have been able to replicate their results. Furthermore, Schachter and Singer may have carried the cognitive interpretation of emotion too far; more recent research indicates that variations in physiological response as well as situational factors may influence the subjective feeling of emotion.

III. 1. Three basic but unproven assumptions govern the common person's beliefs about coping with crisis situations: (1) There are universal reactions to crisis; (2) people go through stages in their coping with crisis; and (3) crisis is ultimately resolved.

2. Research data, however, suggest that these assumptions may be unwarranted. First, individuals vary greatly in their reactions to crisis. Second, theories that

propose a series of stages in coping with crisis tend to be based on weak data; recent research does not validate such a notion. Indeed, the stage concept may actually be harmful if professionals expect a patient coping with crisis to progress in ways not consistent with the patient's actual progress. Finally, patients often take very long to recover from crisis, and some never fully recover. Again, this causes problems when health care professionals expect the patient to progress at a particular rate.

IV.

1. Stress is the body's response to any demand placed on it, regardless of whether that demand is perceived as being positive or negative.

2. According to Selye's general adaptation syndrome theory, all types of stress evoke a similar pattern of physiological responses. The general adaptation syndrome postulates three stages in a stress reaction: alarm, in which the sympathetic nervous system supplies additional energy; resistance, in which the body appears normal but is being gradually weakened; and exhaustion, in which the body's ability to combat stress begins to break down. According to Selye, stress can result in death. Selye's research is based on observation of animals, and recent research indicates that it may be only somewhat applicable to humans.

3. Stress is related to physical illness, especially heart disease. Type A people, whose coping styles involve excess competitiveness, aggressiveness, and impatience, are twice as likely to suffer from heart disease as type B people, who are calmer and more relaxed. Stress also appears to be related to survival rates from cancer, bronchial asthma, and diabetes. Stress may be related to illness because a person has inadequate coping mechanisms, which prolong stress, or because stressful situations demand increased coping, or for both these reasons.

4. Holmes and Rahe developed the Social Readjustment Rating Scale (SRRS) to measure the amount of stress in a person's life. If the total amount of stress in a person's life becomes too high, physical illness is likely to result.

5. There are, however, individual variations in how much stress an individual can healthfully accommodate. Individuals react differently to stressful situations. Some people have more social support than others, which allows them to cope with stress more effectively. Some people seem hardier and can more easily cope with stressful situations.

6. Explanations for these variations in stress reaction suggest that other variables may mediate between stress and illness. Perhaps some people respond to stress by neglecting their self-care. Perhaps certain emotional states, such as depression, are hormonally linked to physical symptoms. Finally, it is possible that those people who suffer most from stress may attach more importance to those stress-producing aspects of their lives than do people who do not get ill as often.

IV.

1. Happiness can generally be described as a positive, enduring state that consists of positive feelings, peace of mind, and active pleasures and joy.

2. Several theories have been proposed to explain what causes happiness. The comparative theory of happiness posits that if our situation is better than that of others around us, we will be happy. This theory has been supported by research that indicates that people who compare themselves to the more fortunate are less happy than those who compare themselves to the less fortunate. However, this theory cannot explain why some advantaged people are unhappy or some disadvantaged people are happy.

3. Adaptation theory argues that people become accustomed to their average circumstances, and it is the deviations from this average that produce unhappiness or happiness. Pessimistically, this theory would suggest that one must continu-

ally improve one's lot to be happy. Optimistically, it suggests that external circumstances (such as money or power) actually have little to do with our happiness.

4. Still other researchers believe that adaptation theory should be supplemented with a trait theory in which happiness is viewed as an outcome of personality stability. A problem with trait theory is that traits associated with happiness are not necessarily the opposite of those associated with unhappiness.

5. A fourth theory holds that happiness is achieved by escaping comparison with others and absorbing oneself in a challenging task that demands one's undivided attention. Thus, a truly happy person is not even aware of his or her happiness.

6. At present, little research has been conducted to assess the predictions of these theories.

7. Psychologists have, however, attempted to identify events that are typically associated with happiness. One of the most consistent factors is a satisfying intimate relationship. The quality (not quantity) of sex also appears to contribute to happiness. Married couples are happier than those living together, and both are happier, overall, than single people. Factors that are generally not related to happiness include wealth, age (although the elderly are less happy), having a happy childhood, religious commitment, and place of residence. Care should be taken in interpreting these results; much further research is needed to document the issues addressed.

☐ Self-Test

A. Matching Questions

_____ 1. Part of the nervous system that responds in a crisis

_____ 2. Part of the limbic system associated with emotional response

_____ 3. Technique involving destruction of brain tissue

_____ 4. Theory statng that patterns of physiological change produce emotion

_____ 5. Actual drug administered by Schachter in his research

a. Cannon-Bard
b. Psychosurgery
c. Sympathetic division
d. Schachter's two-theory factor
e. Epinephrine
f. James-Lange
g. Parasympathetic division
h. Amygdala
i. Suproxin

_____ 6. Researcher who postulates a five-step process in coping with terminal illness

_____ 7. The stage of the general adaptation syndrome in which the body seems to be in control

_____ 8. People who are more likely to have heart disease

_____ 9. Method of measuring the amount of stress in one's life

_____10. The notion that happiness is affected by increases or decreases in one's state of affairs

a. Alarm
b. Selye
c. Type B
d. SRRS
e. Kübler-Ross
f. Adaptation theory
g. Resistance
h. Type A
i. Comparative theory

B. Multiple-Choice Questions Testing Factual Knowledge

1. By recording a person's heart rate, blood pressure, and breathing rate, you are measuring which component of emotion?
   a. overt behavior
   b. subjective feeling
   c. physiological change
   d. all of the above
   Objective 1.1

2. Generally speaking, the sympathetic division of the nervous system dominates during _____; the parasympathetic dominates during _____.
   a. sleep; wakefulness
   b. emergency; relaxation
   c. work; play
   d. job; anger
   Objective 1.2

3. In times of emergency, which of the following would *not* typically occur?
   a. Blood moves from your stomach to your skeletal muscles.
   b. Sugar is released into the bloodstream.
   c. Pupils of your eyes dilate.
   d. Your breathing becomes shallower and slower as you concentrate your attention on the emergency.
   Objective 1.2

4. When various emotions are activated, there appear to be physiological changes in which of the following processes?
   a. digestion
   b. breathing
   c. blood pressure
   d. all of the above
   Objective 1.2

5. Stimulation of the sympathetic nervous system is associated with _____, whereas stimulation of the parasympathetic system is associated with _____.
   a. excitement; aggression
   b. anger; depression
   c. anxiety; depression
   d. aggression, anger
   Objective 1.2

6. According to research presented in the text, depression may be associated with a lack of:
   a. suproxin
   b. norepinephrine
   c. epinephrine
   d. adrenalin
   Objective 1.2

7. The results of a study conducted on the emotionality of men with severed spinal cords indicated that:
   a. emotions are unrelated to the somatic nervous system
   b. emotions are unrelated to the autonomic nervous system
   c. a fully functioning nervous system contributes to emotion
   d. spinal cord injuries intensify negative emotions and reduce positive emotions
   Objective 1.3

8. According to recent evidence, which part of your brain is probably *not* directly involved in emotion?
   a. thalamus
   b. hypothalamus
   c. limbic system
   d. amygdala
   Objective 1.3

9. If psychosurgery is undertaken to relieve a patient of excessive violence, the part of the brain usually removed or destroyed is the:
   a. amygdala

b. cerebral cortex–frontal lobe
c. hypothalamus
d. pons   Objective 1.3

10. Which of the following was *not* one of Cannon's criticisms of the James-Lange theory?
    a. No evidence existed for different physiological responses.
    b. Physiological change occurs too slowly.
    c. Injections of epinephrine alone do not produce emotion.
    d. There are only a few basic emotions, all others being modifications of these.
                                                                       Objective 2.1

11. According to the Cannon-Bard theory, which of the following parts of the nervous
    system is activated in an emotional response?
    a. thalamus
    b. sympathetic nervous system
    c. cerebral cortex
    d. all of the above   Objective 2.1

12. In Schachter and Singer's experiment with the placebo vitamins, which group of sub-
    jects became aroused?
    a. informed
    b. misinformed
    c. placebo
    d. all of the above   Objective 2.2

13. Which of the following is *not* a criticism of Schachter and Singer's research?
    a. Epinephrine does not produce arousal.
    b. They may have failed to use the double-blind technique.
    c. Subjects may have responded according to demand characteristics.
    d. Subjects may have assumed their arousal resulted from the injection.   Objective 2.2

14. According to the text, which of the following beliefs about crisis reactions is probably
    true?
    a. There are universal reactions to crisis.
    b. People go through stages as they respond to crisis.
    c. Responses to crises vary widely from person to person.
    d. Crises are ultimately resolved.   Objective 3.1

15. According to Selye, the ultimate response to exhaustion is:
    a. death
    b. depression
    c. stress
    d. resistance   Objective 4.1

16. Selye's research was based on work done with:
    a. terminally ill cancer patients
    b. blue-collar workers
    c. men (not women)
    d. animals   Objective 4.1

17. Research has demonstrated that type A persons are more likely to:
    a. have heart disease
    b. be intelligent
    c. score higher on the SRRS
    d. have large families   Objective 4.2

18. The SRRS (Social Readjustment Rating Scale) assigns stress to events in one's life that
    involve:
    a. positive change
    b. negative change
    c. both a and b
    d. none of the above   Objective 4.3

19. The comparative theory of happiness says you are happiest when:
    a. you have less than others
    b. you have the same amount as others
    c. you have more than others
    d. you can cause others to lose what they have   Objective 5.1

20. Which of the following traits is most typically associated with happiness?
    a. youth
    b. high quality sex
    c. money
    d. being single   Objective 5.2

C. Multiple-Choice Questions Testing Conceptual Knowledge

21. Suppose you are driving in a car when a truck coming toward you crosses the center line and looks as if it is going to hit you. The part of your nervous system immediately activated is:
    a. the sympathetic division
    b. the parasympathetic division
    c. both a and b
    d. none of the above   Objective 1.2

22. Suppose you were measuring the physiological response of psychopaths. According to research in the text, you might expect their ratio of norepinephrine to epinephrine to be:
    a. higher than normal
    b. lower than normal
    c. about normal
    d. widely different from one person to another   Objective 1.2

23. Extrapolating from evidence presented in the text, if your best friend suddenly developed violent outbursts of temper, you might suspect the presence of a tumor in his:
    a. sympathetic nervous system
    b. parasympathetic nervous system
    c. amygdala
    d. thalamus   Objective 1.3

24. Bob believes that different situations produce different physiological response patterns. These, in turn, arouse their corresponding emotions. Bob's theory most closely corresponds to:
    a. Schachter's two-factor theory
    b. Cannon-Bard theory
    c. Selye's general adaptation syndrome
    d. James-Lange theory   Objective 2.1

25. Marlene believes that emotion is produced by the combination of physiological factors and situational cues. Her theory most closely corresponds to:
    a. the Cannon-Bard theory
    b. Selye's theory
    c. the James-Lange theory
    d. Schachter's two-factor theory   Objective 2.2

26. Suppose you are shown a series of twenty erotic pictures and are given false feedback regarding your physiological arousal level. According to Valins, which pictures would you like best?
    a. those accompanied by fake arousal feedback
    b. those not accompanied by fake arousal feedback
    c. those accompanied by real arousal
    d. no clear preference   Objective 2.2

27. Suppose you are coping with a crisis but are not following the stages that health care professionals believe to be beneficial. According to the text, you are likely to be labeled:
    a. normal
    b. retarded
    c. deviant
    d. needing help   Objective 3.1

28. You just find out you are going to be called on in class to give a twenty-minute lecture on material you hardly understand. You are in which stage of Selye's general adaptation syndrome?
    a. panic
    b. alarm
    c. resistance
    d. exhaustion   Objective 4.1

29. Suppose Jim is a type B personality. Which characteristic would probably most accurately describe him?
    a. impatient
    b. relaxed
    c. aggressive
    d. competitive   Objective 4.2

30. Mary was just divorced. John just got fired. Bob just borrowed some money. Judy just started working the night shift. According to the SRRS, who is under the most stress?
    a. Mary
    b. John
    c. Bob
    d. Judy   Objective 4.3

31. Mathilde has just been raped. Her recovery will probably be most enhanced if:
    a. she doesn't report the rape
    b. she lies about the rape
    c. she has a supportive group of friends to talk to about the rape
    d. she never gets married   Objective 4.4

32. John believes that happiness is only achieved when you are so involved that you are not aware of it. He would probably subscribe to which theory?
    a. comparison theory
    b. adaptation theory
    c. trait theory
    d. "stepping off the hedonistic treadmill"   Objective 5.1

D. Short Essay Questions

1. Suppose you want to conduct an experiment to measure emotion. How would you do this?   (Objective 1.1)

2. What evidence cited in the text supports the James-Lange theory? What evidence supports the Cannon-Bard theory?   (Objective 2.1)

3. Do you think Schachter's two-factor theory of emotion is useful? Why or why not? (Objective 2.2)

4. How might stress be associated with physical illness? (Objective 4.4)

5. Four theories of happiness are mentioned in the text. Which theory do you believe best explains happiness, and why? (Objective 5.1)

The
Dynamics of
Motivation

□ **Preview of the Chapter**
Major Concepts and Behavioral Objectives

CONCEPT 1   Motivation comprises the variables that arouse, sustain, and direct behavior toward the attainment of a goal.

   1.1   Define motivation.

   1.2   Compare and contrast the explanation of motivation in instinctive theories, Freudian theory, drive-reduction theories, and incentive theories.

CONCEPT 2   The cues that motivate us to eat are complex; they issue predominantly from the brain, not the stomach or the taste buds.

   2.1   List and discuss the factors involved in the regulation of hunger and eating.

   2.2   Discuss Schachter's and Nisbett's theories of obesity.

   2.3   Discuss the success of the various kinds of diets mentioned in the text.

CONCEPT 3   Human sexual response is even more complex than eating behavior, involving external stimuli, hormones, and brain activity.

   3.1   Discuss the role of hormones and situational factors in the sexual behavior in animals and in man.

   3.2   Describe the research conducted by Kinsey and by Masters and Johnson regarding human sexual responsiveness.

   3.3   Describe male and female sexual dysfunction and briefly discuss their treatment.

CONCEPT 4   The concept of an optimal level of arousal suggests that we typically seek moderate levels of cortical stimulation. Different levels of cortical arousal could explain the differences between introverts and extroverts. Unusual motivations—such as those involved in risk taking—are explained by other, more specific theories.

   4.1   Describe the optimal level of arousal theory and the research that supports it.

   4.2   Discuss the opponent process model, which attempts to account for risk taking.

CONCEPT 5   In addition to physiologically regulated motivations, we have learned motivations—for example, the need for achievement. Learned motivations are acquired in social interactions, and they therefore show culture–specific patterns.

   5.1   Compare and contrast people high in achievement motivation with those low in achievement motivation.

   5.2   Describe and compare the fear of failure and fear of success motivation.

☐ **Chapter Summary**

I. 1. Motivation can be defined as those variables that arouse, sustain, and direct behavior toward attainment of some goal. These variables may include physiological changes that encourage goal-directed activity as well as external stimuli that initiate approach or avoidance. Such a general definition has limits, however, and the definition of motivation is still controversial, being defined according to specific historical traditions.

2. Darwin's theory of evolution prompted man to view himself as part of the animal world. It was this tradition that led McDougall to propose in 1908 that humans possessed a variety of instincts that served as motivators. However, such instinct-oriented theories soon lost popularity because hundreds of instincts were never clearly defined.

3. Freud proposed that all human instincts could be categorized as Eros (the urge for individual and species survival) or Thanatos (a tendency toward death). Eros and Thanatos continually conflict. Also, some instinctive drives conflict with moral standards and are consequently repressed, or pushed into the unconscious. Although repressed, these impulses could still direct behavior, sometimes being translated into a more socially acceptable form. This process is called sublimation and is responsible for creating a civilized society.

4. Drive theories define a primary drive (for example, hunger) as a state of physiological tension that automatically arises when the body's balance (called homeostasis) is upset. Secondary drives (such as curiosity) are learned from their association with primary drives. Both primary and secondary drives motivate the organism to perform some behavior that will reduce the drive state.

5. However, on some occasions, animals will not initiate behavior that would reduce an active drive state. In other cases, goal-directed behavior occurs when no drive state exists. Thus, some psychologists have postulated that goal-directed behavior occurs not as the result of a physiological drive but rather as the result of the expectation of receiving a reward. These expectations are called incentives. Often, an interaction between drives and incentives underlies goal-directed responses.

II. 1. One of the most impressive characteristics of weight control is the remarkably fine balance the body maintains between food intake and energy expenditure. Generally, body weight is maintained at a relatively constant level.

2. Hunger and eating are probably controlled by several different systems. People feel less hungry when their stomachs are full, regardless of whether they are full of food or something else. Recent evidence, however, suggests that stomach cues are of secondary importance in regulating hunger and eating.

3. Taste also affects hunger and eating. An initially pleasant-tasting food becomes less pleasant as more of it is consumed. Taste, however, is also secondary in regulating hunger. Subjects control their intake of food even when no taste cues are available.

4. Satiation (fullness) signals are carried by the bloodstream to brain sites that are especially susceptible to hunger cues. For instance, electrical or chemical stimulation of the lateral hypothalamus can cause a satiated animal to drastically overeat. If this same region is surgically destroyed, the animal will refuse to eat. On the other hand, the ventromedial hypothalamus has nearly opposite results: When stimulated, the animal will refuse to eat; when lesioned, the animal will overeat to the point of extreme obesity. Thus, these two regions of the hypothalamus work together to control eating behavior, although other parts of the neural system are also involved in the regulation of this highly complex process.

5. Other factors that seem to play some sort of role in regulating eating include glucose levels in the blood and the level of fat already present in the body.

6. Overweight humans share some behavioral characteristics in their eating patterns with rats whose ventromedial hypothalami have been lesioned. For instance, both eat more than subjects of normal weight, both eat more rapidly, and both overeat only when foods are very appealing. Both are also reluctant to work for food reward. Schachter has suggested that both are extremely sensitive to eating cues. Indeed, he has demonstrated that many aspects of overweight subjects' behavior are subject to interference from situational intrusions. This indicates that overweight people are more sensitive to environmental events than normal-weight people.

7. Nisbett has proposed a different theory to account for obesity. He believes that overweight people are in a nearly continuous state of hunger. As evidence he points out that obese people react similarly to normal-weight people who have been starved. The underlying physiological mechanism for this theory is the presence of high levels of free fatty acids in an obese person's blood, indicating to that person's hunger centers a chronic state of energy deficit. Nisbett also believes that biological normal weight varies from one person to another, perhaps relying on insulin production levels or the number of fat cells developed early in life.

8. Obesity is considered unattractive in our society. Consequently, many people turn to dieting to reduce their body weight. Restrained eaters are those people who are nearly constantly dieting and who are also more prone to eating binges. Indeed, a number of researchers have concluded that the stress encountered by restrained eaters in near constant dieting and hunger may outweigh the disadvantages of being overweight.

9. Gain or loss of fat depends entirely on the number of calories consumed. It has nothing to do with their source. Although popular diets can help a person lose weight over the short run, they generally are not linked to long-term weight reduction and may actually be harmful. Behavior modification seems to be the most successful solution to long-term weight control. Many questions regarding hunger and eating remain to be answered.

III.   1. Factors regulating human sexual behaviors are extremely complex, in that they are influenced by drives and incentives as well as societal practices.

2. Hormones are the major influence in sexual behavior of lower animals. Female rats are sexually responsive only when their ovaries are secreting high levels of estrogen. Males are unresponsive when their testes, and consequently their supply of testosterone, are removed. In humans, sex hormones may help initiate sexual responsiveness, but environmental factors play a more significant role in sexual behavior, especially if hormonal influences were normal through the period of puberty (sexual maturation).

3. Hormones interact with the central nervous system. In the sexual response, the hypothalamus stimulates the anterior pituitary gland to release the hormones that stimulate the secretion of sex hormones by the gonads. These sex hormones travel via the bloodstream to the hypothalamus (especially the preoptic region) where they activate the sexual arousal mechanism.

4. In addition to hormones, external stimuli are needed to expand the original arousal into a sexual response. Sensory input (such as taste, smells, and sights) stimulate neural circuits that are channeled through the hypothalamus. A variable that increases sexual responsiveness in animals is variety in partners (the "Coolidge effect"). Thus sexual responsiveness is dependent on the interaction of external stimuli, secretion of sex hormones, activation of sexually related neural circuits in the hypothalamus, and the cerebral cortex. The influence of

the cerebral cortex increases as animals become evolutionarily more advanced. In humans, for instance, sexual responsiveness can be increased or decreased through the use of appropriate fantasies.

5. Alfred Kinsey conducted some of the first research on human sexual responsiveness in the 1940s and 1950s. His interviews with men and women revealed more widespread experience with premarital sex and homosexuality than expected. His methods were criticized on the basis of his sample (white and middle-class) and the possibility of subjects misrepresenting themselves.

6. Masters and Johnson conducted observations and physiological measures of people engaging in sexual relations. They found that the sexual response for both men and women could be divided into four phases: the excitement phase; the plateau phase; orgasm; and the resolution phase. Most women are capable of having another orgasm during the resolution stage, but most men experience a refractory period during which they are unresponsive to sexual arousal.

7. Sexual dysfunction refers to any problem that prevents a person from successfully engaging in sexual relations or reaching orgasm. Among men, the most common problems are impotence, premature ejaculation, and nonemissive erection. Among women, the most common complaint is inability to have an orgasm. Another female problem is vaginismus, which makes penetration painful or impossible. Most researchers believe sexual dysfunction usually stems from psychological rather than physiological problems. Treatment programs are available for people suffering from sexual dysfunction, some programs reporting success rates of 80 percent or more.

IV. 1. As indicated earlier, the drive-reduction view came to dominate the field of motivation in the early twentieth century, but it failed to answer many questions that arose.

2. The optimal level of arousal concept is based on knowledge that sensory information activates two neural pathways—one to the thalamus, the other to the reticular formation—that eventually activate the cerebral cortex in a general way. Too much stimulation induced by the reticular formation causes inappropriate behavior; too little is associated with coma or deep sleep. This research has been generalized into the optimal level theory of motivation, which specifies that for appropriate behavior to take place, the amount of cortical stimulation must be within a certain optimal range.

3. Subjects subjected to sensory deprivation find it very unpleasant. This result is consistent with optimal level theory, but inconsistent with drive-reduction theory. Studies of the inappropriate behavior shown by disaster victims also provide support for optimal level theory.

4. The optimal level of arousal for effective performance varies with task complexity; complex tasks have narrower ranges of optimal levels of motivation than do simpler tasks.

5. Optimal level of arousal also varies with the individual. Eysenck suggested that introverts have high internal levels of cortical arousal; therefore, they require less external stimulation to reach an optimal level than do extroverts whose internal cortical arousal level is lower. This hypothesis has been experimentally supported; extroverts tolerate high levels of external stimulation better than introverts. Further research is needed to determine if optimal level theories will successfully explain motivation.

6. Currently, optimal level theories do not explain why some people take great risks. Solomon and Corbit have suggested that when a strong emotional response disrupts the natural balance of a person, an "opponent process" is acti-

vated. An opponent process is a response opposite to the initial response. Generally, these positive and negative responses cancel each other out, but if one response (say, the negative one) is suddenly eliminated, the other takes over and causes the person to associate that response (say, elation) with the situation. Furthermore, repetitions of the opponent process strengthen it. Although this theory is supported by both observations and experimental results, it cannot explain emotions that persist over a long period of time or why some people are more attracted to risk than others. Eysenck suggests that those individuals who are more attracted to risk are extroverts, people who need much external cortical stimulation to achieve their optimal level. Indeed, research has shown that risk-taking seems to be a general characteristic that extends into many areas of such a person's life.

V. 1. Achievement motivation is one of several learned motivations. It is generally measured with the TAT (Thematic Apperception Test), in which subjects project their own motives onto people in ambiguous pictures.

2. Persons with high need for achievement are more likely to persist longer at tasks, do better on exams, select occupations that require individual initiative, and set challenging but realistic goals. Those with low need for achievement are more likely to set goals that are either too easy or too difficult, and they also score high in their fear of failure. They tend to attribute their failures to lack of ability and their successes to external factors. Those with high need for achievement are more likely to attribute personal failure to insufficient effort and success to their own ability.

3. In McClelland's research and in the Kakinada project adults were taught to have fantasies of their own success. The businessmen who participated in these projects became more successful, thus indicating that motivation is essential for altering behavior.

4. Achievement motivation predicts the behavior of men better than that of women. Matina Horner suggests that because women play two roles in our society (achievement versus femininity), they are motivated by a fear of success as well as a fear of failure. Indeed, her research has indicated women fear success more than men. Unfortunately for Horner's theory, her results have not always been replicated. Instead of measuring fear of success, she seems, in reality, to have measured the subject's assessment of the negative consequences associated with deviations from traditional sex roles (women executives and men nurses, for example). Successful women, however, do seem to be punished by men in our society at present.

☐ **Self-Test**

A. Matching Questions

_____ 1. Those variables that arouse, sustain, and direct behavior toward goal attainment

_____ 2. Freud's term for the life instincts

_____ 3. Freud's explanation for civilization

_____ 4. Our body's automatic tendency to maintain internal equilibrium

_____ 5. An expectation of receiving a reward

a. Repression

b. Eros

c. Homeostasis

d. Primary drive

e. Thanatos

f. Sublimation

g. Incentive

h. Motivation

_____ 6. Region of the brain that, when lesioned, produces gross overeating

_____ 7. Hormone closely related to female sexual functioning

_____ 8. Linked to the idea that variability in partners enhances sexual performance

_____ 9. Sex researcher(s) whose studies were based on observation

_____ 10. Brain structure closely tied to optimal level theories

a. Lateral hypothalamus
b. The Coolidge effect
c. Masters and Johnson
d. Ventromedial hypothalamus
e. Testosterone
f. Reticular formation
g. Estrogen
h. Kinsey

_____

_____ 11. Time during which no orgasm can occur

_____ 12. Eysenck's term for people with high levels of internal stimulation

_____ 13. Theory suggesting that strong emotions are generally accompanied by their opposite emotions

_____ 14. A person likely to choose realistic yet challenging goals

_____ 15. Matina Horner's concept originally attributed primarily to women

a. Opponent process
b. Extroverts
c. Refractory period
d. High need achiever
e. Introverts
f. Fear of success
g. Low need achiever
h. Optimal level of arousal

B. Multiple-Choice Questions Testing Factual Knowledge

1. Which of the following people proposed a long list of human instincts?
   a. Sigmund Freud
   b. William McDougall
   c. Stanley Schachter
   d. Richard Nisbett   Objective 1.2

2. Freud categorized human instincts into two basic groups, the instincts of:
   a. primary drives and secondary drives
   b. drives and incentives
   c. emotion and motivation
   d. life and death   Objective 1.2

3. An incentive differs from a drive in that it involves:
   a. an expectation
   b. humans, not animals
   c. animals, not humans
   d. primary drives, not secondary drives   Objective 1.2

4. Eating behavior and hunger have been found to be related to:
   a. distention of the stomach
   b. changes in the sensation of taste
   c. glucose levels in the blood
   d. all of the above   Objective 2.1

5. A lesion in which part of the brain will suppress (stop) eating behavior?
   a. ventromedial hypothalamus
   b. reticular formation
   c. lateral hypothalamus
   d. all of the above   Objective 2.1

6. Obese humans and rats with lesions in their ventromedial hypothalamus are somewhat similar. Which of the following is *not* characteristic of their eating behavior?
   a. They eat more than normal subjects.
   b. They eat rapidly.
   c. They work hard to get food.
   d. They eat more if food tastes good.   Objective 2.2

7. Schachter believes that people are overweight primarily because:
   a. they have more fat cells
   b. they have slower metabolism
   c. they are more responsive to external cues
   d. they constantly feel hungry   Objective 2.2

8. According to the text, the best long-term weight loss technique is:
   a. psychotherapy
   b. behavior modification
   c. hypnotism
   d. fad diets, especially Stillman's diet   Objective 2.3

9. A female rat is sexually responsive:
   a. any time an interested male is present
   b. only during ovulation
   c. when her testosterone levels are high
   d. when her estrogen levels are low   Objective 3.1

10. Which of the following is *not* directly involved in sexual behavior?
    a. hypothalamus
    b. pituitary gland
    c. gonads
    d. reticular formation   Objective 3.1

11. Compared to that of animals, the human sexual response is more controlled by:
    a. hormones
    b. the preoptic region of the hypothalamus
    c. reticular formation
    d. cerebral cortex   Objective 3.1

12. Kinsey's studies' most controversial findings included all of the following *except*:
    a. homosexuality was more common than expected
    b. sexual dysfunction was more common than expected
    c. premarital sex was more common than expected
    d. extramarital sex was more common than expected   Objective 3.2

13. The refractory period occurs in which of Masters and Johnson's stages?
    a. plateau
    b. orgasm
    c. resolution
    d. excitement   Objective 3.2

14. Masters and Johnson believe that most cases of sexual dysfunction are caused by:
    a. hormone imbalances
    b. psychological factors
    c. improper exercise
    d. damage to sensitive genital tissue   Objective 3.3

15. The optimal level of arousal concept is based on the finding that all of the following parts of the brain are stimulated in arousal *except* the:
    a. hypothalamus
    b. thalamus
    c. cerebral cortex
    d. reticular formation   Objective 4.1

16. The Hebb experiment on sensory deprivation reported in the text was _____ drive-reduction theories and _____ optimal level theories:
    a. supportive of; supportive of
    b. supportive of; contradictory to
    c. contradictory to; supportive of
    d. unrelated to; supportive of   Objective 4.1

17. According to Eysenck, as compared to introverts, extroverts have _____ levels of internal stimulation and seek _____ levels of external stimulation:
    a. higher; the same
    b. lower; the same
    c. higher; lower
    d. lower; higher   Objective 4.1

18. According to Solomon and Corbin's opponent process model, the activation of a strong emotion is accomplished by:
    a. fear
    b. desire to reduce the emotion to a normal level
    c. the opposite response
    d. increased levels of arousal   Objective 4.2

19. In playing a ring-toss game, people with a high need for achievement generally:
    a. stand close to the target
    b. stand at an intermediate distance
    c. stand far from the target
    d. refuse to play   Objective 5.1

20. Matina Horner's explanation for women's tendency to set less challenging goals is their fear of:
    a. failure
    b. success
    c. strange places
    d. competition   Objective 5.2

C. Multiple-Choice Questions Testing Conceptual Knowledge

21. Mary was raped by her father when she was seven years old. Now, at age fourteen, she has no memory of this traumatic event. This is an example of:
    a. repression
    b. sublimation
    c. an incentive
    d. Thanatos   Objective 1.2

22. Which of the following is an example of a secondary drive rather than a primary drive?
    a. food
    b. warmth
    c. creativity
    d. water   Objective 1.2

23. Bob always seems to be on a diet, and he constantly feels hungry when he diets. He fits the pattern of:
    a. an unrestrained eater
    b. a restrained eater
    c. a grossly obese person
    d. a person with a tumor in the ventromedial hypothalamus   Objective 2.2

24. Kelly maintains a normal body weight by her near-constant dieting. She is forced in an experiment to eat a large piece of chocolate cream pie, after which she can eat as many pieces of other kinds of pie as she wishes. According to research presented in the text, you expect her to:
    a. eat no more pie
    b. eat a little more pie
    c. eat about as much more pie as a normal eater
    d. eat much more pie than normal eaters   Objective 2.2

25. Jack decides to ask people to fill out a questionnaire about their sexual behavior and preferences. His research is most similar to that of:
    a. Masters and Johnson
    b. Schachter
    c. Kinsey
    d. Nisbett   Objective 3.2

26. In order to replicate Masters and Johnson's studies, you would have to:
    a. lesion the brains of experimental animals
    b. observe human couples during intercourse
    c. prepare and administer questionnaires
    d. work with hormone balances and imbalances   Objective 3.2

27. Jean has just become sexually active, and she finds that her first partner is unable to have a second erection and orgasm for quite some time after his first. She accurately concludes her partner is:
    a. suffering from premature ejaculation
    b. suffering from nonemissive erection
    c. suffering from impotence
    d. normal   Objective 3.2

28. Which of the following behaviors is most easily explained by a drive-reduction theory of motivation?
    a. A hungry person gets food from a refrigerator.
    b. A religious person fasts for weeks before eating.
    c. Students stay up all night watching old movies on cable television.
    d. None of the above behavior can be explained by a drive-reduction model.
                                                                                Objective 4.1

29. You are going to take a very important test and want to achieve the level of arousal that will maximize your performance. You conclude the level of arousal you should strive for is:
    a. zero
    b. a low level (to reduce tension)
    c. a moderate amount
    d. a high level   Objective 4.1

30. Suppose you have been on a bland diet for several weeks. According to optimal level theory, when you are taken off the bland diet, the food you would probably first prefer is:
    a. bland food, since that is what you've been used to
    b. food just a little more interesting than the bland
    c. the same kind as you usually ate before being on the bland diet
    d. exotic food   Objective 4.1

31. Suppose a fire begins in your classroom and everyone just stands paralyzed, watching it grow. This situation is _____ optimal level theory.
    a. supportive of
    b. contradictory to
    c. unrelated to
    d. both supportive of and contradictory to   Objective 4.1

32. Suppose you are asked by a psychologist to look at some pictures and write a story about each one. The test you are probably taking is the:
    a. Rorschach
    b. TAT
    c. MMPI
    d. Schachter Scale of Motivational Responses   Objective 5.1

D. *Short Essay Questions*

1. What is motivation?   (Objective 1.1)

2. Suppose you were working in a treatment center for overweight people. What advice would you give them regarding weight reduction?   (Objective 2.3)

3. How does sexual responsiveness differ in man as compared to animals?   (Objective 3.1)

4. Explain the opponent process model as it accounts for risk taking. Compare it to the optimal level theory.   (Objective 4.2)

5. How do people with a high need for achievement differ from people with a low need for achievement? What can be done to raise a person's need for achievement? (Objective 5.1)

The
Nature of
Consciousness

■ 12

□ **Chapter Summary**

I. 1. No completely satisfactory definition of *consciousness* has been derived, due to its personal and highly subjective nature. Generally, consciousness is defined as the awareness of the thoughts, images, sensations, and emotions that flow through one's mind. Its definition has changed as different psychological traditions have investigated its processes and content.

   2. Most people would agree, however, that consciousness is limited—that is, we are not aware of all internal or external events. Our consciousness is limited by our ability to sense some kinds of physical stimuli, by the amount of information we can attend to at any one time, and by our inability to be aware of our own conscious processes.

   3. Most psychologists would also agree that consciousness is related to brain activities. Penfield demonstrated that stimulation of the brain aroused recall of specific conscious experiences. Brain activity and consciousness seem to interact, each influencing the other.

II. 1. Perhaps the most familiar characteristic of consciousness is its variability. One state of consciousness may be very different from other states. Drugs can induce altered states of consciousness; however, some consciousness states are natural and very familiar.

III. 1. Although many people believe no mental processing goes on during sleep, research shows that mental activity continues throughout the night and that everyone dreams. Such research is usually conducted by connecting subjects to an EEG (electroencephalograph) and recording their brain waves as they drift into sleep. Different types of brain waves are typically recorded at different stages of sleep. Beta waves (14 + cycles per second) are fastest and are typical in a fully awake person. Alpha waves (8–13 cycles per second) are characteristic of relaxation. As a person falls asleep, theta waves (5–7 cycles per second) also become evident. As sleep becomes deeper, delta waves (4 or fewer cycles per second) become predominant.

   2. There are four stages of sleep, 1, 2, 3, and 4, each progressively deeper. Although stage 4 is characterized by deep relaxation, this is the stage (along with stage 3) during which most episodes of sleepwalking, sleeptalking, and intense nightmares occur.

   3. In a typical night's sleep, you progress from stage 1 to stage 4, and back to stage 1 about every 90 minutes. At this time, you are likely to enter REM sleep, the stage of sleep associated with dreaming. You dream about four or five times each night. REM sleep differs greatly from non-REM sleep.

   4. The scanning hypothesis speculates that the eye movements in REM are due to the dreamer's "watching" the dream's activity. This hypothesis is supported by the finding that people blind from birth have no REMs or visual images; those blinded later in life dream in the same way as sighted people.

   5. REM sleep is paradoxical in that it appears to be both a lighter stage of sleep (as indicated by EEGs and physiological measures) and a deeper stage of sleep (as evidenced by lack of muscle tone).

   6. If subjects are deprived of REM sleep, they will spend more time in REM sleep on the following night. Several hypotheses have been proposed to explain the possible value of REM sleep. Perhaps it is the time the brain adapts to disturbing life events. Perhaps REM sleep plays a role in consolidating information into long-term memory. Since people need less REM sleep as they grow older (new-

borns spend about 50 percent of their sleep in REM; old people, less than 5 percent), some researchers speculate that dreams enhance the growth and maintenance of neural tissue.

7. Some psychologists believe that the content of dreams may be influenced by environmental stimuli. Sigmund Freud believed that dreams have two meanings: the manifest content being the story the dreamer remembers; the latent content being the deeper, underlying meaning of the dream, which can be analyzed to reveal unconscious psychosexual conflicts. Most psychologists who use dream analysis favor interpretation of the dream's direct meaning (manifest content). Some psychologists are working to develop "dream management" techniques, which will allow the subjects to control their dreams; however, no real success can be reported at this time.

IV.　1. Although hypnosis seems somewhat like sleepwalking, it is an entirely different state, characterized by EEGs resembling those of waking persons. There is at present no clear explanation of what hypnosis is.

Most people (about 95 percent) can be hypnotized to some degree if they so desire. Several scales or tests, including the Stanford Scale, have been devised to measure a person's hypnotic susceptibility. People who are highly susceptible to hypnosis tend to have histories of daydreaming, imaginary companions, and absorption in their activities.

2. There is currently no way to measure when a person is in a hypnotic state. Hilgard suggests that we will eventually be able to monitor this state objectively. Hilgard's neodissociation view posits that in hypnosis a split occurs in consciousness, allowing certain thoughts, feelings, and behaviors to operate independently of one another. As evidenced, source amnesia (in which the person can remember facts but not the context in which they are learned) occurs in subjects under hypnosis, but not in subjects who are "faking."

Barber argues that hypnosis is not an altered state of consciousness but merely a state of compliance with the hypnotist's suggestions. This role enactment view suggests that the hypnotist's function is to clearly define the role the subject is to play. Both the neodissociation and role enactment views are currently being investigated.

V.　1. Through meditation, yogis are able to achieve the state called samadhi, in which awareness is separated from the senses. This and similar experiences in meditation and biofeedback differ from dreaming and hypnosis since here the subject himself regulates his state of consciousness.

2. Meditation is a retraining of attention that induces an altered state of consciousness. Although it is a part of all major religions, three forms of meditation are especially common in the United States: transcendental meditation (TM), yoga, and Zen. Meditation involves the letting go of thoughts and feelings that intrude on one's attention, often using techniques of concentration such as focusing on a mantra (sound), mandala (symmetrical design), or other object or body process.

3. Meditation produces physiological changes associated with deep relaxation. These changes differ from those associated with either hypnosis or sleep.

4. Biofeedback is the use of monitoring instruments to give a person continuous information about his or her biological state. By trial and error, the subject gradually learns to control these internal states and regulate a variety of physiological processes, such as heart rhythms, body temperature, and muscle tension. Biofeedback has been found to be a successful technique for coping with heart arrhythmia, tension headaches, and Raynaud's syndrome. Much further

research will be necessary to determine the full usefulness of biofeedback. One thing it apparently will not do is to help the subject emit more alpha EEG waves. Biofeedback is a more specific technique than meditation, in that it helps the subject to regulate a particular physiological function.

VI.

1. Drugs are substances that can alter the functioning of a biological system. Psychoactive drugs interact with the central nervous system and alter a person's mood, perception, and behavior.

2. Alcohol is the most widely used psychoactive drug in the United States. Alcohol is a depressant and as such it suppresses nerve impulses. People sometimes feel elated when drinking a small amount of alcohol because it slows down the brain centers that normally control social inhibitions. With increased doses, other central nervous system functions deteriorate. Blood alcohol levels of .05 percent cause drunkenness, levels of .3 percent to .4 percent may cause coma, and levels exceeding about .5 percent cause death.

3. Alcohol consumption has little effect on short-term and long-term memory, but it does affect the transfer of information from short-term to long-term memory. Alcoholic blackout is the loss of memory for events that occurred while drinking. State-dependent memory also influences recall, such that a person can recall incidences experienced under alcohol's influence when drinking, but not when sober.

4. About 10 percent of those seeking help for alcoholism have suffered from chronic brain damage. Korsakoff's psychosis, a severe form of damage, results in virtually no memory for events occurring since the disorder's onset. Those who indulge in drinking binges run a greater risk of damaging their health than those who regularly drink in moderation.

5. Although use of marijuana is a fairly recent development in the United States, it has been used as an intoxicant in other cultures for centuries. *Cannabis sativa* (Indian hemp) is dried to produce marijuana. Hashish is made from the flowers of the hemp plant. Both contain THC (tetrahydrocannabinal) as their active ingredient and can be smoked or eaten.

6. Although the effects of marijuana vary from person to person, they typically include heightened sensory experiences, elation, an enhanced sense of meaning, and time distortion. Drug experiences with marijuana can be pleasant or unpleasant. About 50 million Americans have used marijuana; 13 million are regular users. Marijuana is now being used to treat glaucoma and to reduce the nausea caused by chemotherapy.

7. Inexperienced users of marijuana suffer more short-term cognitive and motor impairment than long-time users. Early studies indicated that marijuana, like alcohol, impairs transfer of learning from short-term to long-term memory. In high doses, it seems to impair short-term memory as well. More research is needed to further clarify marijuana's effects.

8. Stimulants produce physiological and mental arousal and include drugs as mild as caffeine or as powerful as cocaine and amphetamines. Cocaine, once an ingredient in Coca-Cola, is today illegal, although it is becoming increasingly popular in middle-class America. It can be "snorted" or injected. It produces euphoria, and users report that it improves performance, although users overestimate their abilities. Since energy is expended without replenishing the source, when the drug effects wear off the user "crashes" with exhaustion. Chronic use damages the mucous membranes and can generally poison the system. Large doses can produce hallucinations and even death. One especially horrifying hallucination is formication, the sensation of bugs crawling under one's skin.

9. The amphetamines, such as Dexadrine and Benzedrine, were once prescribed to help people stay awake and lose weight. Under their influence, people feel wonderful and unlimited in their potential. Extended use of amphetamines leads to tolerance, with increasingly larger doses needed to produce the same euphoria. Overuse can lead to paranoia, meaningless wandering of thought, and periods of depression when the drug wears off. Amphetamine abuse can cause brain damage.

10. Hallucinogens, or "psychedelic" drugs, have been extracted from plants and used since earliest human history. They probably work to produce hallucinations by mimicking the activity of certain neurotransmitters in the brain.

11. LSD (lysergic acid diethylamide) is much stronger than natural hallucinogens such as psilocybin and mescaline. It produces a series of hallucinations and feelings of increased awareness and knowledge. In fact, LSD impairs thinking ability as measured by performance on simple tasks. Panic reactions sometimes occur when taking LSD. Apparently LSD works by blocking the effects of serotonin (a neurotransmitter) on brain tissue.

12. Research on the relationship between drug usage and creativity is inconclusive, with some studies indicating beneficial effects, some indicating inhibitory effects. The tentative conclusion is that drugs can stimulate new ideas, but it takes a highly skilled person to use the ideas in a creative way.

□ **Self-Test**

A. Matching Questions

_____ 1. Awareness of the thoughts, images, sensations, and emotions in the mind

a. Manifest content

b. Consciousness

_____ 2. State of sleep associated with dreaming

c. REM

_____ 3. Stage of sleep that shows the greatest proportion of alpha waves

d. Neodissociation theory

e. Scanning hypothesis

_____ 4. Notion that eye movement during dreams indicates watching of the dream's action

f. Stage 4

g. Latent content

_____ 5. The deeper meaning of a dream

h. Stage 1

_____ 6. Notion that hypnosis is the result of conscious suggestion

a. Mantra

b. Neodissociation theory

_____ 7. Sound used in meditation and on which attention is focused

c. Alcohol

d. Zazen

_____ 8. Process of monitoring and changing one's bodily functions

e. Biofeedback

f. Zen

_____ 9. Drug that is a central nervous system depressant

g. Role enactment theory

h. LSD

_____10. Aspect of memory that is usually damaged by taking drugs

i. Transfer

B. Multiple-Choice Questions Testing Factual Knowledge

1. Consciousness is limited by all of the following *except:*
   a. the size of long-term memory
   b. the ability to access one's own cognitive processes
   c. the restricted range of our sensory equipment
   d. selective attention

Objective 1.1

2. The "position effect" in consumer behavior refers to the finding that:
   a. people will buy more when their financial position is strong
   b. people will buy more when their financial position is weak
   c. people buy most items from an intermediate price range, neither cheap nor expensive
   d. people are influenced in buying by the placement of the product   Objective 2.1

3. "A qualitative alteration in overall mental functioning" is the definition of:
   a. consciousness
   b. hypnosis
   c. altered state of consciousness
   d. meditation   Objective 2.1

4. EEG patterns during REM sleep are most similar to those of a person who is:
   a. awake
   b. in stage 1
   c. in stage 2
   d. in stage 4   Objective 3.1

5. The average person goes through about how many sleep cycles in a typical night's sleep?
   a. one
   b. five
   c. eight
   d. hundreds   Objective 3.1

6. Which of the following statements regarding REM sleep is *true*?
   a. REM deprivation enhances memory consolidation.
   b. As you get older, you spend more time in REM sleep.
   c. When deprived of REM sleep, our bodies get used to functioning on less of it.
   d. None of the above are true.   Objective 3.2

7. About what percentage of the population can be hypnotized?
   a. 10 percent
   b. 50 percent
   c. 90 percent
   d. 100 percent   Objective 4.2

8. According to Hilgard's neodissociation view, hypnosis is:
   a. an illusion
   b. an altered state of consciousness
   c. a hoax
   d. an extreme form of persuasion   Objective 4.3

9. According to role enactment theory, hypnotism is most similar to:
   a. being awake
   b. stage 1 sleep
   c. stage 4 sleep
   d. REM sleep   Objective 4.3

10. Which of the following is *not* a technique or tool used to help a meditator center his or her attention?
    a. mantra
    b. zazen
    c. mandala
    d. bodily sensations   Objective 5.1

11. Which of the following physiological changes does *not* occur during meditation?
    a. Breathing slows.
    b. Skin resistance to electrical conductivity rises.
    c. Blood pressure falls.
    d. Oxygen consumption increases.   Objective 5.1

12. The person using biofeedback learns to control target responses by:
    a. aversive conditioning

    b. classical conditioning
    c. trial and error
    d. systematic desensitization   Objective 5.2

13. Biofeedback has been found to be effective in controlling all of the following *except:*
     a. tension headaches
     b. alpha wave output
     c. heart arrhythmias
     d. constriction of blood vessels in the hands and feet   Objective 5.2

14. According to the text, the most widely used mind-altering drug in the United States is:
     a. cocaine
     b. marijuana
     c. Thorazine (chlorpromazine)
     d. alcohol   Objective 6.1

15. The major difference between stimulants and alcohol is that stimulants:
     a. are stronger
     b. are more dangerous
     c. are pleasant to use
     d. produce central nervous system arousal   Objective 6.1

16. Formication is the hallucination that:
     a. "I am dead."
     b. "There are bugs crawling under my skin."
     c. "I see wonderful shapes and colors."
     d. "I can't control myself."   Objective 6.1

17. Amphetamines have been used by people for all of the following *except:*
     a. losing weight
     b. staying awake
     c. reducing anxiety
     d. getting "high"   Objective 6.1

18. Alcohol seems to have the greatest effect on:
     a. short-term memory
     b. long-term memory
     c. transfer from short-term to long-term memory
     d. all of the above about equally   Objective 6.2

19. Regarding memory loss, low doses of marijuana act much like:
     a. alcohol
     b. cocaine
     c. LSD
     d. amphetamines   Objective 6.2

20. According to the text, what is the relationship between drug use and creativity?
     a. Drugs usually produce creativity.
     b. Drugs almost never produce creativity.
     c. Drugs can lay the groundwork for creativity.
     d. Drugs are a detriment to creativity.   Objective 6.2

C.   Multiple-Choice Questions Testing Conceptual Knowledge

21. Suppose you observe a person whose EEG shows a very high level of alpha waves.
     You would guess that person was:
     a. relaxed but not asleep
     b. in stage 2 sleep
     c. in stage 4 sleep
     d. dreaming   Objective 3.1

22. You observe that a sleeper's eyes move up and down repetitively. You wake the sleeper and find that she has been dreaming about watching cliff divers. This experience would support:
    a. neodissociation theory
    b. the scanning hypothesis
    c. role enactment theory
    d. none of the above   Objective 3.2

23. Max has a dream of being chased by a snake. He is sure that this dream represents his insecurity with women. He would be interpreting the dream's:
    a. irregular content
    b. hypothetical content
    c. manifest content
    d. latent content   Objective 3.2

24. Generalizing from an experiment described in the text, if you hypnotized a person and suggested to the person that he was blind in his left eye, you would expect him to:
    a. be truly blind in that eye
    b. be able to see with that eye only when his right eye was closed
    c. be able to see with that eye but deny the sight
    d. admit to being able to see if confronted with evidence that the eye was working
                                                             Objective 4.2

25. Bob recalls that the last person he met named Tommie was a girl, but he has no notion about how he knows that. This is an example of:
    a. neodissociation
    b. role enactment
    c. free association
    d. source amnesia   Objective 4.3

26. A recent television program showed a yogi fit his large body into a very small box, which was then submerged in water. A normal person would have suffocated, but the yogi emerged unharmed. How does this feat differ from dreaming or hypnosis?
    a. It is a true, not a fictional, state of conscious.
    b. It was self-regulated.
    c. In this case, consciousness was not limited.
    d. It did not differ.   Objective 5.1

27. Pamela complains of headaches to her doctor. The doctor attaches electrodes to her head and instructs her to do anything she wants that will produce a green light on the far wall. Her doctor is using:
    a. hypnotism
    b. Zen
    c. biofeedback
    d. transcendental meditation   Objective 5.2

28. Which of the following would be considered a psychoactive drug?
    a. caffeine in coffee
    b. aspirin
    c. penicillin
    d. hormone injections   Objective 6.1

29. You are working in a lab and you analyze a blood sample that contains .6 percent alcohol. You conclude that the person it was drawn from probably:
    a. had a drink before a routine physical
    b. got picked up for drunk driving
    c. passed out from drinking too much alcohol
    d. died from drinking too much alcohol   Objective 6.1

30. Suppose you drink fifteen ounces of alcohol per week. According to research presented in the text, to stay the healthiest:
    a. you should drink about two-and-a-half ounces per day

    b. you should drink it only on weekdays, not weekends

    c. you should drink it all in one day

    d. your drinking pattern does not matter; the total amount you drink does

Objective 6.1

31. Your friend says he has baked some brownies with a drug in them. Furthermore, eating the brownies will make you "high." You conclude the drug he must be talking about is:

    a. alcohol

    b. marijuana

    c. cocaine

    d. any of the above

Objective 6.1

32. Every time you get drunk, you remember your past sexual conquests. When you're sober, you don't remember any of them. This is an example of:

    a. transfer of memory

    b. consolidation of memory

    c. state-dependent memory

    d. proactive interference

Objective 6.2

D. *Short Essay Questions*

1. What is meant by "altered states of consciousness"? (Objective 2.1)

2. Describe a normal night's sleep. (Objective 3.1)

3. How are hypnosis and sleep alike? How do they differ? (Objective 4.1)

4. What is hypnosis? (Hint: compare neodissociation theory to role enactment theory.) (Objectives 4.2, 4.3)

5. According to the text, would taking drugs enhance your creativity? Why or why not? (Objective 6.2)

Personality Theories and Research

■ 13

☐ **Chapter Summary**

I.   1.   Personality can be defined as a fairly stable set of characteristics and tendencies that determine the individuality of a person's responses to a variety of environmental circumstances. This definition addresses two key questions: Why do different people behave differently in the same situation, and what accounts for an individual's consistency across situations?

2. Personality results from the interplay of biological and environmental factors. Different personality theorists emphasize different aspects of personality and its development.

II. 1. Sigmund Freud was the founder of the psychoanalytic approach to personality, although other theorists have modified and expanded his concepts. All such theorists believe that powerful unconscious motives exist and that conflict between motives produces anxiety and defense mechanisms.

2. As a practicing neurologist, Freud treated many patients suffering from psychosomatic symptoms. After studying hypnosis with Charcot and the "talking cure" with Breuer, Freud developed his own procedure—now known as free association—for treating psychosomatic "hysteria." In free association the patient says whatever comes to mind. When the patient shows anxiety, it is assumed that the topic being discussed is related to an unconscious conflict.

3. Freud believed that early experiences, especially those of a sexual nature, produced adult problems. Because of their unacceptable nature, such experiences were often buried in the unconscious. Freud used the procedure called psychoanalysis to bring these thoughts and feelings to consciousness.

4. According to Freud's theory, the unconscious contains both instinctive drives and thoughts that could cause conflict if they were to become conscious. The unconscious is the major motivating force in human behavior. Although we cannot directly experience the contents of the unconscious, the contents can reveal themselves in unguarded moments through such things as slips of the tongue, accidents, and revealing jokes.

5. Freud divided the human psyche into three separate but interacting motivational forces: the id, ego, and superego. The unconscious id contains the psychic energy and biological drives. The id (or "it") operates according to the pleasure principle, seeking immediate reduction of tension, regardless of circumstances. The ego begins developing soon after birth and helps the innate id to realistically reduce tension. The ego (or "I") is present in the conscious and functions according to the reality principle, seeking rational solutions to satisfy the id's demands. The superego (or "over the I") develops in childhood and represents the moral standards of society as conveyed to the person by his or her parents. The superego, commonly referred to as our conscience, functions to prohibit the expression of the id's instinctive drives. Thus, the id and superego are often in conflict, and it is the ego's task to mediate this conflict.

6. When the ego is losing its struggle to reconcile the demands of the id, superego, and reality, anxiety develops. There are three types of anxiety: reality anxiety (brought on by a threat in the outside world), morality anxiety (arising from the superego, which threatens to overwhelm the person with guilt), and neurotic anxiety (caused by the id's threat to burst through ego controls).

7. Anxiety, especially neurotic anxiety, can be reduced by using defense mechanisms. Repression is the most basic defense mechanism; it operates by pushing unacceptable id impulses back into the unconscious. All other defense mechanisms involve repression. Regression reduces anxiety by allowing the person to behave as he or she did at an earlier, less conflict-oriented stage of life. In reaction formation, a person replaces an anxiety-producing impulse or feeling (e.g., hate) with its opposite (e.g., love). Projection occurs when a person unknowingly attaches his or her own objectionable attributes to other people. Displacement is the transfer of unacceptable feelings from their appropriate target to a

much safer object, and sublimation is a kind of displacement in which forbidden impulses are diverted toward socially desirable goals.

8. Since Freud believed that early life experiences laid the groundwork for adult personality, he developed an elaborate theory of personality development. Freud argued that at different stages in a child's life the id's drive for sexual pleasure centers around different body parts, and that adult personality is shaped by the way the child resolves the conflicts between these early sexual urges and the restrictions imposed by society. Failure to resolve a conflict results in fixation, characterized by the symbolic expression of this confict throughout life.

9. The stages in normal development are: the oral stage (where anxiety can result from withholding food when hungry), the anal stage (where anxiety can result from inappropriate toilet training), the phallic stage (in which pleasure focuses on masturbation and conflict comes from inadequate resolution of the oedipal conflict), the latent stage (in which the sexual impulses remain in the background), and finally the genital stage (in which sexual intercourse provides pleasure). Although society was shocked at Freud's suggestion of childhood sexuality, Freud believed that sex was one of the powerful impulses that shaped personality.

10. According to Freud, women are morally inferior to men because they are jealous of men's penises (penis envy) and because they cannot undergo the same oedipal conflict as a boy (which involves castration anxiety). Because the superego develops from the oedipal conflict, women are also culturally inferior. Other psychoanalytic theorists, most notably Karen Horney, have objected to this conclusion. She believes that men, not women, perceive the anatomical difference and create a self-fulfilling prophecy that produces female inferiority.

11. Post-Freudian psychoanalytic theorists have tended to give increased emphasis to the ego rather than the id. They have also tended to deemphasize the importance of sexual and aggressive drives and emphasize the process of social interactions in explaining personality development.

12. Jung and Adler both broke their ties with Freud over disagreements about psychoanalytic theory. Jung objected to Freud's pessimistic view of the unconscious. Adler believed that the great human motivation is striving for superiority; he emphasized the importance of early social relationships. Horney believed that children felt "basic anxiety" when their parents were indifferent to them. The "basic hostility" or resentment that develops is repressed and later expresses itself in one of three modes of social interaction: moving toward others (looking for approval), moving against others (finding security in dominating others), or moving away from others (becoming withdrawn).

13. Freud is often criticized for not attempting to test his theory. Others have attempted to verify his concepts; however, their studies have yielded mixed results. Another criticism is that Freud's concepts are too general; although they can explain behavior, they cannot predict it. This is a serious weakness in the theory. A third criticism is that Freud's theory is culture-bound and applies only to Western society. His concepts have been tested in other cultures with mixed results. Despite these criticisms, Freud's theory and concepts have been of enormous importance in establishing a theory of personality.

III. 1. About the same time that Freud was developing his theory of psychoanalysis in Vienna (the early 1900s), behaviorists in the United States were formulating a different theory of personality—one that focused on learning rather than conflict between unconscious motives.

2. Miller and Dollard, in their psychodynamic behavior theory, attempted to use learning principles to explain many of Freud's concepts. They believed, as

Freud did, that organisms are motivated by a variety of drives that seek reduction. When placed in a situation where a pleasurable drive-reducing response (such as eating) is associated with a negative consequence (such as electric shock), an approach-avoidance conflict—similar to Freud's id–ego conflict—develops. Thus, using rats as subjects Miller and Dollard demonstrated Freud's concepts in a laboratory and explained them as learned responses. They similarly explained defense mechanisms as learned responses that work to avoid or reduce anxiety. Although Miller and Dollard have been criticized for basing a theory of human personality on experiments with rats, they have shown that Freudian theory was not out of step with either a research emphasis or American behaviorism.

3. B. F. Skinner formulated another behavioristic approach, called "radical behaviorism." Skinner denies free will and argues that all our actions are shaped and controlled by environmental events, especially reward and punishment. To change behavior, he argues, you eliminate the external events maintaining it. Skinner's radical behaviorism is an extreme position, and some critics find it frightening or unlikely.

4. Social learning theorists differ from Skinner in that they believe learning can take place through observation and imitation. Reinforcement may strengthen a response, but it is not necessary for learning that response.

IV. 1. Traits are defined as relatively enduring ways in which one individual differs from another. Furthermore, traits are dimensions of personality along which any person can be assessed. Trait theorists emphasize and try to explain the consistency of human behavior (Freud, in contrast, used traits to explain and verify his theory). Trait theory is more a descriptive theory of personality than an explanatory one. An important question for the trait theorist is, which behaviors are correlated?

2. Gordon Allport believed that traits existed somewhere in the nervous system. For Allport, traits could be organized hierarchically: Cardinal traits direct a major portion of a person's behavior; central traits are less inclusive and represent characteristic ways of dealing with the world; and secondary traits or attitudes are the most specific and susceptible to change. Allport also believed that traits are unique to an individual, although people in similar environments may develop common traits that produce similar behavior.

3. Factor analysis is a statistical technique used to identify traits that underlie various behaviors. Raymond Cattell used factor analysis on data collected from self-reports, objective tests, and life records (clusters of behavior that go together). This technique allowed him to identify source traits, the underlying, fundamental elements of personality. Cattell identified sixteen source traits.

4. Hans Eysenck also used factor analysis to support his theory that the traits in personality can be reduced to two major dimensions: neuroticism versus emotional stability and introversion versus extroversion. He believes that brain activity differences underlie these dimensions; for example, extroverted people have low levels of arousal in the cerebral cortex, causing them to seek more stimulation from the environment.

5. Trait theorists assume that behavior is relatively consistent since the underlying traits that produce it are fixed. However, Mischel found that behavior does not seem to be as consistent as the trait theories would suggest. Mischel argues that traits do not exist as part of personality; rather, they exist as a way of explaining the behavior of others. Due to the primacy effect (first impressions are important) and to the tendency to observe another person in only one role, we simplify that person's behavior by assigning a trait to it. Furthermore, our own

behavior probably helps elicit the expected behavior in that person. Mischel's ideas have been challenged by Bem and Allen, who believe that traits exist and operate consistently in most situations. Considering all the research, both traits and situational factors would seem important in interpreting the cause of behavior. Indeed, many psychologists believe further research will be directed at the interactions of these two factors.

V.

1. The phenomenological approach to personality stresses the individual's unique perception of the world and suggests that all people are free to fulfill their own potential. Phenomenological approaches thereby contradicted both psychoanalysis and behaviorism, both of which hold that our behavior is determined by forces beyond our control.

2. Carl Rogers believes that all humans strive toward self-actualization, the fulfillment of one's capabilities and potential. He found, however, that his clients (patients) had trouble doing this due to "conditional positive regard," the distortion of feelings produced by the withholding of parental love. In order to gain praise from others, the child incorporates into himself "conditions of worth," ideas that the child believes will bring positive regard. Rogers believes children will either become fully functioning or their self-actualization will be blocked. To help the latter, Rogers developed client-centered therapy. In this therapy, the therapist does not judge the client and offers the client *un*conditional positive regard, enabling the client to confront conflicts and feelings in an atmosphere of support. Rogers suggests that children should be raised in an atmosphere of *un*conditional positive regard. Some research supports his belief that this method produces cooperative children, but other research has demonstrated that the same techniques can produce selfish children.

3. Abraham Maslow also believed that a person's primary motivation was self-actualization, but that before a person could reach this stage, a hierarchy of needs must first be satisfied. This hierarchy begins with the fundamental physiological needs, then safety needs, then psychological, social, and love needs, and finally self-actualization. Maslow analyzed healthy people, both historical figures and present-day persons, to develop his ideas.

4. Humanists, such as Rogers and Maslow, have encouraged us to study the positive aspects of personality.

5. When one considers all the theories of personality, several important themes emerge—conflict, external influences on thought and behavior, continuity and consistency of behavior, and self-fulfillment. Although personality theories each have a different focus, they all address these fundamental concepts.

☐ **Self-Test**

A. Matching Questions

____ 1. A fairly stable set of characteristics that determines an individual's response to a variety of situations

____ 2. The "talking cure"

____ 3. The process by which unconscious thoughts and feelings are raised into consciousness

____ 4. The Freudian component of personality that embodies society's moral code

____ 5. Describes the operation of the ego

a. Psychoanalysis
b. Defense mechanism
c. Reality principle
d. Personality
e. Ego
f. Pleasure principle
g. Free association
h. Superego

_h_ 6. Pushing back of unacceptable id impulses into the unconscious

_e_ 7. The transfer of unacceptable feelings to a ''safer'' object

_b_ 8. Time in which the oedipal conflict unfolds

_i_ 9. Horney's name for a child's feelings of helplessness and insecurity

_f_ 10. Miller and Dollard's concept to explain anxiety

a. Regression
b. Phallic stage
c. Projection
d. Basic hostility
e. Displacement
f. Approach–avoidance conflict
g. Anal stage
h. Repression
i. Basic anxiety

_f_ 11. According to Allport, a trait that directs a major portion of a person's behavior

___ 12. Mathematical techniques for finding underlying traits

___ 13. Cattell's notion of the fundamental elements of personality

___ 14. Stresses the individual's unique perception of the world

___ 15. Rogers's term for the parental withholding of praise and love

a. Surface trait
b. Cardinal trait
c. Unconditional positive regard
d. Factor analysis
e. Conditional positive regard
f. Central trait
g. Phenomenology
h. Source trait
i. Humanism

B. Multiple-Choice Questions Testing Factual Knowledge

1. Before becoming an analyst, Freud was a:
   a. teacher
   b. neurologist
   c. plumber
   d. rabbi   Objective 2.1

2. According to Freud, which of the following is the major motivating force in personality?
   a. unconscious
   b. conscious
   c. ego
   d. conscience   Objective 2.1

3. To Freud, a slip of the tongue represented:
   a. a neurological disorder
   b. an unhealthy childhood
   c. an unconscious conflict
   d. a simple mistake   Objective 2.1

4. According to the discussion of Freud's theory in the text, the id, ego, and superego are:
   a. physical divisions in the brain
   b. different ways of processing information
   c. various biochemical processes in the brain
   d. strong motivational forces   Objective 2.1

5. Which of the following is present at birth?
   a. superego
   b. id
   c. ego
   d. all of the above   Objective 2.1

6. Which of the following defense mechanisms underlies all others?
   a. projection
   b. fixation
   c. regression
   d. repression   Objective 2.2

7. Sublimation is a special kind of:
   a. repression
   b. regression
   c. displacement
   d. projection   Objective 2.2

8. The intense desire to take the place of the same-sex parent in the affections of the parent of the opposite sex is called:
   a. the oedipal conflict
   b. reaction formation
   c. sublimation
   d. the pleasure principle   Objective 2.3

9. Freud felt that women, as compared to men, were:
   a. inferior
   b. envious of the male penis
   c. unable to make substantial contributions to society, except in the task of weaving
   d. all of the above   Objective 2.3

10. Horney's major objection to Freud's theory was:
    a. his notion of unconscious desires
    b. the emphasis he placed on the ego
    c. his bias about female inferiority
    d. his emphasis on childhood sexuality   Objective 2.4

11. Most of the psychoanalytic theorists who broke away from Freud came to place more emphasis than Freud on which of the following?
    a. ego
    b. id
    c. unconscious
    d. conscience   Objective 2.4

12. According to the text, a major problem with Freudian theory is that it cannot:
    a. describe behavior
    b. predict behavior
    c. explain behavior
    d. all of the above   Objective 2.4

13. Which of the following Freudian concepts have been heavily criticized?
    a. penis envy
    b. anxiety
    c. repression
    d. defense mechanisms   Objective 2.4

14. Miller and Dollard placed a hungry rat in a runway in such a way that to reach food, the rat had to receive shock. This produced what they called:
    a. anxiety
    b. a drive state
    c. an approach–avoidance conflict
    d. punishment–reward   Objective 3.1

15. Miller and Dollard attempted to apply the principles of learning to the theory proposed by:
    a. Miller and Dollard
    b. Skinner

c. Rogers
d. Freud   Objective 3.1

16. According to Skinner, the causes of behavior are:
    a. drives
    b. outside the organism
    c. basic anxieties
    d. unconscious conflicts   Objective 3.1

17. Social learning theorists believe that reinforcement is very important in:
    a. learning a behavior
    b. maintaining a behavior
    c. both a and b
    d. none of the above   Objective 3.1

18. Which of the following was *not* a technique used by Cattell to gather information about a person's traits?
    a. free association
    b. self-reports
    c. objective tests
    d. life records   Objective 4.1

19. Eysenck concluded that personality structure varies on two dimensions: neuroticism versus emotional stability and introversion versus extroversion. Underlying these traits are differences in:
    a. drive
    b. genetic composition
    c. brain stimulation
    d. early experiences in the environment   Objective 4.1

20. Which of the following theorists has done his work primarily with normal adult humans?
    a. Rogers
    b. Skinner
    c. Freud
    d. Maslow   Objective 5.2

C. Multiple-Choice Questions Testing Conceptual Knowledge

21. Maria is continually worrying about whether her actions are going to be socially acceptable. You might say her personality was being controlled by her:
    a. ego
    b. id
    c. superego
    d. defense mechanisms   Objective 2.1

22. Jack finds any mention of male femininity offensive. His therapist suggests that, in actuality, this may be Jack's method of reducing anxiety from his true fear of being a homosexual. If so, Jack is using the defense mechanism of:
    a. reaction formation
    b. displacement
    c. projection
    d. regression   Objective 2.2

23. If fixation occurs during the first year of a person's life, you might expect that, as an adult, this person would be:
    a. homosexual
    b. excessively neat
    c. a compulsive smoker
    d. all of the above   Objective 2.3

24. James believes that the major motivation in a person's life is to strive for perfection. In this respect, he is most like:·
    a. Sigmund Freud
    b. Alfred Adler
    c. Carl Jung
    d. Karen Horney   Objective 2.4

25. Sally's roommate is continually doing favors for people—to a point where she gets frustrated because she has no time of her own. According to Horney, she is moving:
    a. against people
    b. toward people
    c. away from people
    d. with people   Objective 2.4

26. Which of the following is an example of an approach–avoidance conflict?
    a. Mary cannot decide which of two dresses to buy.
    b. If Mary goes out with Bill (her current heartthrob) tonight, she will flunk the math test tomorrow.
    c. Mary does not want to go to the dentist, but she also does not want to get cavities.
    d. none of the above   Objective 3.1

27. Jeremy believes that the major purpose of a personality theory is to explain the consistency of human behavior. Your best guess as to which type of personality theory describes his views is:
    a. phenomenological theory
    b. radical behaviorism
    c. social learning theory
    d. trait theory   Objective 4.1

28. Suzanne has recently acquired a taste for spicy foods. According to Allport, this preference would best be considered a:
    a. secondary trait
    b. cardinal trait
    c. central trait
    d. source trait   Objective 4.1

29. Bob is outgoing, sociable, excitement-seeking, and loves a good time. He also has a good job and a stable family life. According to Eysenck, he would be especially high on which of the following dimensions?
    a. neuroticism
    b. introversion
    c. psychoticism
    d. extroversion   Objective 4.1

30. As presented in this chapter, Mischel's research on the consistency of personality would be most threatening to which of the following theoretical positions?
    a. psychoanalytic theory
    b. phenomenological theory
    c. trait theory
    d. behavioral theory   Objective 4.1

31. Marty believes that humans have an inborn potential for growth, creativity, and spontaneity. He would best be classified as advocating which of the following approaches?
    a. psychoanalytic
    b. trait
    c. social learning
    d. phenomenological   Objective 5.1

32. Joe's wife always treats him with respect and is warm, accepting, and sympathetic. Furthermore, she encourages Joe to speak his mind on whatever is troubling him. According to Rogers, she is offering Joe:
    a. unconditional positive regard
    b. conditional positive regard
    c. self-actualization
    d. phenomenological worth   Objective 5.2

D. Short Essay Questions

1. Why do you think psychologists study personality?   (Objective 1.1)

2. What role do the defense mechanisms play in Freud's theory of personality? (Objective 2.2)

3. Compare and contrast the behaviorist theory of Miller and Dollard, Skinner, and the social learning theorists.   (Objective 3.2)

4. What is a trait? How do trait theorists explain personality?   (Objective 4.2)

5. Why can Rogers and Maslow be called phenomenologists? Why can they be called humanists?   (Objective 5.2)

■ 14
Assessment and Individual Differences

□ **Chapter Summary**

I. 1. Tests have existed throughout history. They can serve many purposes—measuring students' mastery of content, comparing one group of students to others, diagnosing specific problems, developing appropriate instructional plans, selecting students with special abilities, and others. Testing can also be misused, and it has been criticized because it reveals controversial differences among people.

   2. A good test must have reliability—that is, it must measure a particular trait or ability with consistency. Several kinds of reliability can be assessed. Test–retest reliability is determined by administering the same test to the same individual on more than one occasion. If reliability is high, the individual's scores on both occasions should be similar. To remove the possibility that a person might remember the answers from the previous taking of the test, another form of reliability—alternate forms reliability—can be used. Alternate forms reliability compares a student's score on one form of a test to his or her score on another, similar form. Split-half reliability, also called internal consistency, is often used when it is difficult to develop an alternate form of the test or when retesting is undesirable. In split-half reliability, the test items on a particular test are randomly divided into two groups and performances on the two halves are compared. In tests that are subjectively scored (in which there is no one correct answer), interjudge reliability is important. High interjudge reliability means that two judges independently score the tests the same way. Thus, the type of reliability that is most appropriate is determined by the type of test used and the type of trait being measured.

   3. Validity reveals whether the test is measuring what it is intended to measure. Content validity measures whether the test covers a representative sample of the material that is being tested. Criterion-related validity refers to the relationship between a person's test score and some other criterion. Two kinds of criterion validity are commonly used: concurrent validity, which compares test performance to other scores presently available; and predictive validity, which compares test performance to performance on some future task. Construct validity reveals how well a test measures the hypothethical traits or constructs it is intended to measure.

   4. A test score is not very meaningful until we compare it to its norm, the range of scores attained on the test by other similar people. Before a test is put into general use, it is given to a well-defined and representative group of people, called a standardization group. Their scores make up the normative distribution to which other test results can be compared.

II. 1. In the early 1900s, Alfred Binet developed the first tests of mental ability (intelligence tests) designed to predict who would be successful in school. He reasoned that since older children could typically answer more difficult questions than younger children, individual children can be characterized by their mental age. The IQ, or intelligence quotient, is the ratio of a child's mental age as determined by Binet's test to the child's chronological age (how old the child is) multiplied by 100.

   2. The revision of Binet's original intelligence test currently in use is the Stanford-Binet test. This test contains items from a number of verbal and performance subtests arranged in order of their difficulty. Starting at the basal age (the highest mental age at which all questions can be answered correctly) the child is asked progressively more difficult questions until he or she can no longer answer them correctly. Thus, the child's performance is compared to typical performance for children at various ages. A mental age of 10 means that the child could

answer questions that the average ten-year-old could answer. A child's mental age is compared to his or her chronological age multiplied by 100 to yield IQ. In 1960 a change was made in calculating IQ. It is no longer calculated by the mental age–chronological age ratio. Instead, a score is compared to a norm group to see how far the score deviates from the norm (average) for children the same age. The Stanford-Binet test has also been expanded for use with preschool children and adults.

3. The other frequently used intelligence tests are the Wechsler Adult Intelligence Scale (WAIS) and the Wechsler Intelligence Scale for Children (WISC). The Wechsler tests report separate scores for each of the several subtests and yield two intelligence scores (verbal and performance), unlike the Stanford-Binet, which yields only one. The Wechsler tests are less biased toward verbal skills, and they use the same items for subjects of all ages. The Wechsler tests encourage the view that intelligence is composed of a number of different abilities.

4. Paper-and-pencil tests of intelligence can be administered to large groups of people. Representative tests are the Army Alpha, the Army Beta, and the Scholastic Aptitude Test (SAT). Although group tests are less expensive and easier to administer and score, they are not as accurate in predicting school success as are individual tests. Both the verbal and mathematical subtests of the SAT are good predictors of college success, especially when combined with high school performance. Whether or not coaching can improve a student's score on the SAT remains a controversial issue.

5. Of the total population 68 percent score in the average range on intelligence tests (between 85 and 115); 95 percent fall between 70 and 130; and 99.7 percent fall between 55 and 145.

6. Levels of retardation correspond to IQ test scores: 67 to 52 is considered mild retardation; 51 to 36, moderate retardation; 35 to 20, severe retardation; and less than 19, profound retardation. These categories are not absolute, however, and depend somewhat on the individual's adaptive skills. The mentally retarded constitute 2 to 3 percent of the population (6 million people). Retardation is caused by many factors, including the chromosome abnormality called Down's syndrome. Down's syndrome can be detected before birth by amniocentesis. Since social and perceptual limitations can cause a person of normal intelligence to seem retarded, careful screening must be done for an accurate diagnosis to be made.

7. Among the many misconceptions about children who are intellectually brilliant are beliefs that their brilliance fades with age, and that they are unhealthy, mentally unstable, and socially inept. In 1921 Terman began studying child geniuses and found that such beliefs were not valid. Terman also found that a good environment has a favorable effect on intelligence. One problem that gifted children do have is maximizing their potential in our traditional school systems.

8. Intelligence is different from creativity, although a certain amount of intelligence is necessary for creative thought. Creative people tend to follow their own ideas and to be independent, self-confident, motivated to succeed, enthusiastic, open to new experience, intuitive, and introverted. Tests of creativity are relatively new and generally consist of open-ended questions.

III. 1. Because the genetic component of intelligence cannot be measured directly, there is considerable disagreement about how influential it is.

2. Arthur Jensen in 1969 published an article in which he argued that intelligence was highly heritable; hence, racial differences in IQ were due to differences in gene distribution in the population. To understand genetic influence, one must

know that heritability is the extent to which an observed individual variation of a trait can be attributed to genetic differences and that the reaction range is the range of possible effects the environment can have. Jensen's claims were based on data collected by Sir Cyril Burt that showed that identical twins separated at birth and placed in different environments still had remarkably similar IQs. The implications from Jensen's article were that intelligence is fixed at birth and, therefore, compensatory education would be useless.

3. Jensen's work has been heavily criticized. First, Burt's statistics may have contained errors. Also, blacks differ from whites on socioeconomic factors that could contribute to IQ differences. IQ tests are affected by many factors (disease, motivation, etc.) that Jensen did not address. Finally, Jensen's critics claim that he does not attend to reaction range considerations.

4. More recent studies and opinions suggest that both heredity and environment play a significant role in determining intelligence. Apparently, intelligence has a fairly wide reaction range, and the differences within any racial or ethnic group far exceed differences between groups. It seems unlikely that a definitive answer to the nature–nurture question for intelligence will be completely attained.

5. The public is concerned about IQ testing for several additional reasons. Some people claim that IQ tests are biased toward the language and culture of the middle class. Although cultural bias is most obvious on verbal tests, it is present in performance tests as well. Psychologists are working at the difficult job of developing culture-free intelligence tests. The best known of these is SOMPA (System of Multicultural Pluralistic Assessment), which includes a standard IQ test, an interview with the child's parents, and a medical examination to identify possible physical problems.

6. Another criticism is that, although IQ tests can predict school success, they do not predict success in life. Sometimes IQ tests are inappropriately used as job selection criteria. They have also been used to "track," or group, students according to intelligence scores. This practice has largely been discontinued since the passage of a 1977 law that requires that assessment of intelligence for class placement include more than the simple administration of an IQ test. IQ tests do, however, provide a means of identifying students who might benefit from special programs. New kinds of intelligence tests are emerging to test such skills as "social intelligence" or "learning potential." Such tests may change the definition of intelligence.

IV. 1. Personality assessment developed from differential psychology (the study of individual differences) and abnormal psychology. The free-association test was one of the first personality tests developed. It requires the subject to respond to a stimulus word with the first word that comes to his mind in order to reveal unconscious personality conflicts. Since then, many personality tests have been developed.

2. Projective tests of personality ask the subject to interpret ambiguous material and in so doing reveal his own conflicts and emotions. The Rorschach Inkblot Test asks subjects to report what they see in each of ten inkblots. Their responses are scored according to location (the part of the inkblot they interpret), determinants (the form, color, or shading of the blot they emphasize), and content (what the subject claims to see). Subject response can vary depending on how and by whom the test is administered. Meaningful results depend strongly on the skill of the test giver. The Thematic Apperception Test (TAT) requires the subject to tell a coherent story about each of twenty pictures of people doing different things. Originally intended to reveal the impact of a person's "internal needs" and "environmental presses (forces)," it is now often used as a general personality test in both clinical and research settings. It has many of the same disadvantages as the Rorschach.

3. Objective tests attempt to measure how much of a particular group of traits a person has. One type of objective test is developed by using factor analysis statistics to disclose which test items best measure these basic traits. Other tests like the MMPI (Minnesota Multiphasic Personality Inventory) are developed empirically, by administering the test to various groups of subjects and comparing their responses. Both types can have problems with validity. The MMPI is composed of 550 true-false items that may pertain to a person's self-image. An individual's pattern of answers is compared to typical answers given by various groups of diagnosed psychiatric patients. A high score on one set of items (or scale) could indicate personal characteristics similar to those typical of the group from which the scale was drawn (for example, victims of depression). The ten clinical scales (such as depression) are supplemented with three validity scales, the L scale (which indicates lying), the F scale (which picks out highly unusual answers), and the K scale (which reveals the subject's evasiveness in answering the questions). The MMPI is useful for identifying and diagnosing psychopathology but not for measuring normal personality.

4. Interest tests are useful in educational and vocational counseling. The Strong-Campbell Interest Inventory (SCII) presents 325 items, and the subject reports whether he or she likes, dislikes, or is indifferent about each item. Results are reported on six general occupational scales, which are broken into 23 basic scales and two additional scales indicating the subject's likelihood of continuing advanced education and a preference for working with people or alone. Other vocational tests can be administered to measure specific aptitudes (such as finger dexterity) or performance abilities (such as typing). Some employers also use certain kinds of personality tests to predict job success. Other personnel assessment methods include collecting biographical information on an application blank and holding personal interviews. The best strategy in hiring is probably to use a variety of assessment instruments.

V. 1. Tests, like other tools, are not always properly used and interpreted. Common pitfalls include overgeneralizing the results and failure to understand possible sources of error and bias. A test is only valid when it is being used for the specific purpose for which it was intended. Although tests are designed to help people, they can also hurt them, so ethical issues must be carefully considered and monitored.

☐ **Self-Test**

A. Matching Questions

_____ 1. General term for the consistency of test results

_____ 2. Process of collecting normative information about a test

_____ 3. Comparison of one administration of a test to a second administration with the same group of subjects

_____ 4. General term for whether a test is measuring what it is intended to measure

_____ 5. Relationship of a test score to another piece of information

_____ 6. Assesses whether a test measures the underlying trait it is supposed to be measuring

a. Split-half reliability
b. Construct validity
c. Standardization
d. Validity
e. Test-retest reliability
f. Alternate forms reliability
g. Content validity
h. Reliability
i. Norms
j. Concurrent validity

_____ 7. $\dfrac{\text{Mental age}}{\text{Chronological age}} \times 100$

_____ 8. An individual intelligence test

_____ 9. A group intelligence test

_____ 10. A culture-free test of intelligence

_____ 11. A projective test of personality

_____ 12. An interest test

a. SAT

b. L scale

c. IQ

d. TAT

e. SCII

f. WISC

g. MMPI

h. SOMPA

B. Multiple-Choice Questions Testing Factual Knowledge

1. A group of scores against which an individual's test score is compared is called a:
   a. norm
   b. reference group
   c. positive reference group
   d. construct

   Objective 1.2

2. Binet's original intelligence test was developed to:
   a. measure IQ
   b. predict success in school
   c. discriminate between racial groups
   d. prove the superiority of the upper socioeconomic group's children   Objective 2.1

3. Which of the following tests measures intelligence individually and reports both a verbal and a performance IQ?
   a. Stanford-Binet
   b. Scholastic Aptitude Test
   c. Wechsler Intelligence Scale for Children
   d. Army Alpha

   Objective 2.2

4. According to the text, which of the following is the best predictor of success in college?
   a. high school grades
   b. SAT scores
   c. a combination of a and b
   d. student self-reports of motivation

   Objective 2.4

5. About 95 percent of the American population scores between _____ and _____ on a standardized intelligence test.
   a. 85 and 115
   b. 70 and 130
   c. 55 and 145
   d. 30 and 170

   Objective 2.4

6. "Mild retardation" has been associated with an intelligence test score of about:
   a. 85
   b. 75
   c. 65
   d. 45

   Objective 2.4

7. With inappropriate diagnosis, which of the following problems is sometimes erroneously diagnosed as mental illness?
   a. coming from a non-English speaking home
   b. emotional disturbance
   c. physical or perceptual difficulties
   d. all of the above

   Objective 2.4

8. According to Terman's study of genius, children with exceptionally high IQs are more likely to:
   a. become alcoholics
   b. turn to a life of crime
   c. attain a superior income level
   d. get divorced
   Objective 2.4
9. According to the text, one of the problems that gifted children face is:
   a. being bored in school
   b. being unpopular
   c. being physically unhealthy
   d. all of the above
   Objective 2.4
10. According to the text, what is the relationship between intelligence and creativity?
    a. They are very strongly correlated.
    b. They are unrelated.
    c. Intelligence is necessary but not sufficient for creativity.
    d. Creativity is necessary but not sufficient for intelligence.
    Objective 2.4
11. According to the text, intelligence tests measure:
    a. genetic influences
    b. environmental influences
    c. both a and b
    d. neither a nor b
    Objective 3.1
12. According to the text, the reaction range for intelligence as measured by an intelligence test is about:
    a. 3 to 5 points
    b. 10 to 15 points
    c. 20 to 25 points
    d. 40 to 50 points
    Objective 3.1
13. Arthur Jensen argued that individual and racial differences in IQ come predominantly from:
    a. cultural differences
    b. impoverished environments
    c. test biases
    d. genetic differences
    Objective 3.1
14. According to the text, the current status of the issue Jensen raised is:
    a. resolved in favor of Jensen
    b. resolved in favor of Jensen's opponents
    c. no longer considered important
    d. still controversial
    Objective 3.1
15. SOMPA (System of Multicultural Pluralistic Assessment) is a recently developed intelligence test that attempts to control for:
    a. cultural biases in intelligence testing
    b. genetic differences in intelligence
    c. environmental differences in intelligence
    d. all of the above
    Objective 3.2
16. The federal law PL 94–142 that deals with rights of retarded and disabled children specifies that:
    a. children cannot be assigned to special-education classes solely on the basis of an IQ score
    b. colleges cannot discriminate in student selections on the basis of IQ scores
    c. intelligence tests can no longer be used in placing children in special-education classes
    d. different intelligence tests must be used with retarded or disabled children
    Objective 3.2

17. Selecting test items that are answered differently by "normal" and "mentally ill" people and using them to test for possible mental illness is the rationale behind which of the following tests?
    a. Rorschach Inkblot Test
    b. MMPI
    c. free-association tests
    d. TAT   Objective 4.1

18. According to the text, which of the following tests would most typically be used by a vocational counselor?
    a. TAT
    b. MMPI
    c. Stanford-Binet
    d. SCII   Objective 4.2

19. According to research presented in the text, the best job-selection policy would involve routinely making hiring decisions on the basis of:
    a. personal interviews by a staff of trained interviewers
    b. application blank information
    c. specific aptitude tests
    d. a combination of all of the above   Objective 4.2

20. The authors of the text believe that the use of tests:
    a. is generally good
    b. is generally bad
    c. can be either good or bad
    d. is neither good nor bad   Objective 5.1

C. Multiple-Choice Questions Testing Conceptual Knowledge

21. Suppose you wish to know whether the test you have developed to place children in an advanced math class is consistently measuring the same characteristic. You would want to assess your test's:
    a. norms
    b. validity
    c. standardization
    d. reliability   Objective 1.1

22. If time for test development is limited and the answers on the test(s) is (are) easily remembered, the preferred measure of reliability would be:
    a. alternate forms reliability
    b. test-retest reliability
    c. split-half reliability
    d. interjudge reliability   Objective 1.1

23. Suppose you have three trained observers recording aggressive behaviors exhibited by a particular child. The kind of reliability that you would be most interested in is:
    a. alternate forms reliability
    b. interjudge reliability
    c. split-half reliability
    d. test-retest reliability   Objective 1.1

24. A personnel director wants to develop a test to use for placing job applicants in jobs where they will do well. She would be most interested in:
    a. predictive validity
    b. criterion-related validity
    c. content validity
    d. concurrent validity   Objective 1.1

25. Janet is ten years old. Her IQ is 120. According to Binet's original IQ formula, what is Janet's mental age?
    a. six
    b. eight
    c. ten
    d. twelve   Objective 2.1

26. You are taking a test in which you arrange the following letters into as many words as possible: AGBDFCEGDF. You conclude that this test is probably measuring:
    a. creativity
    b. intelligence
    c. personality
    d. interest   Objective 2.4

27. Suppose you determine that genes are responsible for 90 percent of the individual variation of a particular trait, such as eye color. You are here considering eye color's:
    a. reaction range
    b. heritability
    c. normative distribution
    d. Jensen factor   Objective 3.1

28. You are taking a personality test and are asked to respond to the words the tester says by saying the first related word that comes into your mind. You are probably taking:
    a. the MMPI
    b. an intelligence test
    c. a projective test
    d. an interest test   Objective 4.1

29. You are walking outside with your friend when he asks, "What does that cloud look like to you?" You know that this situation is very much like which of the following tests?
    a. MMPI
    b. TAT
    c. Rorschach Inkblot Test
    d. unconscious nonverbal cues   Objective 4.1

30. Probably the most severe problem of the projective tests concerns the assessment of the tests':
    a. norms
    b. validity
    c. test-retest reliability
    d. split-half reliability   Objective 4.1

31. You take the MMPI and are given several assertions such as "I never think bad thoughts about other people." You answer all these statements with the "applies to me" response. You would probably score unusually high on:
    a. the L scale
    b. the depression scale
    c. the hypochondria scale
    d. all the clinical scales   Objective 4.1

32. You are taking a test that asks you whether you like, dislike, or are indifferent to activities such as playing with children, working with your hands, and so on. You conclude you are taking the:
    a. Strong-Campbell Interest Inventory
    b. Wechsler Adult Intelligence Scale
    c. Thematic Apperception Test
    d. System of Multicultural Pluralistic Assessment   Objective 4.2

D. *Short Essay Questions*

1. Which do you think is more important, test reliability or test validity? Why? (Objective 1.1)

2. How does the Stanford-Binet test currently in use differ from Binet's original test? How does it differ from Wechsler's tests?   (Objectives 2.1, 2.2)

3. Is IQ the only factor related to genius and retardation? What other factors might be related?   (Objective 2.4)

4. Briefly summarize the Jensen controversy about intelligence.   (Objective 3.1)

5. What differences do you see between projective and objective personality tests? Which are more useful?   (Objective 4.1)

6. Do you think the advantages of testing outweigh the disadvantages? Defend your answer. (Objective 5.1)

Exploring
Abnormal Behavior ■ 15

I. 1. Abnormal behavior can be defined in many ways. The statistical criterion is simplest; it specifies that abnormality is any substantial deviation from the average. The social norms criterion defines abnormal behavior as that which differs significantly from the norms of society. The absolute criterion suggests that abnormality is defined by comparing behavior to an absolute standard of mental health. All three definitions have advantages and disadvantages, and all three can be used in diagnosis.

2. Several theories have been proposed to account for abnormal behavior, each applying to different cases and each suggesting different causes and cures.

II. 1. The medical model has probably been the most influential theory. It likens psychological disorder to physical illness: Symptoms are used to diagnose the underlying "mental illness," which results from a physical problem. *The Diagnostic and Statistical Manual of Mental Disorders* (DSM) lists hundreds of mental disorders, each classified by their associated symptoms. Thomas Szasz criticizes the medical model, claiming that treating people as if they were ill causes them to become ill.

2. The psychoanalytic perspective, first proposed by Sigmund Freud, holds that unresolved conflicts in early childhood set the stage for psychological disorders later in life. If such a conflict produces fixation very early in life, psychosis (any severe disturbance) would be the result. If the fixation occurs later, after the ego has developed, neurosis (a milder disturbance characterized by anxiety) would result. The neurotic would overuse defense mechanisms to control the excessive anxiety, and behavior would become abnormal. The psychoanalytic perspective is similar to the medical model in that symptoms are seen as being produced by underlying disorders, and treatment is offered by medical doctors trained in psychoanalysis.

3. The learning perspective differs sharply from the medical and psychoanalytic models. It proposes that psychological disturbances arise from learning abnormal responses. Thus, maladaptive behavior can be learned at any time of life. Treatment usually consists of trying to extinguish the maladaptive behavior and teach more normal methods of living through processes of classical and instrumental conditioning. Thus, when symptoms disappear, treatment is successful. The cognitive approach in the learning perspective suggests that the interpretations a person places on an event can also be significant determinants of how he or she will respond to that event.

4. The family, or systems, approach suggests that the source of a psychological disturbance may not be entirely within the person: The relationships the person has with others may also be the cause of maladaptive behavior. Thus, maladaptive behavior can be seen as a normal response to a bad situation.

5. The sociocultural perspective looks for the source of psychological disturbances in the society in which a person lives. It suggests that conditions such as overcrowding and poverty may produce undesirable behavior.

6. The humanistic-existential perspective views humans as being born with a drive to "actualize," or fulfill, themselves. Psychological disturbances are thought to result from a failure to actualize one's potential. Therefore, this theory specifies that we must take responsibility for our lives and make good choices for our future. This perspective is very optimistic, emphasizing the positive aspects of human potential.

7. None of these theories provides perfect answers for therapy, but each contributes a different perspective for the study of psychological disturbances.

8. In evaluating a psychological disorder, a person's symptoms are classified into a cateogry, allowing specification of treatment. Some people, however, object to classification, claiming it is unreliable, causes people to be treated according to their diagnosis rather than their actual behaviors, and produces a negative stigma. When Rosenhan conducted a study in which normal people faked symptoms to get into a mental institution, he found support for these criticisms. Others defend diagnosis as having more assets than liabilities. Obviously, there is still controversy regarding the appropriateness of classification.

9. The DSM has been the preeminent system of classification for many years. It has gone through three revisions, the most recent in 1980. Changes in the DSM reflect new information about disorders and their treatment as well as social changes in attitudes about mental illness.

III. 1. The neurotic disorders are characterized by inappropriate fear.

2. The anxiety disorders include anxiety, phobias, obsessions, and compulsions. Free-floating anxiety is a generalized fear with no identifiable cause. The anxiety may interrupt sleep and eating cycles. Panic attacks are episodes of extreme, uncontrollable anxiety. A phobia is an extreme and irrational rear focused on a particular object. An obsession is a recurring, irrational thought that intrudes continuously, even though the person tries to avoid thinking about it. A compulsion is an uncontrollable, repetitive behavior such as excessive handwashing.

3. Somatoform disorders include those physical problems caused by psychological factors. The conversion disorder usually involves the loss of some body function following a traumatic event. For example, in glove anesthesia, a hand becomes paralyzed, even though there is no physical cause. The conversion disorder arises to protect the person from being forced to confront a high-anxiety situation.

4. The dissociation disorders involve the splitting of the personality into component parts. Amnesia, the forgetting of past experiences, involves the dissociation of present memories from certain memories of the past. In a fugue state, people leave their identity and take up a new life, having entirely forgotten their past. Multiple personality is the dissociation of the mind into several "people," each with different characteristics.

IV. 1. Affective disorders are characterized by disturbances in mood. Depression involves a general feeling of sadness and inactivity. When depression takes on the extreme characteristics of psychosis, the person may have hallucinations (imagined sensory experiences) or delusions (irrational beliefs). Depression seems to be a persistent disorder; people who have experienced one episode stand a 50 percent chance of having another.

2. Mania is a state of elation and feverish activity. As such, it is in many respects the opposite of depression. Mania often occurs in conjunction with depression. This manic-depressive disorder involves alternating periods of mania and depression.

3. Different theories have attempted to explain depression in a variety of ways. Freud suggested that depression resulted from the loss of a loved one toward whom one had ambivalent feelings. Lewinsohn, a learning theorist, proposes that depression occurs because a person is no longer receiving any pleasurable reinforcement from life. Beck, a cognitive theorist, believes that depressed people make errors in their thinking, which leads them to put a consistently negative interpretation on nearly everything. Seligman, another learning theorist, suggests depression is a learned response of inactivity that arises when a person feels that he has no control over what happens to him. When a person interprets a negative event as permanent and due to his or her personal failing, depression is a likely result.

Weiss's biological theory suggests that depression results from a reduction of norepinephrine in the brain. Other biological theories have proposed that depression arises from higher levels of sodium in the body or from disruptions in the amount of neurotransmitters such as serotonin or norepinephrine.

The family, or systems, approach specifies that depression results from disturbed interactions among family members. Integrative theories propose that depression arises from a complex combination of these above-mentioned theories.

V.   1. Schizophrenia is considered the most severe of the mental disorders since schizophrenics are generally unable to function in normal life. Symptoms include disordered thought, delusions, hallucinations, nonsensical speech, and inappropriate expressions of emotion.

2. Most schizophrenics exhibit a split between various ideas and emotions. Often, their language indicates the inappropriate shifting from one thought to the next as they ramble through meaningless and unrelated phrases. Their speech is characterized by poverty of content—lots of words but almost no meaning.

3. Schizophrenics also have a distorted view of reality, seeing, feeling, and hearing things that have no existence in reality. They may also display bizarre and inappropriate behaviors. Sometimes, when in a catatonic stupor, the schizophrenic displays no behavior at all, just remaining motionless for long periods of time.

4. Different theories propose various explanations of the cause of schizophrenia. Schizophrenia is more common in low than in high socioeconomic classes; thus, the sociocultural theorists believe it is the result of environmental stress, genetic predisposition, or overanxious diagnosis. Learning theorists suggest that the schizophrenic is rewarded for acting crazy; therefore, the crazy behavior persists.

Family, or systems, theorists believe that schizophrenia is produced by inappropriate family functioning. The "schismatic family" produces schizophrenia by setting up a situation in which parental strife divides the family. In the "skewed family," strife is avoided by total submission of the one spouse to the other. Another possible cause is the double-bind hypothesis: the child receives two contradictory messages and never learns to make sense out of this confusing situation.

The humanistic-existential approach argues that schizophrenia is a normal reaction to an unlivable and disturbed society. Biological approaches have suggested that schizophrenia may result from a genetic predisposition (schizophrenia is positively correlated with similarity of genetic makeup), too much dopamine in the brain (drugs that block dopamine absorption reduce schizophrenic symptoms), too many dopamine receptors in critical brain locations, too many endorphins, or too much of some other substance in the body. The vulnerability theory proposes that several factors contribute to one's tendency toward schizophrenia.

VI.   1. Personality disorders are deep-seated patterns of maladaptive behaviors that cause distress to others. Unlike the anxiety disorders, the personality disorders produce little or no guilt or anxiety.

2. Antisocial personalities, or sociopaths, are people who follow their impulses without guilt and without considering the consequences of their behaviors for others. These people often commit crimes and feel no guilt or sorrow. Sociopaths are incapable of friendship or love. Psychoanalytic theorists explain sociopathy as the result of rejecting parents. Learning theorists suggest that the sociopath receives reinforcement when he or she commits sociopathic acts. Biological theorists suggest such a person may suffer from autonomic underarousal, committing crimes to get a thrill. The treatment a therapist chooses for a sociopath depends on which theory he or she believes best explains the behavior, although no highly successful method of treatment has been developed.

□ **Self-Test**

A. Matching Questions

_____ 1. A set of related symptoms

_____ 2. Theory that considers mental illness to be similar to physical illness

_____ 3. According to Freud, a fixation during superego development would produce this

_____ 4. Advocates treating symptoms rather than underlying problems

_____ 5. Traces mental illness to our making of poor choices in achieving self-actualization

a. Neurosis
b. Family or systems approach
c. Medical model
d. Humanistic-existential perspective
e. Learning theory
f. Syndrome
g. Psychosis
h. Sociological perspective

_____ 6. A common problem associated with classification of symptoms

_____ 7. Fearfulness without a recognizable cause

_____ 8. Fearfulness focused on a particular object or situation

_____ 9. A recurring irrational thought

_____10. Specific kind of conversion disorder

a. Compulsion
b. Labeling
c. Fugue state
d. Obsession
e. Amnesia
f. Free-floating anxiety
g. Glove anesthesia
h. Phobia

_____11. Another word for mood

_____12. Sensory perception unrelated to external stimuli

_____13. A characteristic of the communication of a schizophrenic

_____14. A discrepancy between overt and covert feelings

_____15. Characterized by neither emotion nor guilt

a. Delusion
b. Hallucination
c. Obsession
d. Double bind
e. Sociopathic personality
f. Affect
g. Poverty of content
h. Schizophrenic

B. Multiple-Choice Questions Testing Factual Knowledge

1. Applying the term _abnormal_ to some behaviors that are "statistically frequent" but which one may not wish to consider as subject for concern is _not_ a problem with which criterion for abnormality?
   a. statistical criterion
   b. absolute criterion
   c. social norms criterion
   d. all of the above criteria   Objective 1.1

2. Many agents have been proposed to account for mental illness through history. Centuries ago, mental illness was thought to be caused by:
   a. stress
   b. brain disease
   c. heart disease
   d. possession by the devil   Objective 1.2

3. The theory of mental illness that proposes that abnormal behavior has an organic cause that produces a specific set of symptoms is the:
   a. psychoanalytic perspective
   b. learning-theory perspective
   c. medical model
   d. humanistic-existential perspective   Objective 1.2

4. Thomas Szasz's main criticism of the medical model is that:
   a. it is based on outdated ideas
   b. because it casts patients in the role of "sick" people, patients behave "sick"
   c. psychiatrists and neurologists have not been successful in locating specific brain pathologies
   d. it cannot account for many illnesses that we know are caused by stress
                                                                          Objective 1.2

5. According to the psychoanalytic perspective, neurosis and psychosis are produced by:
   a. brain injury
   b. biochemical imbalances in the brain
   c. the isolation produced by modern society
   d. fixations in childhood   Objective 1.2

6. According to learning theorists, which factors most directly account for abnormal behaviors?
   a. modeling and conditioning
   b. id, ego, and superego
   c. poor family structure
   d. a stressful society   Objective 1.2

7. The therapist most likely to treat the symptoms rather than an underlying problem is the:
   a. psychoanalytic therapist
   b. family, or systems, therapist
   c. learning theory therapist
   d. medical model therapist   Objective 1.2

8. The therapist most likely to consider the whole network of relationships in which the patient is involved would be the:
   a. family, or systems, therapist
   b. learning therapist
   c. medical model therapist
   d. psychoanalytic therapist   Objective 1.2

9. According to the text, which of the following is currently the perspective for looking at mental disorders?
   a. sociocultural perspective
   b. learning theory perspective
   c. psychoanalytic perspective
   d. none of the above   Objective 1.2

10. The standard guide for diagnosing mental illness is:
    a. *The Mental Measurements Yearbook*
    b. *The Diagnostic and Statistical Manual of Mental Disorders*
    c. *The Guide to Psychiatric Illness*
    d. *The Etiology, Diagnosis and Prognosis of Mental Disease*   Objective 2.1

11. According to Rosenhan, the problem with diagnosis of mental illness is:
    a. it diminishes the patient's humanity
    b. it influences subsequent treatment
    c. it encourages psychiatrists to ignore normal behavior
    d. all of the above   Objective 2.2

12. Which of the following statements regarding use of the DSM for diagnosis of mental illness is *false*?
    a. Its usefulness probably outweighs the hazards of its use.
    b. It currently views homosexuality as a category of abnormal behavior.
    c. Its categories change with changing times and attitudes.
    d. Its new edition will try to be more specific in describing the various disorders.
    Objective 2.2

13. A senseless but recurring irrational thought that a person tries to suppress is a(n):
    a. phobia
    b. compulsion
    c. obsession
    d. panic attack
    Objective 3.1

14. The dissociation of a healthy personality into two or more complete and distinct behavior organizations is called:
    a. multiple personality
    b. depression
    c. schizophrenia
    d. an affective behavior
    Objective 3.1

15. The holding of irrational beliefs despite evidence that they have no basis in reality is called:
    a. a fugue state
    b. a hallucination
    c. a delusion
    d. glove anesthesia
    Objective 3.1

16. The disorder characterized by extreme swings in mood from sadness to elation is called:
    a. schizophrenia
    b. a dissociative disorder
    c. depression
    d. manic-depressive disorder
    Objective 4.1

17. "Learned helplessness" is a possible explanation for:
    a. depression
    b. schizophrenia
    c. affective disorders
    d. dissociative disorders
    Objective 4.2

18. Disordered thought, delusions, hallucinations, nonsensical speech, and inappropriate expressions of emotions are symptoms associated with:
    a. schizophrenia
    b. paranoia
    c. affective disorders
    d. anxiety disorders
    Objective 5.1

19. According to the text, which of the following is the most disabling of the common disorders?
    a. depression
    b. multiple personality
    c. schizophrenia
    d. anxiety
    Objective 5.1

20. Sociological theorists have found that schizophrenia is most common among which socioeconomic class?
    a. upper class
    b. lower class
    c. middle class
    d. none of the above; it is equally represented in all three classes
    Objective 5.2

C. Multiple-Choice Questions Testing Conceptual Knowledge

21. A person who is seven feet, eight inches, tall would be considered abnormal according to which of the following criteria?
    a. statistical
    b. absolute
    c. neurotic
    d. deviation from social norms   Objective 1.1

22. Jennifer is treated by a therapist who believes that her abnormal behavior consists of a series of symptoms caused by an underlying physical problem. This therapist probably subscribes to which tradition?
    a. humanistic-existential perspective
    b. family or systems perspective
    c. medical model
    d. sociocultural perspective   Objective 1.2

23. Gene's therapist says his neurosis stems from childhood conflicts with an overprotective mother. Gene's therapist is probably most influenced by:
    a. the sociocultural perspective
    b. the humanistic-existential perspective
    c. the medical model
    d. the psychoanalytic perspective   Objective 1.2

24. The theoretical perspectives which would most agree that normal and abnormal behavior are caused by the same variables would be the:
    a. psychoanalytic perspective
    b. learning theory perspective
    c. psychoanalytic perspective
    d. family, or systems, approach   Objective 1.2

25. Jack believes that the causes of most mental illness are poverty, poor nutrition and education, and overcrowding. He would probably prefer the:
    a. learning theory perspective
    b. humanistic-existential perspective
    c. family, or systems, approach
    d. sociocultural perspective   Objective 1.2

26. Matt's therapist believes that her job is to help Matt recognize his potential for positive growth. This therapist probably subscribes to the:
    a. psychoanalytic approach
    b. humanistic-existential approach
    c. sociocultural approach
    d. learning theory approach   Objective 1.2

27. Bart is jumpy, irritable, fearful, has trouble sleeping, and cannot concentrate on his work. An amateur diagnosis would be that Bart suffers from:
    a. generalized anxiety disorder
    b. obsessions
    c. paranoia
    d. a phobic disorder   Objective 3.1

28. Julia is so afraid of riding in an elevator that she will shop only in stores on the ground level. She would be classified as:
    a. obsessive-compulsive
    b. paranoid
    c. phobic
    d. schizophrenic   Objective 3.1

29. Judy sees her mother raped and killed by a violent man. She then develops a psychically induced blindness. This disorder is called:
    a. a conversion disorder
    b. depression
    c. obsession
    d. glove anesthesia   Objective 3.1

30. Mark believes that his wife's depression exists because she gets reinforcement and pleasure from being depressed. His theoretical position is similar to that of the:
    a. psychoanalytic perspective
    b. learning theory perspective
    c. biological perspective
    d. family, or systems, approach   Objective 4.2

31. Little Janie's mother sometimes treats her lovingly and sometimes treats her hatefully. Janie develops the symptoms of schizophrenia. This condition is an example of:
    a. learned helplessness
    b. a fugue state
    c. a double-bind situation
    d. a manic-depressive environment   Objective 5.2

32. Bill is arrested for murdering his mother, wife, and two children and for trying to kill himself. He reports that he feels no sadness or guilt over his actions. Your diagnosis of Bill's condition is:
    a. manic depressive
    b. schizophrenia
    c. suicidal depression
    d. sociopathic personality   Objective 6.1

D. Short Essay Questions

1. Which method of defining abnormal behavior do you prefer? Why?   (Objective 1.1)

2. Describe the changes that have occurred through the three editions of the DSM. (Objective 2.1)

3. How does a phobia differ from free-floating anxiety?   (Objective 3.1)

4. How does depression differ from mania? How are they alike? (Objective 4.1)

5. Why is schizophrenia considered the most severe psychological disorder? (Objective 5.1)

6. What symptoms characterize a sociopath? How can a sociopath be treated? (Objectives 6.1, 6.2)

Approaches to ■ 16
Treatment

☐ **Preview of the Chapter**
Major Concepts and Behavioral Objectives

CONCEPT 1   Freudian psychoanalysis, behavior therapy, family–systems therapy, and humanistic-existential therapy all use different techniques to help a patient regain a normal way of life.

    1.1 Define psychotherapy and discuss the background of the various professionals who use it.

    1.2 Discuss the following types of psychotherapy: psychoanalysis, ego analysis, behavior therapy, cognitive therapy, family–systems therapy, and humanistic-existential therapy.

CONCEPT 2   Group therapies, which borrow from all these traditions, treat several people at once, thereby reducing costs.

    2.1 Suggest why group therapies have recently become more popular.

    2.2 Discuss and compare transactional analysis, encounter groups, and self-help groups.

CONCEPT 3   Research on the effectiveness of the various therapies suggests no clear "winner," but it does indicate that therapy facilitates improvement in patients.

    3.1 Report Eysenck's conclusion regarding the helpfulness of psychotherapy.

    3.2 Discuss current reports of the utility of psychotherapy.

CONCEPT 4   Drug therapy has become very common since the 1950s. Before then, electroconvulsive therapy and psychosurgery were the primary methods of controlling violent behavior.

    4.1 List and describe the effects of the various psychoactive drugs discussed in the text.

    4.2 Discuss the current status of electroconvulsive therapy and psychosurgery.

    4.3 Cite problems associated with biological treatment methods.

    4.4 Formulate an opinion about the various biological therapies discussed in the text.

CONCEPT 5   The community mental health movement attempts to bring psychological help to the underprivileged and to establish moral and legal guidelines in the field of mental health.

    5.1 Describe the purposes of the community mental health movement.

    5.2 Describe the community mental health programs discussed in the text.

    5.3 Discuss various ways in which values can influence the treatment of mental illness.

☐ **Chapter Summary**

I. 1. Psychotherapy is a series of interactions between a trained therapist and a troubled person. Therapists can be trained in different traditions. A psychiatrist is a medical doctor (M.D.) who specializes in the diagnosis and treatment of mental illness. A psychoanalyst has had advanced training in psychoanalysis and has also been analyzed. A clinical psychologist holds a Ph.D. in clinical psychology and has completed a one-year internship. A psychiatric social worker has earned an M.A. in social work and has specialized in psychiatric social work. A psychiatric nurse holds a nursing degree and has specialized in psychiatric nursing.

2. Therapists differ in their theoretical orientation as well as their training. Although several distinct traditions for treatment exist, most therapists borrow ideas from several approaches in formulating a treatment program for a patient.

3. Psychoanalysis focuses on the interplay between conscious and unconscious forces first outlined by Freud. The psychoanalyst tries to bring the patient's repressed memories into the consciousness where they can be confronted and understood. Sometimes dreams are analyzed to help the therapist understand the nature of unconscious conflict. Every dream has a manifest content (what the person dreams) and a latent content (the underlying meaning of the dream). Because confronting one's repressed feelings is unpleasant, patients sometimes engage in resistance, an attempt to block treatment. In transference, the patient may direct emotions about some other person onto the therapist. Psychoanalysts also use Freud's technique of free association (talking about whatever enters one's mind) to help uncover the source of patients' problems. Psychoanalysis is a long (several years) and costly procedure and, because it relies on the patient's verbal abilities, works best for those who are well educated. Thus, as a general treatment strategy, its usefulness is limited.

4. As you remember from the previous chapter, some of Freud's original associates broke away to form a new group. These theorists, most notably Carl Jung, Alfred Adler, Karen Horney, Harry Stack Sullivan, Erich Fromm, and Erik Erikson, formed a group that advocated ego analysis. Ego analysis attempts to strengthen the patient's ego so the patient can better control his or her environment. This therapy differs from psychoanalysis in that it involves a face-to-face confrontation between the therapist and patient, it places greater emphasis on present events, the therapists take a more active role in guiding discussion, and it is shorter and less intensive.

5. Behavior therapists believe that the same basic principles of learning govern all behaviors, normal and deviant. They also believe that the environment plays a crucial role in determining which behaviors will be exhibited. They analyze the behavior they see and generally do not concentrate on unconscious sources of pathology. Classical conditioning is the principle that underlies systematic desensitization, a technique pairing relaxation with mildly fearful events to relieve the patient of an irrational fear. Aversive conditioning, also modeled after classical conditioning, pairs an aversive (negative) stimulus with the unwanted behavior until the mere thought of the unwanted behavior becomes associated with an avoidance response. Aversive conditioning has been successfully used to treat bedwetting, alcoholism, and certain kinds of sexual deviations.

In therapies based on operant conditioning, reward or punishment is used to increase or decrease the occurrence of a particular behavior. Token economies involve giving patients tokens (which can be exchanged later for privileges) when they exhibit the desired behavior. Such systems are effective in classrooms as well as for juvenile offenders and the mentally retarded.

Learning through observation, called modeling, is also useful in therapy. Participant modeling, in which the therapist performs an act the patient fears and then guides the patient through the same act, seems to be a helpful technique in extinguishing phobias. It is more effective than symbolic modeling (showing the patient pictures) or systematic desensitization.

Several therapies are based on a cognitive approach. Cognitive restructuring is aimed at changing the patient's way of thinking. For example, in Ellis's rational-emotive therapy, subjects are helped to construct a more accurate and positive view of themselves. In Beck's cognitive therapy, the therapist questions the patient in a way that helps the patient discover the irrational basis of negative self-evaluations. In Meichenbaum's version of cognitive therapy, self-instructional training, clients are instructed to think rational and positive thoughts when they encounter an anxiety-producing situation.

6. In the family, or systems, approach, the therapist focuses on changing negative patterns of interaction within the family. Sometimes patients are "ordered" to perform their disruptive activity, thereby bringing the patient under the control of the therapists. In this double-bind technique, the patient either disrupts the session as directed or allows the session to proceed; both are positive outcomes. Family therapies are especially useful with children or in homes where social and economic problems are also present.

7. Humanistic-existential therapies all focus on leading the client toward self-fulfillment and personal growth. Perhaps the most famous of these theories is Carl Rogers's client-centered or nondirective therapy. Here, the therapist seeks to arrange a situation in which the client feels free to express and get in touch with his or her own feelings. The therapist's role is to communicate warmth and empathy, called unconditional positive regard. Fritz Perls, the founder of Gestalt therapy, believes that a client must get rid of defenses and release pent-up feelings in order to become a whole person.

II. 1. Group therapies arose after World War II to help the large number of people who had become disturbed during this period. Its major strength is promotion of better interpersonal relationships. It also costs less than more traditional therapies. Group therapies exist that borrow from all of the previously described traditions. However, three forms of therapy have become especially prominent: transactional analysis, encounter groups, and self-help groups.

2. Transactional analysis (TA) was developed during the 1950s and '60s by Eric Berne. In this approach, every person is thought to have three parts in his or her personality: the satisfaction-oriented Child, the rule-imposing Parent, and the rational, mature Adult. TA attempts to analyze the client's personality and prescribe how to build up the adult aspect of personality.

3. Rather than helping solve a particular problem, encounter groups help people grow by encouraging them to increase their spontaneity and release positive feelings. Under the direction of a trained group leader, participants engage in exercises that encourage the lowering of defensive barriers. Unfortunately, people with problems may have a traumatic negative reaction to so much openness and might be better advised to seek a different type of therapy.

4. Recently, the number of self-help groups has increased dramatically. These groups have no trained therapist; they consist of people who all have a similar problem—alcoholism or overweight, for example. Generally, these groups set up a communication system whereby any member can call another for help if he or she seems likely to give in to temptation. These groups also allow for discussion of feelings with an understanding group and provide emotional support for the members.

5. Unfortunately, little research has been conducted to establish the effectiveness of the various types of group therapies.

III. 1. In 1952 Eysenck published a review concluding that psychotherapy produced no better results than no treatment whatsoever. Other researchers reacted to Eysenck's report, and further research aimed at identifying treatment success was undertaken.

2. The Temple study, for instance, revealed that both behavioral therapy and psychoanalytic therapy were helpful, although behavioral therapy worked best under different conditions.

3. It seems likely that no one therapy will be found to be most effective in all situations. Rather, research may help tell us which types of treatment are most appropriate for particular problems.

IV. 1. In addition to psychoanalytic and behaviorally oriented therapies, biological therapies have been used to treat psychological disorders. Psychopharmacology, or the science of drug therapy, has been successfully used with all kinds of patients and many kinds of disorders. Drugs are generally grouped into categories, as follows:

2. The antianxiety drugs, or minor tranquilizers, are used to reduce excitability and cause drowsiness. Common brand names include Miltown, Librium, and Valium. These pills are the most widely prescribed drugs in the world. They act by depressing the activity of the central nervous system.

3. The antipsychotic drugs, or major tranquilizers, are used to reduce extreme symptoms of agitation in psychotic patients. This category includes Thorazine (chlorpromazine) and Stelazine. Originally introduced as more humane alternatives to psychosurgery and electroconvulsive therapy, these drugs have become widely used, especially in the treatment of schizophrenia. Estimates indicate that 87 percent of all psychiatric inpatients are given these drugs. Unfortunately, these drugs have some drawbacks: They can be misused to dope troublesome patients, and they sometimes produce harmful and irreversible side effects such as tardive dyskinesia and pseudoparkinsonianism.

4. The antidepressant drugs, including the tricyclics Tofranil and Elanil, are used to elevate the patient's mood. Lithium is currently used to relieve symptoms of manic-depressive psychosis. As with the major tranquilizers, prolonged use may produce negative side effects.

5. Electroconvulsive therapy, or "shock treatment," relieves severe depression, although no one understands how it works to provide relief. Over a period of several weeks the patient is given a series of 70–130-volt electrical shocks, which produce convulsions. Although the patient experiences little or no discomfort, the shocks frequently cause temporary memory loss. Since treatment gives immediate relief, it is especially useful for suicidal patients.

6. In psychosurgery portions of brain tissue are permanently destroyed. While the effectiveness of early surgeries was debatable, psychosurgery now involves "fractional operations" that destroy very small amounts of tissue in specific locations. Such surgeries seem to be reasonably effective last-resort measures to bring relief from depression. Approximately four hundred patients in the United States receive such surgery each year.

7. The effective use of drugs to treat mental illness has been a phenomenon of only the last few decades. While almost replacing the more hazardous technique of electroconvulsive therapy and psychosurgery, drug therapies also have their problems: Side effects occur, the drugs may produce addiction, and the patient may become dependent on them for security. Refined techniques of electroconvulsive therapy and psychosurgery are still used but generally as last-resort measures after other therapies have produced no beneficial effects.

V.

1. The community mental health movement is an attempt to decentralize and deinstitutionalize the treatment of middle- and lower-class mentally ill. The Community Mental Health Center Act of 1963 authorized a health center offering outpatient services for every 50,000 people. Such centers often employ paraprofessionals who come from backgrounds similar to the patients'.

2. Halfway houses, which are becoming more common, provide an intermediate step between institutionalization and independent living.

3. Crisis hot lines are being set up to provide help in emergency situations such as suicide, drug overdose, rape, and with social problems such as battered wives and children and runaways. These networks give support and information to people in need.

4. The basic goals of the mental health movement are primary prevention (prevention of the development of the disorder), secondary prevention (prevention of the worsening of the disorder), and tertiary prevention (prevention of the severe effects of disorder on the individual and on society). Primary prevention is, of course, the most difficult to achieve.

5. Personal values impact many aspects of treatment of the mentally ill. The values held by a therapist, for instance, are bound to influence his or her treatment of patients. Patients who exhibit extreme symptoms may be involuntarily committed to an institution. Indeed, the ratio of involuntary to voluntary commitments in the United States is about two to three. Patient's rights must be protected, but sometimes such protection ensures that behavioral therapies that might relieve the patient's symptoms cannot be used because they violate the patient's rights. The proposed patient's right to refuse treatment is a highly complex issue.

6. In response to such difficult moral issues, committees and boards have been established to consider cases involving patients' rights, therapists, and treatment strategies.

☐ **Self-Test**

A. Matching Questions

_____ 1. A medical doctor who diagnoses and treats mental illness

_____ 2. Type of therapy that follows most directly from Freud's theories

_____ 3. Verbalizing one's thoughts without ordering or censoring them

_____ 4. The patient's blocking of treatment

_____ 5. Therapy based on the idea that you cannot be both relaxed and nervous at the same time

_____ 6. A technique that involves imagining an unpleasant event

a. Psychoanalysis
b. Clinical psychologist
c. Resistance
d. Aversive conditioning
e. Psychiatrist
f. Free association
g. Covert sensitization
h. Ego analysis
i. Systematic desensitization

_____ 7. Therapy that rewards appropriate behavior with poker chips or slips of paper

_____ 8. Therapy in which the therapist performs the feared activity before the patient

a. Transactional analysis
b. Participant modeling
c. Double-bind
d. Rational-emotive therapy

_____ 9. Therapy in which clients are urged to recognize the irrational nature of certain unpleasant beliefs

_____ 10. A situation in which any response the patient makes will in some way be appropriate

_____ 11. Therapy that focuses on helping the client fulfill his or her potential.

e. Symbolic modeling
f. Client-centered therapy
g. Self-instructional training
h. Token economy
i. Self-help group

_____ 12. One of the most prescribed antianxiety drugs

_____ 13. A permanent side effect of prolonged use of antipsychotic drugs

_____ 14. Used in the treatment of manic-depressive psychosis

_____ 15. The kind of psychosurgery currently being conducted in the United States

_____ 16. The prevention of the development of mental illness

_____ 17. Places in the community used to ease a previously institutionalized patient back into society

a. Tertiary prevention
b. Valium
c. Primary prevention
d. Lithium
e. Half-way houses
f. Thorazine
g. Fractional operation
h. Tardive dyskinesia
i. Crisis intervention programs

B. Multiple-Choice Questions Testing Factual Knowledge

1. Psychotherapy refers to:
   a. Freudian analysis
   b. behavioral therapy
   c. group therapy
   d. all of the above   Objective 1.1

2. The "vocalization of whatever thoughts come to mind in whatever order, without self-censorship, logical structure, or interruption from the therapist" is called:
   a. free association
   b. transactional analysis
   c. client-centered therapy
   d. psychoanalysis   Objective 1.2

3. In psychoanalysis, transference refers to:
   a. repression
   b. projection of feelings about others onto the therapist
   c. psychoanalysis
   d. free association   Objective 1.2

4. Freud's followers who later broke away (such as Jung, Adler, Horney, Sullivan, Fromm, and Erikson) placed much more emphasis than Freud on the concept of:
   a. unconscious
   b. superego
   c. ego
   d. id   Objective 1.2

5. The therapy technique based on reducing the frequency of an unwanted response by pairing it with a negative stimulus is called:
   a. systematic desensitization

b. aversive conditioning
c. covert sensitization
d. participant modeling   Objective 1.2

6. In a token economy system, behavior is maintained by giving the patient:
   a. electric shocks
   b. praise
   c. drugs
   d. conditioned reinforcers   Objective 1.2

7. One therapy consists of helping clients recognize the irrational nature of long-held, negative beliefs about themselves. This therapy is called:
   a. rational-emotive therapy
   b. psychoanalysis
   c. transactional analysis
   d. participant modeling   Objective 1.2

8. The "double-bind" technique involves:
   a. pairing an aversive stimulus with a maladaptive stimulus
   b. getting the client to imagine a positive self-image
   c. putting the client in a forced-positive interaction
   d. imagining the feared object   Objective 1.2

9. Family, or systems, therapy would be especially useful in treating which kind of problems?
   a. those arising from a "generation gap"
   b. those based on fear of objects
   c. those based on fear of people
   d. those involving generalized anxiety   Objective 1.2

10. Gestalt therapy emphasizes:
    a. being in touch with one's feelings
    b. escaping depression caused by a bad environment
    c. repressing unacceptable urges
    d. strengthening the ego   Objective 1.2

11. Group therapies are almost exclusively based on the principles of:
    a. behaviorism
    b. psychoanalysis
    c. family–systems analysis
    d. none of the above   Objective 2.2

12. Alcoholics Anonymous (AA) is an example of therapy based on:
    a. transactional analysis
    b. encounter groups
    c. self-help groups
    d. systematic desensitization   Objective 2.2

13. From a study conducted in 1952, Hans Eysenck concluded that psychotherapy was about:
    a. as effective as drug therapy
    b. twice as effective as no therapy
    c. three times more effective than no therapy
    d. as effective as no therapy   Objective 3.1

14. According to the Temple study, which of the following forms of therapy is generally the most effective?
    a. behavioral therapy
    b. psychoanalytic therapy
    c. group therapy
    d. participant modeling   Objective 3.2

15. Which of the following is *not* an antianxiety drug?
    a. Librium
    b. Thorazine
    c. Valium
    d. Miltown
    Objective 4.1

16. The antipsychotic drugs have largely replaced:
    a. minor tranquilizers
    b. psychoanalysis
    c. electroconvulsive therapy
    d. antidepressants
    Objective 4.1

17. The major side effect of electroconvulsive therapy is:
    a. speech difficulty
    b. respiratory difficulty
    c. uncontrollable facial movements
    d. memory loss
    Objective 4.2

18. Community mental health centers have arisen mainly to:
    a. provide better facilities for electroconvulsive therapy
    b. provide a place to train young psychiatrists
    c. provide an alternative to sending people to large institutions
    d. make it easier for relatives to visit inpatients
    Objective 5.1

19. An intermediate step between the hospital and the community in which people live in a supportive environment is a:
    a. self-help group
    b. halfway house
    c. primary care facility
    d. crisis intervention facility
    Objective 5.2

20. The Supreme Court has ruled that mental patients have certain rights that cannot be violated. Which is *not* one of their guaranteed rights?
    a. adequate meals
    b. to be outdoors regularly
    c. to have visitors
    d. to refuse treatment
    Objective 5.3

C. Multiple-Choice Questions Testing Conceptual Knowledge

21. On her therapist's wall, Julie notices a diploma from a medical college granting her therapist an M.D. degree. She concludes her therapist must be:
    a. a clinical psychologist
    b. a psychiatrist
    c. a psychoanalyst
    d. none of the above
    Objective 1.1

22. Jack dreams that he is eaten by a snake. He insists that this dream signifies his homosexual preferences. The latent content of this dream involves:
    a. the snake
    b. being eaten
    c. the homosexual interpretation
    d. finding out what he ate before he went to sleep
    Objective 1.2

23. John believes that abnormal behaviors are governed by the same principles as normal behaviors and that the environment plays a crucial role in determining behavior. His theory would be most similar to that of:
    a. Sigmund Freud
    b. transactional analysis
    c. an environmentalist
    d. behavioral therapists
    Objective 1.2

24. Suppose you are terribly afraid of spiders. Your therapist suggests you try to relax as she brings increasingly more fearful "spider-related things" before you. This therapy is most similar to:
    a. systematic desensitization
    b. psychoanalysis
    c. a token economy
    d. behavior modification   Objective 1.2

25. Mack is afraid of snakes. His therapist leads him through a series of gradual steps in which he approaches snakes more and more closely. This technique is called:
    a. participant modeling
    b. covert sensitization
    c. aversive conditioning
    d. symbolic modeling   Objective 1.2

26. In client-centered therapy, the role of the therapist comes closest to that of:
    a. rewarder and punisher
    b. question asker
    c. problem solver
    d. problem identifier   Objective 1.2

27. Martha says, "I'm not going to work today because I'm tired and I just want to have some fun." A transactional analyst would conclude that her behavior is being controlled by:
    a. reinforcement
    b. her Child
    c. her Adult
    d. anxiety   Objective 2.2

28. John attends a group therapy session in which the participants are encouraged to touch each other, tell others what they think of them, and be honest about themselves. This type of therapy is most similar to:
    a. Gestalt therapy
    b. self-help groups
    c. transactional analysis
    d. encounter groups   Objective 2.2

29. Genie is having trouble sleeping at night and feels anxious most of the time. If a drug is prescribed for her condition, it will probably be:
    a. an antianxiety drug
    b. an antipsychotic drug
    c. an antidepressant
    d. a major tranquilizer   Objective 4.1

30. John has been diagnosed as suffering from manic-depressive psychosis. The drug most likely to be prescribed for him would be:
    a. Thorazine
    b. an antidepressant
    c. lithium
    d. Valium   Objective 4.1

31. You walk into a mental hospital and see a person making grotesque facial movements. You conclude that this results from prolonged use of:
    a. Valium
    b. electroconvulsive therapy
    c. Thorazine
    d. antidepressants   Objective 4.3

32. Suppose a school system undertakes a program to help children cope with unusual situations at home and to raise their self-esteem. This would be an example of:
    a. primary prevention

    b. secondary prevention
    c. tertiary prevention
    d. crisis intervention

Objective 5.2

D. *Short Essay Questions*

1. Why have group therapies become popular? (Objective 2.1)

2. Is one form of psychotherapy likely to be more effective than others? Why or why not? (Objective 3.2)

3. Do you believe that electroconvulsive therapy should be discontinued in the United States? Why or why not? (Objectives 4.2, 4.3)

4. What are some of the problems associated with the use of biologically based treatments? (Objective 4.3)

5. What is the community mental health program, and why has it developed? (Objectives 5.1, 5.2)

6. In what ways do society's values influence the treatment of mental illness? (Objective 5.3)

Attitudes and Social Perception

■17

□ **Preview of the Chapter**
Major Concepts and Behavioral Objectives

CONCEPT 1   Attitudes, with their thinking, feeling, and behavior components, are learned tendencies to respond favorably or unfavorably.

   1.1   Define an attitude and describe how it can be measured.

CONCEPT 2   Attitudes can be changed in two ways: by persuasive argument or by reducing the inconsistency between conflicting views.

   2.1   Discuss how attitudes can be changed through persuasive arguments.

   2.2   Describe consistency models of attitude change and the research that supports them.

   2.3   Compare and contrast cognitive dissonance theory with self-perception theory.

   2.4   Describe reactance theory.

CONCEPT 3   First impressions can substantially determine our subsequent attitudes. For example, people's physical attractiveness often affects our perceptions of them.

   3.1   Discuss the impact of the primacy effect on the formation of attitudes.

   3.2   Describe how physical attractiveness affects attitude formation.

CONCEPT 4   When we analyze people's characters, we generally make attributions about their personality on the basis of their behavior—but we attribute their behavior to different causes than we do our own.

   4.1   Explain in general terms how causal attributions are made.

   4.2   Describe the actor–observer bias and the self-serving bias in making causal attributions.

CONCEPT 5   Friendship and love, which are special cases of attribution, are the subject of much current research and theorizing.

   5.1   Describe the situational factors that are influential in liking and loving.

   5.2   Explain the theories that attempt to account for falling in love and describe supporting research.

CONCEPT 6   Prejudice, such as sexism and racism, also involves attribution—negative attribution. Prejudice can be reduced in situations in which participants *must* cooperate for their common welfare.

   6.1   Define prejudice and cite evidence which supports its existence.

   6.2   Discuss how prejudices might be formed and how they might be eliminated.

☐ **Chapter Summary**

I. 1. The "Stanford County Prison" experiment conducted by Philip Zimbardo consisted of randomly assigning young men to the role of "guard" or "prisoner." Within six days the experiment had to be discontinued because the students were taking their roles too seriously. This indicates the strong influence of learning in attitude formation.

2. Not all psychologists agree on a standard definition of *attitude,* but most do agree that an attitude has four characteristics: It is learned, it persists over a long period of time, it motivates us to act, and it is evaluative. Other psychologists add that attitudes are based on cognitions or beliefs. They believe that any attitude has three components, the cognitive (thinking), the affective (feeling), and the behavioral (acting).

3. Attitudes can be measured in several ways: by questionnaires exploring both the directions and strength of the subject's attitude, by physiological measurements, and by actual behavior. Each method has advantages and disadvantages.

II. 1. Persuasive communications are constructed so as to change the recipient's attitudes. One-sided communications are most effective with people who are initially in favor of the argument presented and with people who are poorly educated. Presenting both sides of an issue is more effective with an audience that opposes the argument and is well educated. The two-sided presentation also prepares the audience to withstand future counterarguments.

2. Fear-arousing campaigns can also produce attitude change, although studies do not agree on the amount of fear that produces greatest attitude change. It seems that increased fear produces the appropriate action only if the fear does not become excessive and if steps to avoid the feared consequences are clearly specified.

3. Another approach to attitude change involves cognitive consistency. Consistency theorists believe that incompatible thoughts and actions put us in a physiological drive state. We seek to reduce the resulting tension by changing either our thoughts or our actions so we can perceive them as compatible.

4. Cognitive dissonance theory is a consistency theory that focuses on perceived differences between one's thoughts and behaviors. Persons who believe they have done something contrary to their beliefs ("I'm a good person and I just robbed a bank.") will reduce the dissonance aroused by this inconsistency by changing their attitudes about some aspect of this situation.

5. Cognitive dissonance theory is strengthened by experiments showing that when subjects are induced to tell a lie for either a small amount or a large amount of money, more attitude change occurs when the subjects are paid the small amount. Apparently, the subjects who were paid a large sum could justify their lying and thus did not feel the greater dissonance felt by the subjects who lied for less. Similar research shows that punishment operates in a similar fashion: If you want to induce another person to dislike an object, *mildly* punish the person for approaching the object. (Although strong punishment will also prevent approach, it will not produce the long-lasting attitude change.)

6. Cognitive dissonance theory is not without its critics, however. Daryl Bem points out that the results of cognitive dissonance experiments could be explained in another way. He believes that people are not routinely aware of their own attitudes. When asked what they believe, people reflect on their behavior and conclude what their attitude must have been for that behavior to have been appropriate. ("Why did I lie for a little money? I must not have lied to begin with.") Thus, although dissonance theory and Bem's self-perception theory both make the same predictions, they explain these results in different ways.

Both theories have received considerable support. Bem's theory, however, can explain the result that when people are paid a large sum to do something they like to do, their attitude about the task becomes less positive. Dissonance theory cannot account for this result, since the two original attitudes are not discrepant and should therefore arouse no dissonance. Both theories have been extremely useful in generating research regarding processes of attitude change.

7. The phenomenon of psychological reactance results when a person's choice is eliminated. If told you can't eat an ice cream cone, you would then come to value eating the cone more highly. The "Romeo and Juliet" effect is a reactance example: If parents forbid their child to date a particular partner, that partner becomes all the more attractive.

III.
1. Dissonance theory, self-perception theory, and reactance theory all attempt to explain attitude change. The theories about person perception and attribution explain how attitudes are initially formed.

2. The primacy effect is a label for our tendency to place more value on the first information we receive than on later information. Consequently, first impressions are often very influential in determining our attitudes about a person.

3. Physical attractiveness also has a powerful effect on how we evaluate another person. Indeed, in an experiment disguised as a dance with a computer-matched dating, only attractiveness (not intelligence or personality) had an impact on how favorably dates were evaluated. Apparently, a person who is beautiful is also assumed to have many additional positive traits. Moreover, people who associate with beautiful people reap the benefits of positive traits being attributed to them. These effects even hold for children.

4. A self-fulfilling prophecy involves one's acting as one is expected to act. Thus, when we expect a person to possess certain characteristics (say stinginess), we act toward him as if he were stingy, and he in turn reacts with stingy behavior. First impressions are indeed important in establishing attitudes.

IV.
1. First impressions, however, do not account for all our inferences about people. As we get to know someone better, we begin to make causal attributions based on the person's behavior: we either attribute the behavior to the person's disposition (personality) or to some situational factor (the environment). We infer underlying personality traits only when we attribute behavior to the person's disposition.

2. Jones and Davis argue that unexpected behaviors are especially useful in making causal attributions. Kelley, however, argues the opposite—that even repetitive or initial behaviors are informative if we have time to compare them to other things. The consistency factor is generally examined first: Is the behavior repeated in many similar situations? If consistency is high, distinctiveness may be considered: Is the response distinct to this one narrowly defined situation? Finally, consensus is examined: Do others respond the same way in this situation? If not, the behavior may be attributed to a personality trait.

3. This may also account for the actor–observer bias, our tendency to attribute our own behavior to environmental causes rather than personality factors. The observer has less information than the actor and is therefore more likely to attribute behavior to personality traits. This bias is most pronounced when the effects of the behavior are negative and least pronounced when they are positive. This self-serving bias operates when the actor takes credit for his good deeds and finds situational excuses for bad ones. The self-serving bias is most evident when the actor is highly involved and has a choice in engaging in the behavior and when the behavior is public.

4. Various theories have been proposed to explain the self-serving bias. Perhaps it

arises from a need to protect one's self-esteem or perhaps from being exposed to one-sided positive evaluations of oneself by one's friends. Both factors probably play a role, combining motivational and cognitive input to produce this effect.

V.
1. Physical proximity is the single most important factor in forming friendships. Research shows that the closer together two people live and the more they interact, the stronger their friendship. Apparently, people tend to like things to which they are repeatedly exposed.

2. Although Senator Proxmire disagrees, psychologists believe it is worthwhile to study love. Few people report love-at-first-sight reactions, although falling in love appears to be quite different than establishing a friendship. Behaviors such as gazing into each other's eyes, shortening physical distance, and leaning toward one another are correlated with attraction. Physiological psychologists have suggested that falling in love may be related to an abundance of phenylethylamine (a chemical similar to adrenalin) in the brain.

3. Schachter's theory of emotion suggests that falling in love occurs when physiological arousal is labeled with the situational explanation that one must be falling in love. An experiment in which men met a beautiful woman while walking across either a fearfully shaky bridge or a stationary bridge supports this theory. Men were more attracted to women when on the arousing, shaky bridge.

4. Once a relationship is formed, several factors enhance the likelihood that it will last. These include how well matched the couple are (age, intelligence, education, physical attractiveness, etc.) and whether they are equally involved in the relationship. Premarital sexual relations appear to have no effect on the permanence of a match.

VI.
1. Prejudice can be conceptualized as a negative and inflexible attitude based on erroneous or incomplete information. It is generally directed at an entire group as well as individual group members. A negative stereotype, or cluster of preconceived expectations about the group, underlies prejudice. Thus, anyone who exhibits a particular key trait (for example, a female who is emotional) is assumed to have all the expected traits (to be dependent, sensitive, and so on). Discrimination, the behavioral expression of prejudice, is often justified by these erroneous stereotypes. Individuals who violate the stereotype are usually dismissed as exceptions, and in this way the stereotype is maintained. Sexism and racism are two widespread examples of prejudice in our society.

2. Prejudice directed at one sex is called sexism. As throughout history, today women are the victims of sexism, even in the United States.

3. Although there are some innate sex differences (for example, boys are more aggressive than girls), the differences among members of the same sex are far greater than differences between males and females. Most people believe, however, that the differences between the sexes are much greater than they actually are. Furthermore, people of all ages hold essentially the same male and female stereotypes.

4. Sex-related characteristics probably begin to develop shortly after birth through differential treatment of males and females. These messages are reinforced by teachers, TV programs and advertisements, and other socializing agents. Even women view other women as less competent than men: When identical essays were attributed to either a man or woman author, women rated the article lower when they believed it was written by a woman.

5. Racism in the United States has been directed at almost every group that is not white, Anglo-Saxon, and Protestant. Racism lowers the racial group's self-esteem as well as its socioeconomic opportunity and achievement.

6. Several explanations of the causes of racism have been proposed. One argument suggests that economic competition turns prejudice onto the lowest socioeconomic group. In one experiment Muzafer Sherif created prejudice by dividing boys at camp into two groups and placing them in situations involving fierce competition. Other people believe that prejudice is the result of projecting anger and aggression caused by frustration onto a powerless group. Indeed, frustration has been demonstrated to increase subjects' prejudice against a minority group. A third theory accounts for prejudice by suggesting that people with an authoritarian personality are in general more inclined toward prejudice and hatred than others. The authoritarian personality is measured by the potentiality for Fascism test (the F scale). People who score high on the F scale show rigid values about authority and morality and a preference for antidemocratic leaders; they also score high on tests of prejudice. One finding suggests that these people grew up in a family with a domineering, status-oriented father and a punitive mother. Still another view suggests that prejudice may also exist due to conformity to social norms. Indeed, people's prejudices can be seen to change as they move from one area to another.

7. Prejudice is seldom eliminated by information campaigns. It can be reduced by forced encounters in which participants have equal status and are encouraged to get to know each other as individuals, and where friendliness and courtesy, nonstereotyped behaviors, and interdependence among members of the groups are emphasized.

□ **Self-Test**

A. Matching Questions

_____ 1. A learned, relatively enduring predisposition to respond to a given object in a consistently favorable or unfavorable way

_____ 2. Theory that focuses on discrepancies between attitudes and overt behavior

_____ 3. The notion that we infer our own attitudes in the same way we infer those of others

_____ 4. Attitude change produced by the elimination of choices

_____ 5. Describes why first impressions are important in attitude formation

a. Self-perception
b. Self-fulfilling prophecy
c. Cognitive dissonance
d. Psychological reactance
e. Prejudice
f. Propaganda
g. Primacy effect
h. Attitude

_____ 6. The matching of behavior to a person's expectations

_____ 7. The process of assigning traits to persons according to their behavior

_____ 8. Attribution tendency made by actors (ourselves)

_____ 9. Tendency for actors to take credit for their good deeds and find situational excuses for bad ones

_____10. The behavioral expression of prejudice

a. Self-serving bias
b. Environmental cause
c. Stereotyping
d. Fundamental attribution error
e. Self-fulfilling prophecy
f. Personality cause
g. Causal attribution
h. Discrimination

B. Multiple-Choice Questions Testing Factual Knowledge

1. Zimbardo's prison study was terminated because:
   a. he ran out of funding
   b. it was considered unethical
   c. subjects became too involved with the roles they were playing
   d. it obviously was not going to work   Objective 1.1

2. Which of the following is *not* a basic component of an attitude?
   a. cognitive component
   b. behavioral component
   c. affective component
   d. component message   Objective 1.1

3. To an educated audience, which of the following will probably lead to the *least* amount of attitude change?
   a. an expert speaker
   b. a trustworthy speaker
   c. a one-sided message
   d. a two-sided message   Objective 2.1

4. A benefit of a two-sided approach to attitude change is:
   a. it is faster
   b. it is easier
   c. it makes later counterarguments less effective
   d. it works best with a knowledgeable audience   Objective 2.1

5. Cognitive dissonance theory suggests that holding incompatible attitudes produces a state of:
   a. tension
   b. psychological health
   c. mental illness
   d. peacefulness   Objective 2.2

6. Bem, in his self-perception theory, believes we arrive at our attitudes by:
   a. a dissonance reduction
   b. trying to explain our behavior
   c. being reinforced for them
   d. learning them from our parents   Objective 2.2

7. Bem's self-perception theory is different from cognitive dissonance in its:
   a. explanations
   b. experimental support
   c. predicted results
   d. all of the above   Objective 2.3

8. Bem's self-perception theory has the advantage over cognitive dissonance theory of being able to explain:
   a. more attitude change for one dollar than twenty dollars
   b. more attitude change for twenty dollars than one dollar
   c. cognitive factors in attitude change
   d. more decrease in a positive attitude for twenty dollars than one dollar
                                                                            Objective 2.3

9. The "Romeo and Juliet" effect stems from:
   a. cognitive dissonance theory
   b. psychological reactance theory
   c. self-perception theory
   d. all of the above   Objective 2.4

10. According to the "computer dance" study described in the text, which of the following variables predicted how much the "dates" liked each other?
    a. intelligence
    b. physical attractiveness
    c. personality
    d. all of the above   Objective 3.2

11. Jones and Davis argue that the behavior that gives us the most information about making attributions about a person is behavior that is:
    a. unexpected
    b. typical of most people
    c. consistent with your stereotypes
    d. repeated often in various situations   Objective 4.1

12. The factor that makes Kelley's theory of attribution broader than Jones and Davis's is his inclusion of:
    a. personality variables
    b. original expectations
    c. an analysis of the situation
    d. comparisons made over a long period of time   Objective 4.1

13. The "fundamental attribution error" involves:
    a. inferring causation from correlational evidence
    b. overestimating the role of situational factors
    c. overestimating the role of dispositional factors
    d. making totally inappropriate attributions   Objective 4.2

14. Jones and Nisbett argue that we tend to attribute our own behavior to environmental causes, whereas we attribute others' behaviors to some enduring personality trait. This is called:
    a. the actor–observer bias
    b. the fundamental attribution error
    c. causation–correlation confounding
    d. the salience effect   Objective 4.2

15. According to the text, the most important factor in friendship formation is:
    a. similarity of attitudes
    b. similarity of attractiveness
    c. similarity of values
    d. close physical proximity   Objective 5.1

16. According to research presented in the text, how frequently does Jung's "love at first sight" occur?
    a. never
    b. very infrequently
    c. about half of the time
    d. very frequently   Objective 5.1

17. According to the research presented in the text, an abundance of phenylethylamine in the brain may be associated with:
    a. frequent attitude change
    b. reduced resistance to persuasion
    c. the tendency to commit the fundamental attribution error
    d. falling in love   Objective 5.2

18. Which of the following factors is *not* predictive of whether a love relationship will last?
    a. similarity of age of partners
    b. equal involvement by both partners in the relationship
    c. living together before marriage
    d. similarity of physical attractiveness   Objective 5.2

19. "A cluster of preconceived beliefs and expectations about the way members of a group think and act" is the text's definition of:
    a. prejudice
    b. stereotype
    c. the fundamental attribution error
    d. the self-serving bias
                                                                        Objective 6.1

20. Prejudice against a group of people generally results in all of the following *except:*
    a. increased self-esteem for group members
    b. lower incomes
    c. higher mortality rates
    d. poorer nutrition
                                                                        Objective 6.2

C. Multiple-Choice Questions Testing Conceptual Knowledge

21. Martha decides to determine John's attitude about television viewing by recording how many hours of TV he watches per week. What component of attitudes is she measuring?
    a. affective
    b. behavioral
    c. cognitive
    d. message
                                                                        Objective 1.1

22. According to the text, if a doctor is about to give a patient a highly frightening report about the patient's health, he could best reduce the patient's fear by:
    a. giving the patient directions to alleviate the feared condition
    b. projecting expertise
    c. trying to be highly trustworthy
    d. giving the patient a one-sided presentation
                                                                        Objective 2.1

23. Suppose you convince your roommate to call your professor and tell her that you are too sick to take the exam. According to cognitive dissonance theory, your roommate is most likely to believe you are sick if you pay your roommate which of the following sums for making the call?
    a. ten cents
    b. one dollar
    c. ten dollars
    d. fifty dollars
                                                                        Objective 2.2

24. According to cognitive dissonance theory, if you want to convince a small child that it is wrong to climb up on top of the kitchen cupboards, which kind of punishment would you use?
    a. severe punishment
    b. occasional punishment
    c. mild punishment
    d. none of the above
                                                                        Objective 2.2

25. As you are marking your ballot in an election, someone tells you that you *must* vote for candidate A. According to the principle of psychological reactance you will probably:
    a. vote for candidate A
    b. vote for candidate B
    c. vote for your original choice
    d. not vote at all
                                                                        Objective 2.4

26. You see four of Dustin Hoffman's movies. In the first he plays a kind father, in the second an outlaw, in the third a psychopathic murderer, and in the fourth a drug pusher. According to the primacy effect you probably think of him most as:
    a. a psychopath
    b. an outlaw
    c. a drug pusher
    d. none of the above
                                                                        Objective 3.1

27. John has heard that Mary is shy. When he meets her, he treats her as if she were shy, and she responds as if she were shy, even though she is not. This is an example of:
    a. psychological reactance
    b. the "Romeo and Juliet" effect
    c. cognitive dissonance
    d. a self-fulfilling prophecy   Objective 3.1

28. Which of the following is *not* a dispositional attribution regarding why Rex failed his first psychology test?
    a. "The test was too hard."
    b. "The teacher did not cover this material in class."
    c. "I have no aptitude for psychology."
    d. "My roommate would not let me study."   Objective 4.2

29. If Schachter's theory of love is correct, you would be most likely to fall in love with someone:
    a. with whom you had just been trapped in an elevator in a burning building
    b. with whom you had been pen-pals when you were children
    c. your parents chose for you to marry
    d. you find overwhelmingly physically attractive   Objective 5.2

30. Mary believes that women have always been discriminated against and that, even in the United States, women are still the victims of discrimination. After reading the text, you would:
    a. disagree, since women have not historically been victims of discrimination
    b. disagree, because women in the United States are not now the victims of discrimination
    c. disagree; both a and b are correct
    d. agree   Objective 6.1

31. If Jack is a typical American, he would probably believe that women are all of the following *except:*
    a. more aggressive than men
    b. less competitive than men
    c. more submissive than men
    d. poorer decision makers than men   Objective 6.1

32. Suppose you are in charge of a sixth-grade class in which the children are very prejudiced against two Vietnamese in the class. According to the text, the best way to reduce the prejudice is to:
    a. move the two Vietnamese students out of the classroom
    b. lecture the class about the evils of prejudice, especially racism
    c. create a positive situation in which all students are forced to cooperate
    d. ask the students individually to be nice to the Vietnamese students   Objective 6.2

D. Short Essay Questions

1. What are the three components of an attitude? How can each component be measured? (Objective 1.1)

2. How does cognitive dissonance theory explain the result that more attitude change accompanies smaller (rather than larger) rewards?   (Objective 2.2)

3. Does the primacy effect operate in attitude formation? Cite evidence to support your answer.   (Objective 3.1)

4. How are people biased in making causal attributions about their own behavior? About the behavior of others?   (Objective 4.1)

5. How do the situational factors involved in liking differ from those involved in loving? (Objective 5.1)

6. How can prejudice be reduced or eliminated?   (Objective 6.2)

Conflict and Cooperation █ 18

□ **Preview of the Chapter**
Major Concepts and Behavioral Objectives

CONCEPT 1   Social conditions affect our behavior in many ways. In conditions calling for conformity, for example, social pressure produces a tendency to shift our opinions or actions to correspond with those of others.

    1.1   Discuss research that demonstrates conformity effects.

    1.2   Describe conditions that affect conformity.

    1.3   Distinguish between compliance, identification, and internalization.

    1.4   Discuss Milgram's research on obedience.

CONCEPT 2   Membership or participation in a group has important effects on our behavior; our behavior, in turn, can affect the quality of decisions reached by these groups.

    2.1   Define a group and discuss its operation.

    2.2   Discuss how roles and how the presence of other group members can influence a person's behavior.

    2.3   Describe the possible effects a group might have on decision making.

CONCEPT 3   Many factors influence human aggression, including biological influences, social learning influences, and frustration.

    3.1   Describe how psychologists view aggression from the biological, social learning, and frustration-aggression perspectives.

CONCEPT 4   Altruism, or helping behavior, is also affected by several factors, including the number of bystanders present, the demands of the situation, and the costs and rewards of helping.

    4.1   Describe bystander-intervention research.

    4.2   Propose reasons why altruism decreases when the number of bystanders increases.

    4.3   Discuss problems encountered when people do try to help others.

CONCEPT 5   Environmental psychology analyzes the interrelationships between people and their physical and social surroundings. By studying environmental effects in both laboratory and naturalistic settings, environmental psychologists can help in the design of more satisfactory living environments.

    5.1   Discuss the purpose and focus of environmental psychology.

    5.2   Describe the effects that noise and crowding have on behavior.

☐ **Chapter Summary**

I. 1. Conformity is the tendency to shift one's opinions or actions to correspond with those of other people because of implicit or explicit social pressure. Sherif investigated conformity using the autokinetic effect (the illusion that when a person views a stationary point of light in absolute darkness, the light looks as if it is moving). In his experiment he found that subjects alone varied widely in the amount of movement they reported seeing; the amount of movement reported by subjects in groups converged around a group norm.

2. Asch also arranged a conformity experiment by asking group members to judge the length of lines against a standard. He found that when all but one group member were instructed to select an inappropriate line as being a correct match, the last subject often agreed with the incorrect choice of the group, thus conforming. The likelihood of conformity is increased when a person interacts with other group members, when a person is lower in status or self-esteem than other group members, or when a person does not feel he or she fits into the group.

3. Three kinds of conformity can be identified: compliance, in which a person yields outwardly to pressure but doesn't change his true opinion; internalization, in which a person conforms with the expectation of another to maintain a valued relationship; and internalization, in which the person actually comes to accept another's ideas as correct.

4. Conformity can be positive or negative, depending on the particular circumstance.

5. Obedience is compliance with the explicit demands of a person in authority. Milgram has researched the circumstances in which people conform and follow orders, even when obedience involves cruelty to others. In Milgram's experiment, subjects were told they were participating in a learning experiment and were ordered to give increasingly intense electric shocks to another subject. Although no shocks were actually given, Milgram's subjects believed they were hurting and perhaps even harming another person. Psychology students and psychiatrists estimated that few, if any, subjects would give the complete range of shocks to another person. However, the experiment produced startling results: twenty-six of the forty subjects (65 percent) obeyed the experimenter's verbal commands to continue administering the shocks until the highest voltage level on the generator was reached. The subjects who did obey were not sadists; in fact, the procedure caused them severe emotional strain.

6. Several factors affected obedience, as demonstrated by later experiments. Obedience was somewhat decreased by letting the subject see or hear the person receiving the shocks. Obedience also decreased when the experimenter increased his distance from the subject. Regardless of the circumstances, though, a large percentage of the subjects continued to obey Milgram's demands.

7. Milgram's experiment has been criticized as unethical on grounds that the procedure might have been emotionally harmful to those subjects who obeyed Milgram's instructions. Milgram, however, rejects this criticism, adding that most subjects responded that they had found the experiment enlightening. Such research highlights the controversy over whether important questions should be investigated despite possible harm to subjects. Actually, to be performed today, Milgram's experiments would have to be modified to conform to stricter guidelines regarding the ethical use of human subjects.

II. 1. A *group* is defined as two or more people who must interact in a fairly structured way, whose orientation is toward specific goals, and who have a sense of group identity, solidarity, and interdependence. Groups influence our thinking by presenting us with norms, which are sets of shared guidelines and standards. A reference group is a group of people we look to for guidance in formulating our values, beliefs, and attitudes. A positive reference group is one whose outlook we adopt; a negative reference group is one whose views we tend to reject. Parents are typically our first reference group. Later, peers take over this function.

2. In the 1930s, Newcomb investigated the impact that parents and peers had on girls attending Bennington College. Typically, these girls' parents were politically conservative. The school, however, was a liberal environment. By the time they were upperclasswomen, most girls had shifted away from their conservative upbringing, indicating the powerful effect of a positive reference group on attitudes. Even twenty-five years later, the attitude held in college persisted in these women's lives.

3. Brainwashing is an extremely intense persuasion effort backed by various types of pressure: social isolation, physical hardship, and verbal attacks on the subjects' values. Brainwashing has been used in wartime to coerce soldiers. It is currently being used by several religious cults to convert people. If a person who has been converted to a cult through brainwashing techniques later drops out, that person may have difficulty readjusting to a conventional life. He or she may experience depression, difficulty in sex-based relationships, inability to take charge of one's life, and flashbacks to a trancelike state.

4. The role others expect a person to play can also shape that person's behavior. Zimbardo performed an experiment in which he randomly assigned male college students to the role of "prisoner" or "guard" and told them to act out their roles in a mock prison setting. After only six days, Zimbardo was forced to terminate the experiment because subjects were taking their roles so seriously that the situation was potentially dangerous. Zimbardo argues that this experiment demonstrates the power that social roles exert on our personalities.

5. The phenomenon of social facilitation suggests that a person's performance is improved when he or she is in the presence of others. Some research supports this notion; however, other research contradicts it. Zajonc's model attempts to reconcile these disparate results. He believes that the presence of others increases drive or motivation. On an easy task high drive enhances performance, thus producing the social facilitation effect. On difficult tasks, however, high drive interferes with performance.

6. Group decision making typically has many advantages. When a group is both powerful and isolated, however, groupthink may occur, with disastrous results. An example of the dangers of groupthink is the decision-making group that encouraged President Kennedy's disastrous decision to invade Cuba's Bay of Pigs. Groupthink is characterized by an illusion of invulnerability; a compulsion to avoid disrupting group unity, even at the expense of ignoring important information; and a suppressing of doubts, thus creating an illusion of unanimity. Groupthink can be avoided by encouraging group members to express their doubts, to discuss options, and to challenge ideas before they are adopted.

III. 1. Interpersonal aggression is behavior intended to injure another person. Some psychologists, such as Freud and Lorenz, believe that aggression is biologically based. Freud believed aggressive energy built up until it was expressed; Lorenz views aggression as an evolutionary remnant of the "fighting instinct," although humans differ from animals in two respects: We lack an inhibition against killing members of our own species, and we are constantly suppressing our fighting instinct. Lorenz's theory is open to criticism, however: animals also kill members of their own species, and large cross-cultural differences in human aggressiveness are evident.

2. Social learning theories suggest that aggression is learned through reinforcement and observation of violence. Indeed, children will imitate an adult who aggressively beats a Bobo doll. Some theorists believe that watching televised violence increases a child's tendency to behave aggressively; others argue that viewing violence has a cathartic effect, releasing pent-up hostility. Research on this question is still incomplete, but most studies currently support the social learning position that violence should be removed from TV.

3. Dollard and his colleagues proposed that aggression is the result of frustration, defined as interference in goal-directed activity. Although some research evidence supports this view, more recent formulations suggest that frustration probably produces several responses, one of which is aggression. Berkowitz has further clarified this frustration–aggression hypothesis by concluding that frustration produces anger, which can easily instigate aggression if appropriate aggressive cues (such as guns) are present.

IV.
1. Although altruism (helping behavior) may have a genetic base, most social scientists reject such an instinct-oriented theory since it cannot account for large individual differences in altruistic behavior. They instead prefer to consider the environmental factors that can encourage or inhibit altruism.

2. Several factors influence bystander intervention, including determining if an event is an emergency and accepting the responsibility for helping rather than diffusing it to other people. Bystander intervention is less likely to occur if other people are present than if only one person observes an emergency.

3. Latané and Darley have conducted several studies in which subjects who are either alone or with others are subjected to witnessing an emergency. These experiments support the conclusion that helping decreases when bystanders are present.

4. Another factor that apparently influences altruism is the costs and benefits involved in helping. Furthermore, some scientists suggest that crowded and stressful conditions may negatively affect people's attitudes toward helping others.

5. Actually, when people do try to help others, their attempts are often unsuccessful. Contributing to this difficulty is the tendency to assume that the recipient is incompetent, and hence both givers and receivers view improvements as resulting solely from the help, not from the recipient's efforts. As a consequence, the recipient of help often responds in a passive but nongrowing way.

6. People whose jobs involve continually helping others often experience burnout, a syndrome characterized by loss of concern for clients, a tendency to treat clients in a detached or dehumanizing way, rationalizing failure by blaming the clients, a decline in motivation and self-esteem, irritability and anger, and resistance to change. Apparently, burnout is a defense mechanism that provides an escape from frustration and perceived failure. Burnout can be reduced by encouraging workers to form realistic attitudes about their jobs and to discuss their problems with coworkers, and by restructuring the work situation.

V.
1. The relatively new field of environmental psychology focuses on the interrelationships between people and their physical and social surroundings. This field has an interdisciplinary focus and an emphasis on applied research.

2. Noise produces physiological arousal in humans and is a source of stress. It can interfere with task performance and diminish sensitivity to others. The most negative effects seem to come from noise we cannot control. When children from quiet school environments were compared with children from noisy environments, the children from noisy schools had higher blood pressure, were

more easily distracted, and gave up more easily in solving puzzles. Furthermore, rather than adapting to the noise over prolonged periods, these effects intensified. Thus, long-term exposure to noise may have negative long-term effects on cognitive skills.

3. When rats are kept in crowded environments, their behavior becomes inappropriate and aggressive. Since it is difficult to generalize from rats to humans, demographic studies have been conducted to determine the effects of crowding on humans. Early studies indicated that crowding was accompanied by pathology, but these results were unreliable since the studies failed to control economic variables. When crowding was examined in the laboratory, the results proved somewhat contradictory. Recently, psychologists have combined laboratory studies with studies of the same subjects under real-world conditions of crowding. For instance, students living in dorms with long halls had more interactions with neighbors and reacted by withdrawing from social interactions more than did students living in dorms with short hallways. In the laboratory, the subjects from dorms with long halls also were less motivated and had more difficulty making decisions than the comparison group. One theory attempts to explain crowding effects as being due to overstimulation, which produces stress.

4. Environmental psychology will probably become more important as knowledge from several disciplines is brought together to improve human living conditions.

□ **Self-Test**

A.   Matching Questions

_____ 1. The tendency to shift one's opinion or actions to correspond with those of others because of social pressure

_____ 2. When a person's behavior yields to outside pressure but his opinions do not change

_____ 3. Researcher who studied obedience

_____ 4. Shared guidelines or standards

_____ 5. People whose outlooks we tend to adopt

a. Prejudice
b. Conformity
c. Asch
d. Internalization
e. Positive reference group
f. Compliance
g. Norms
h. Milgram
i. Negative reference group

_____ 6. Situation in which the presence of others improves people's performance

_____ 7. Group decision-making strategy that often leads to faulty decisions

_____ 8. Helping behavior

_____ 9. Hypothetical cause of aggression

_____ 10. Can partially explain the bystander intervention effect

_____ 11. Problem for people working in helping occupations

a. Altruism
b. Autokinetic effect
c. Burnout
d. Frustration
e. Groupthink
f. Diffusion of responsibility
g. Social facilitation
h. Interpersonal aggression
i. Crowding

B. Multiple-Choice Questions Testing Factual Knowledge

1. The text describes the My Lai incident as an example of:
   a. conformity
   b. prejudice
   c. the frustration–aggression hypothesis
   d. the autokinetic effect   Objective 1.1

2. The autokinetic effect is:
   a. the reflex involving hand-eye coordination
   b. the tendency to perceive a stationary pinpoint of light as moving
   c. a possible cause of aggression
   d. only experienced when you are in a group of people   Objective 1.1

3. Which of the following increased the conformity Asch revealed in his line-judging experiment?
   a. unanimity of the other group members
   b. previous coaching of the subject
   c. six of the confederates
   d. the amount of frustration the subject felt   Objective 1.2

4. The most long-lasting kind of conformity is:
   a. identification
   b. compliance
   c. obedience
   d. internalization   Objective 1.3

5. In Milgram's obedience experiment, subjects believed that Milgram was studying:
   a. obedience
   b. learning
   c. aggression
   d. all of the above   Objective 1.4

6. When Milgram asked psychology majors and psychiatrists what percentage of subjects would deliver all the shocks, they estimated about _____ percent would. In his experiment, he found that _____ percent in fact delivered all the shocks.
   a. 50; 50
   b. 10; 10
   c. 2; 65
   d. 65; 2   Objective 1.4

7. The predominant criticisms of Milgram's obedience experiment center on:
   a. the kind of subjects he used
   b. the ethical implications of the procedure
   c. the lack of an appropriate control group
   d. the possibility that his results were unreliable   Objective 1.4

8. For a social psychologist, which of the following is *not* a necessary condition in defining a group?
   a. regular interactions of the members
   b. orientation toward a specific goal
   c. a feeling of group identity and solidarity
   d. lack of disagreement among group members   Objective 2.1

9. In a twenty-five-year study of the political attitudes of women at Bennington College, women's attitudes twenty some years after attending Bennington tended to:
   a. match their attitudes as freshmen
   b. match their attitudes as seniors
   c. be a compromise between their freshman and senior attitudes
   d. be unrelated to college attitudes   Objective 2.2

10. In his prison study, Zimbardo demonstrated the importance of _____ on conformity.
    a. groups
    b. brainwashing
    c. obedience
    d. roles   Objective 2.3

11. Zajonc's resolution of the social facilitation contradiction described in the text was to suggest that the presence of others serves to:
    a. increase drive
    b. provide reinforcement
    c. encourage obedience
    d. eliminate distraction   Objective 2.3

12. Which of the following does *not* contribute to groupthink?
    a. an illusion of invulnerability
    b. an illusion of unanimity
    c. strong dissenting opinions among the group members
    d. strong cohesiveness   Objective 2.3

13. According to the text, the major difficulty with biological theories of aggression is their:
    a. reliance on nonhuman subjects
    b. inability to explain large cross-cultural differences
    c. inability to isolate a hormone responsible for aggression
    d. complexity   Objective 3.1

14. Berkowitz argues that frustration and aggression are connected by a third factor. It is:
    a. altruism
    b. hostility
    c. withdrawal
    d. anger   Objective 3.1

15. According to Darley and Latané, one reason that bystanders may fail to help the victim in an emergency is:
    a. diffusion of responsibility
    b. they do not want to get involved
    c. the autokinetic effect
    d. emergencies are so obvious they cannot be mistaken for ordinary events
                                                                 Objective 4.2

16. Milgram's concept of "cognitive overload" suggests that bystander apathy results from:
    a. diffusion of responsibility
    b. a rational response to a crowded and stressful environment
    c. failure to interpret a situation as an emergency
    d. the costs of helping being too high   Objective 4.2

17. Who are the most frequent victims of burnout?
    a. minority group members
    b. people who do not really care about their job
    c. dedicated professionals in help-related careers
    d. people who entered the work force at too early an age   Objective 4.3

18. Which of the following is *not* a characteristic of the field called environmental psychology?
    a. It studies relationships between people and their surroundings.
    b. It is becoming increasingly popular and important.
    c. It focuses on basic rather than applied research questions.
    d. It is an interdisciplinary field.   Objective 5.1

19. According to a study that compared children from quiet and noisy schools under controlled conditions, children from the noisy schools did *not:*
    a. have higher blood pressure

b. give up easier at solving problems
c. prove to be more distractible
d. adapt to the high noise level   Objective 5.2

20. Calhoun's studies of crowded rats indicated that crowding caused:
a. increased aggression
b. inappropriate sexual behavior
c. failure to build satisfactory nests
d. all of the above   Objective 5.2

C. Multiple-Choice Questions Testing Conceptual Knowledge

21. Suppose you are discussing candidates in an upcoming political election. All of the
other group members strongly endorse Candidate A. You wish to vote for Candidate B.
Generalizing from Asch's experiment studying line judging, if your friends asked you
whom you are going to vote for, you would say:
a. Candidate A
b. Candidate B
c. "I haven't decided"
d. "It's none of your business"   Objective 1.2

22. Lisa goes to college and joins a sorority. Now she dresses like the other girls dress,
dates the same kind of boys the other girls date, and takes the same classes the other
girls take. These "other girls" are serving as her:
a. compliance group
b. positive reference group
c. negative reference group
d. brainwashers   Objective 1.3

23. Rudy has undergone a training program in which he was socially isolated, was verbally
attacked about his values, and was forced to participate in the training group's activities. You suspect this situation is similar to:
a. the Asch experiment
b. the Zimbardo prison study
c. brainwashing
d. being exposed to a positive reference group   Objective 1.3

24. Your performance on an assembly line is described as under the control of social
facilitation. This means that you will work harder when:
a. you are rewarded for hard work
b. you are punished for goofing off
c. you are alone
d. other people are working with you   Objective 2.1

25. According to Zajonc, social facilitation would probably occur in which of the following situations?
a. making a difficult shot during an important basketball game
b. sight-reading a piece of music in a symphony audition
c. demonstrating for the thousandth time how to operate a computer terminal
d. all of the above   Objective 2.1

26. Suppose someone accused your decision-making committee of groupthink. To avoid
the groupthink effect, you would be best advised to:
a. call another secret meeting of the group
b. reexamine the group's decisions with additional observers present to challenge the
decision
c. use compliance to prevent the group members from further discussing the decisions
d. act on the decision immediately   Objective 2.3

27. Matt believes that jogging every night after work helps him reduce his aggressive tendencies. According to the text, his theory would probably suggest that aggression stems from:
    a. biological influences
    b. psychological influences
    c. social learning influences
    d. frustration   Objective 3.1

28. Which of the following theorists or groups of theorists would argue most strongly to remove violence from television programming?
    a. Konrad Lorenz (ethologists)
    b. Sigmund Freud
    c. frustration-aggression theorists
    d. social learning theorists   Objective 3.1

29. According to research conducted by Darley and Latané, if you were the victim in an emergency, how many observers would you want present?
    a. 0
    b. 1
    c. 5
    d. 25   Objective 4.1

30. Karen, who works as a public health nurse, has lately been feeling apathetic about her job and has not been very effective with her patients. You suspect she is suffering from:
    a. burnout
    b. depression
    c. bystander apathy
    d. groupthink   Objective 4.3

31. According to research presented in the text, if you were going to work in a noisy environment, the characteristic that would most substantially interfere with your performance would be noise that was:
    a. loud
    b. so soft you can barely hear it
    c. uncontrollable
    d. frequent   Objective 5.2

32. In choosing between moving into a dorm with long hallways and one with short hallways, you consider research suggesting that students in dorms with long hallways:
    a. have more friends
    b. are better decision makers
    c. were less motivated
    d. all of the above   Objective 5.2

D. Short Essay Questions

1. Describe Asch's line-judging experiment and explain why subjects conformed to the group. (Objective 1.1)

2. Describe Zimbardo's prison study. Why did he terminate the study earlier than planned? (Objective 2.2)

3. What can be done to lessen the chances that groupthink will occur?   (Objective 2.3)

4. Discuss the effect that violence on television would supposedly have from a biological perspective; from a social learning perspective; from a frustration–aggression perspective.   (Objective 3.1)

5. What problems occur when people try to help others?   (Objective 4.3)

6. Do you believe that environmental psychology will become increasingly more important? Why or why not?   (Objective 5.1)

1. The major characteristic of a science is its reliance on:
   a. theory
   b. hypotheses
   c. objective rather than subjective methods
   d. empirical data

2. Experimental psychologists generally believe their questions will ultimately be answered through a better understanding of:
   a. human behavior
   b. the methods of science
   c. the principles of conditioning
   d. the brain

3. Freud asked patients to talk about their dreams in order to:
   a. give him symbolic clues to the nature of their unconscious conflicts
   b. put them to sleep
   c. relax them so they would talk about what was really bothering them
   d. be able to observe their natural behavior

4. You meet a woman who tells you she is a psychologist. From this information, you infer that professionally she is probably most interested in:
   a. what you do and the way you think
   b. your personality
   c. your emotional stability
   d. animal (not human) behavior

5. Which of the following research problems would probably *not* be explored by an experimental psychologist?
   a. What is the effect of electric shock on motivation?
   b. Does the display of emotion become less frequent when it is punished?
   c. Does Valium (a tranquilizer) help control hyperactivity in children?
   d. Do young infants prefer sweet foods to salty ones?

6. The task of determining whether the off/on switch on a television should turn or pull would probably be left to which type of psychologist?
   a. social psychologist
   b. developmental psychologist
   c. engineering psychologist
   d. experimental psychologist

7. The method that will allow cause-and-effect inferences to be made is the:
   a. correlational study
   b. survey
   c. experiment
   d. all of the above

8. Which of the following methods of conducting psychological research is best?
   a. survey

b. correlation
c. experiment
d. none of the above; it depends on the circumstances

9. Which of the following is used to determine whether a given set of conclusions can be drawn from a particular set of data?
   a. descriptive statistics
   b. standard deviations
   c. inferential statistics
   d. correlations coefficient

10. In order to replicate an experiment, you would:
    a. reanalyze the data using inferential rather than descriptive statistics
    b. substitute a new independent variable
    c. substitute a new dependent variable
    d. reconduct the experiment much as it was originally performed

11. You decide the best way to study the Ku Klux Klan is to become a member and observe the Klan from the inside. You are using a technique called:
    a. participant observation
    b. naturalistic observation
    c. representative sampling
    d. the self-fulfilling prophecy

12. Suppose you wish to study the effects of room temperature on job productivity on an assembly line. The independent variable in this study would be:
    a. the temperature in the room
    b. the number of people present
    c. the number of goods assembled
    d. how hot or cold people said they felt

13. Suppose I discover that as I eat more vegetables, my body weight decreases. I have demonstrated:
    a. a positive correlation
    b. a negative correlation
    c. a cause-and-effect relationship
    d. random sampling

14. The sympathetic and parasympathetic divisions work by dual control. This means they:
    a. augment (help) one another
    b. work antagonistically
    c. take turns
    d. are located in different areas of the body

15. Which of the following is most clearly responsible for speeding the conduction of a neural impulse?
    a. myelin
    b. glial cells
    c. interneurons
    d. hormones

16. Which of the following brain areas is least involved with vision?
    a. midbrain
    b. occipital cortex
    c. thalamus
    d. cerebellum

17. Which of the following would most typically be controlled primarily by the right cerebral hemisphere?
    a. language
    b. the right half of the body
    c. analytical thinking
    d. spatial relationships

18. If you went to a phrenologist, you would expect him to tell you about your personality by:
    a. giving you an EEG
    b. giving you a series of personality tests
    c. doing a brain scan
    d. feeling the bumps on your head

19. Mary is having problems regulating the production of estrogen and progesterone. If the doctor suspects an endocrine disorder, the first place he would probably examine would be Mary's:
    a. adrenal glands
    b. ovaries
    c. thyroid gland
    d. pons

20. As a result of brain damage, a man loses control over his body movements. The damage is probably in which lobe of his brain?
    a. parietal
    b. occipital
    c. temporal
    d. frontal

21. According to the principle of sensory adaptation, our sensory systems are particularly well designed to detect:
    a. duration
    b. intensity
    c. quality
    d. change

22. Which of the following statements regarding the rods and cones is *false*?
    a. They both transduce light.
    b. There are more types of cones than rods.
    c. Rods are concentrated in the fovea.
    d. None of the above are false.

23. Which of the following is *not* one of the basic skin senses discussed in the text?
    a. warmth
    b. sharpness
    c. cold
    d. pressure

24. Suppose you find that when lifting a fifty-pound barbell, you can just notice the difference when two pounds are added. According to Weber's law, if you were lifting a twenty-five-pound barbell, the just noticeable difference would be:
    a. one-half pound
    b. one pound
    c. two pounds
    d. four pounds

25. The phenomenon of color blindness is _____ trichromatic theory and _____ volley theory.
    a. not supportive of; unrelated to
    b. supportive of; contradictory to
    c. contradictory to; supportive of
    d. contradictory to; not supportive of

26. Suppose I believe that hearing is set up the same way as a harmonica: The note you hear depends on the place you blow. I would probably subscribe to:
    a. trichromatic theory
    b. volley theory
    c. opponent-process theory
    d. place theory

27. Which of the following is a characteristic of learning but not performance?
    a. It is observable.
    b. It is measurable.
    c. It is a mental activity.
    d. All of the above are characteristics of learning.

28. According to Garcia's studies, rats are especially likely to attribute the occurrence of foot shock to:
    a. the taste of the food they were eating when they were shocked
    b. the taste of the food they were eating about two hours before they were shocked
    c. the auditory and visual characteristics of the food
    d. none of the above

29. When an individual mistakenly assumes a contingency between a response and reinforcement when no such contingency exists, the behavior that is produced is called:
    a. superstitious behavior
    b. sporadic behavior
    c. partial behavior
    d. noncontingent behavior

30. How would you extinguish an operantly conditioned response?
    a. stop reinforcement
    b. prevent the response
    c. punish the response
    d. any of the above

31. You teach your dog to sit by giving him a dog biscuit every time he sits on command. This is an example of:
    a. the orienting reflex
    b. habituation
    c. classical conditioning
    d. operant conditioning

32. You are teaching a mentally retarded child to dress herself. When she does something correctly, you give her a poker chip that she can later exchange for food or privileges. This is an example of:
    a. programmed instruction
    b. discrimination training
    c. a token economy
    d. systematic desensitization

33. Recent research has indicated that different people have different "cognitive styles," or ways of thinking about problems. This research would be most consistent with the beliefs of:
    a. Edward Thorndike
    b. B. F. Skinner
    c. Edward Tolman
    d. John B. Watson

34. Humans have a sensory memory that corresponds to their sense of:
    a. taste
    b. smell
    c. vision
    d. all of the above

35. The kind of rehearsal that is especially effective in transferring information from short- to long-term memory is:
    a. effective rehearsal
    b. elaborative rehearsal
    c. maintenance rehearsal
    d. recombinatory rehearsal

36. Distortion in memory can be produced by:
    a. expectations about the outcome

    b. stereotypes

    c. suggestions from other people

    d. all of the above

37. Neurophysiologists believe that temporary circulation of electrical impulses around complex loops of interconnected neurons is responsible for:

    a. confabulation

    b. retrograde amnesia

    c. long-term memory

    d. short-term memory

38. You are talking to a friend at a large party when you hear someone mention your name. You immediately start paying attention to the other conversation. This is called:

    a. dichotic listening

    b. selective attention

    c. sensory gating

    d. shadowing

39. Jack is eighty-seven years old and has good recall of events before his sixty-fifth birthday. However, he remembers virtually nothing since then. He probably suffers from:

    a. anterograde amnesia

    b. retrograde amnesia

    c. repression

    d. consolidation

40. If you delivered electroconvulsive shock to a depressed patient, you would expect the resulting memory loss to be for that period of time:

    a. in the long distant past

    b. just after the patient woke up after the shock treatment

    c. about one to three days after the shock

    d. just before the shock was given

41. The major problem with the method of introspection is that:

    a. people have no insight into their own thoughts

    b. it is not objectively measurable

    c. it can only be used to study algorithmic thought

    d. it can only be used to study heuristic thought

42. If a person has adopted a global focusing strategy, the errors he or she would most likely commit would be errors of:

    a. overextension

    b. underextension

    c. mental set

    d. functional fixedness

43. The tendency to view an object as being usable only for its customary use is called:

    a. mental set

    b. natural construct

    c. an algorithm

    d. functional fixedness

44. Gene goes to Las Vegas and keeps putting his money on red at the roulette wheel as long as red comes up but moves his money to black as soon as black is a winner. His strategy is:

    a. global hypothesis

    b. algorithm

    c. scanning hypothesis

    d. win-stay, lose-shift

45. Suppose you are to construct a suit to allow an astronaut to walk on the moon. You tackle the problem by dividing it into smaller problems, such as fabric choice, life-support, elimination, and so on. This is an example of:

    a. subgoal analysis

    b. means-end analysis
    c. utility analysis
    d. reproductive thinking

46. You meet John and find that he is forty-five years old, intelligent, dedicated, verbal, concerned about other people's welfare, and wealthy. You conclude that he is more likely to be a doctor than a truck driver. You are using the heuristic called:
    a. probabilistic inference
    b. utility analysis
    c. availability
    d. representativeness

47. If a human cell undergoes meiosis, how many single chromosomes normally remain?
    a. twelve
    b. twenty-three
    c. thirty-six
    d. forty-six

48. Sensorimotor intelligence is best characterized by:
    a. action
    b. concept construction
    c. thought
    d. conservation

49. When Harlow's monkeys were deprived of attachment, they eventually:
    a. grew out of the attachment stage into normal adults
    b. died
    c. became withdrawn and apathetic
    d. became more dependent on friendships in their peer group

50. According to Erikson, the crisis encountered in adolescence centers around:
    a. sexual frustrations
    b. establishing an identity
    c. achieving one's goals
    d. evaluating one's contribution to society

51. Jackie is shown a rattle she wants. Her mother partially hides it behind a book. Jackie now acts as if the rattle has ceased to exist. Jackie is probably about how old?
    a. two months
    b. six months
    c. ten months
    d. fourteen months

52. Typing is primarily a speed-related skill. Which age group could generally be expected to be the best typists?
    a. ten- to sixteen-year-olds
    b. twenty- to thirty-year-olds
    c. thirty-five- to forty-five-year-olds
    d. fifty- to sixty-five-year-olds

53. Doris believes that moral reasoning is acquired through reinforcement of sex-appropriate behavior and punishment of sex-inappropriate behavior. She would best be classified as a:
    a. Freudian theorist
    b. biological theorist
    c. cognitive development theorist
    d. social learning theorist

54. Which of the following is *not* a characteristic of language?
    a. It is symbolic.
    b. It is tied to concrete representations.
    c. It can be used to express past, present, and future.
    d. All of the above are characteristics of language.

55. The transformation of a sentence's surface structure into its underlying representation is the process involved in:
    a. talking
    b. writing
    c. listening
    d. translating foreign languages

56. Brain damage can cause difficulty in producing and comprehending speech. A general term for this condition is:
    a. regression
    b. amnesia
    c. stammering
    d. aphasia

57. According to studies reported in the text, parents generally reinforce their children for correct:
    a. grammar
    b. pronunciation
    c. meaning
    d. phrasing

58. You analyze the word *dog* by breaking it into *d* plus *o* plus *g*. You are analyzing this word according to its:
    a. phonology
    b. semantics
    c. morphology
    d. syntax

59. David believes that he analyzes sentences according to the meanings of the major words. His would be considered which kind of approach?
    a. semantic
    b. syntactic
    c. grammatical
    d. verbatim

60. Suppose you stumble onto a culture that has only three basic color terms. According to research, which color term will *not* be one of them?
    a. black
    b. purple
    c. red
    d. white

1. According to your text, psychology is:
   a. a science
   b. an academic discipline
   c. a means of promoting human welfare
   d. all of the above

2. "A quest for knowledge purely for its own sake" is a definition of:
   a. science
   b. basic science
   c. applied science
   d. research

3. The inclusion of the study of animals as well as humans in the discipline of psychology is primarily the result of the work of:
   a. Sigmund Freud
   b. Charles Darwin
   c. Josef Breuer
   d. Wilhelm Wundt

4. Psychologists who use intelligence and personality tests in their work trace the origins of these tests back to:
   a. Wilhelm Wundt
   b. Sir Francis Galton
   c. Sigmund Freud
   d. B. F. Skinner

5. The clearest example of applied research would be studying the relationship between:
   a. cigarette smoking and cancer
   b. colors of light and feelings of stress
   c. order of words on a list and the ability to remember the list
   d. age and problem-solving ability

6. The issue of heredity versus environment as the major determinant of behavior would be most clearly represented by comparing the views of:
   a. Sigmund Freud and B. F. Skinner
   b. Wilhelm Wundt and Ivan Pavlov
   c. John B. Watson and B. F. Skinner
   d. Sir Francis Galton and John B. Watson

7. An attempt to estimate the opinions, characteristics, or behaviors of a particular population by investigating a representative sample is:
   a. a correlational study
   b. a correlational coefficient
   c. a case study
   d. a survey

8. Heart rate, respiration rate, and galvanic skin response are all used as:
   a. physiological measures

b.   psychological tests
c.   rating scales
d.   all of the above, at one time or another

9.   The average extent to which all scores in a particular set vary from the mean is the:
a.   standard deviation
b.   central tendency
c.   probability statistic
d.   statistical significance

10.   According to the American Psychological Association, a researcher cannot:
a.   subject a human to physical pain
b.   subject a human to psychological pain
c.   refuse to let a human subject quit in the middle of an experiment
d.   all of the above

11.   Suppose you go into a laboratory and are asked to taste several different foods and indicate which you like the most and the least. You are being asked to perform:
a.   a psychological test
b.   a physiological measure
c.   a rating scale
d.   a self-fulfilling prophecy

12.   What is the range of the following set of scores?
        3, 4, 5, 5, 6, 6, 6, 7, 10
a.   5
b.   5.9
c.   6
d.   7

13.   Two researchers study the same problem. One finds a significant difference between the experimental and control group; the other does not. A possible cause of this discrepancy is:
a.   the placebo effect occurred in both experiments
b.   the second researcher's measures were not sensitive enough
c.   the variables probably defy measurement
d.   the self-fulfilling prophecy could not have been operating

14.   The major function of the glial cells is to:
a.   manufacture RNA
b.   stimulate hormones
c.   speed neural conduction
d.   nourish and support neurons

15.   In the nervous system the messages conducted are _____; in the endocrine system they are _____.
a.   electrochemical; chemical
b.   chemical; electrochemical
c.   physical; chemical
d.   electrical; physical

16.   Wilder Penfield applied tiny amounts of electric current to the surface of the brain in experiments that seem to support the notion of:
a.   localization of function
b.   mass action
c.   multiple control
d.   evoked potentials

17.   If you compare your neural conduction mechanism to the U.S. Post Office, the nature of the message sent in the neural system would be analogous to what in the postal system?
a.   the route you sent the letter by
b.   the cost of the stamp

    c. how many letters you sent

    d. the weight of the letter

18. A boy is brought into a hospital suffering from head injuries. The most noticeable symptom is his inability to sleep in a regular eight-hour cycle. You suspect brain damage to the:

    a. cerebellum

    b. reticular formation

    c. thalamus

    d. hypothalamus

19. Suppose I believe that any particular part of the brain has many different functions. This belief is essentially that expressed by:

    a. Olds and Milner in their work with pleasure center

    b. Lashley's principle of mass action

    c. the principle of multiple control

    d. the principle of localization of function

20. Signal detection theory is unique in that it accounts for the effects of:

    a. the just noticeable difference

    b. noise

    c. Weber's law

    d. Stevens's power law

21. Jeff can tell red from green but confuses yellow and blue; he is a:

    a. blue-yellow dichromat

    b. red-green dichromat

    c. monochromatic

    d. trichromatic

22. Which of the following is *not* one of our senses?

    a. olfaction

    b. balance and equilibrium

    c. touch

    d. all of the above *are* human senses

23. The fact that some cultures do not see the same illusions as Americans tends to demonstrate the impact on perception of:

    a. motivation

    b. experience

    c. genetics

    d. deformity

24. You go to an optometrist who tells you that you have an abnormally high pressure inside your eyes. You suspect you might be suffering from:

    a. glaucoma

    b. cataracts

    c. presbyopia

    d. a blind spot

25. Which of the following has a function that differs from the others?

    a. auditory canal

    b. ear ossicles

    c. eardrum

    d. Organ of Corti

26. Most people see the letters displayed below as three groups of three As, three Bs, and three Cs. This is consistent with the Gestalt principle of:

AAABBBCCC

    a. similarity

    b. proximity

    c. continuity

    d. subjective contour

27. According to Pavlov, the tendency to react to a previously neutral stimulus as though it were an unconditioned stimulus is called:
    a. stimulus substitution
    b. reflex behavior
    c. refining of the operant
    d. backward conditioning

28. The decrease of the frequency of a response that is followed by a negative consequence is:
    a. systematic desensitization
    b. punishment
    c. negative reinforcement
    d. behavior modification

29. A rat learns that he will be reinforced only when a red light in his cage is lit. This is an example of:
    a. generalization
    b. stimulus control
    c. continuous reinforcement
    d. the Garcia effect

30. You are walking down the street when you hear an explosion off to your left. You immediately turn to the left and devote your attention to trying to figure out what happened. This is an example of:
    a. the orienting reflex
    b. habituation
    c. classical conditioning
    d. operant conditioning

31. You work on an assembly line and you know that every day your work output is checked by a computer. You do not know when it is checked, since the time changes from day to day. You are on which of the following reinforcement schedules?
    a. fixed ratio
    b. fixed interval
    c. variable ratio
    d. variable interval

32. You teach a child to be afraid of the dog next door (who bites little children), but the child becomes afraid of all dogs. This is an example of:
    a. discrimination
    b. generalization
    c. stimulus control
    d. a discriminative stimulus

33. The memory that lasts about twenty seconds and is maintained by acoustic rehearsal is:
    a. sensory memory
    b. long-term memory
    c. short-term memory
    d. acoustic memory

34. Essay tests require _____; multiple choice tests require _____.
    a. recall; recognition
    b. recognition; recall
    c. recall; recall
    d. recognition; recognition

35. Loftus's research on eyewitness testimony indicates:
    a. eyewitnesses often lie to protect themselves
    b. eyewitnesses can distort the truth without realizing it
    c. eyewitnesses are typically accurate in their recall
    d. none of the above

36. The notion that long-term memory storage takes time is called:
    a. consolidation
    b. synaptic rehearsal
    c. enrichment
    d. confabulation

37. Suppose you are asked to remember a list of thirty words. Your short-term memory would facilitate your recall of:
    a. the first words on the list
    b. the middle words on the list
    c. the last words on the list
    d. both the first and last words but not the middle words

38. A memory expert remembers long lists of words by imagining herself walking down a familiar street and at each step placing an object on the sidewalk. To remember the list, she simply walks down the street and picks up the objects. This technique is an example of:
    a. déjà vu
    b. method of loci
    c. key word system
    d. eidetic imagery

39. Suppose you conceptualize learning as building a complex system of roads in your brain; consequently, forgetting involves taking the wrong road. This theory is similar to:
    a. repression
    b. decay
    c. motivated forgetting
    d. interference

40. The categories that we use every day such as *furniture* and *dogs* are called:
    a. constructs
    b. arranged constructs
    c. predetermined concepts
    d. natural concepts

41. A sudden perception of the solution to a problem is called:
    a. insight
    b. incubation
    c. satisfactory solution
    d. revealed solution

42. The inclination to repeat a solution that has worked in the past, even though it is not helpful in the particular situation, is called:
    a. mental set
    b. functional fixedness
    c. fixation
    d. incubation

43. One way to deal with making a difficult decision is to put it off to a later date. This is called:
    a. rationalization
    b. buck-passing
    c. subgoal analyses
    d. procrastination

44. Suppose you volunteer for a psychology experiment in which you are asked to describe your thought processes. This experimental method would be similar to:
    a. an algorithm
    b. a heuristic
    c. introspection
    d. subgoal analysis

45. Suppose someone asks you to list all the possible uses of a brick you can generate. This would most likely be a test of your:
    a. prototype knowledge
    b. creative thinking
    c. ability to use algorithms
    d. reproductive thinking

46. Suppose I tell you that to calculate the mean of a distribution, you must always add the scores and divide the total by the number of scores. This is an example of:
    a. a subgoal analysis
    b. a heuristic strategy
    c. an algorithmic strategy
    d. a means–end analysis

47. Which of the following is a newborn *not* capable of?
    a. 20/20 vision
    b. depth perception
    c. locating the direction from which a sound comes
    d. discriminating different sounds

48. The increased memory capacity that older children have is probably related to all of the following *except:*
    a. greater familiarity with commonly used items
    b. more highly developed short-term memories
    c. better learning strategies
    d. increased use of memory cues

49. Which of the following appears to be a major difference between infants in day care and infants raised at home?
    a. Day-care infants formed attachments to their teachers rather than their mothers.
    b. Day-care infants formed weaker attachments to others.
    c. Day-care infants formed attachments later in their development.
    d. None of the above are true.

50. According to research and theory presented in the text, the period of greatest stability in the typical person's life is:
    a. age twenty to thirty
    b. age thirty to forty
    c. age fifty to sixty
    d. age seventy to eighty

51. Suppose your friend has a baby who is diagnosed as having the genetic defect called PKU (phenylketonuria). You would assume that treatment will consist of:
    a. genetic engineering
    b. drug therapy (chemotherapy)
    c. eating a special diet
    d. none of the above; there is no treatment for this disorder

52. Gelman's research that tested children's conservation skills using toy mice is _____ Piaget's theory.
    a. supportive of
    b. contradictory to
    c. unrelated to
    d. essentially the same as research conducted according to

53. Jerry believes that children acquire their gender roles through a process of coping with a deep affection for the opposite sex parent, which ultimately cannot be realized. To compensate, a child identifies with this parent and internalizes his or her gender role. Jerry's theory would be most like that of:
    a. social learning theorists
    b. biological theorists

    c.   cognitive development theorists

    d.   Freudian theorists

54. Which of the following is *not* one of the basic levels of structural analysis for language?
    a.   morphology
    b.   syntax
    c.   linguistic relativity
    d.   phonology

55. Which of the following human languages would a chimp be best able to learn?
    a.   Ameslan
    b.   English
    c.   Spanish
    d.   Chinese

56. Which of the following develop first?
    a.   babbling phonemes of foreign languages
    b.   intonation patterns
    c.   simple words for objects
    d.   simple words for commands

57. Which of the following consists of a single bound morpheme?
    a.   th
    b.   re
    c.   dog
    d.   undone

58. Which of the following is an example of telegraphic speech?
    a.   I must have it now (accompanied by a gesture)!
    b.   I'd like that.
    c.   Doggy bye-bye.
    d.   Please give me my dolly.

59. Which of the following is an obvious example of an error of overregularization?
    a.   Me, too.
    b.   I goed, too.
    c.   Mommy likes me.
    d.   Daddy bye-bye.

60. Jackie's mother is verbally approving of her attempts to learn to play the violin, but every time Jackie makes a mistake, her mother has a horrible, pained expression on her face. This situation is an example of:
    a.   evolutionary influences
    b.   the linguistic relativity hypothesis
    c.   linguistic universals
    d.   a double-bind situation

1. Generally speaking, the sympathetic division of the nervous system dominates during _____; the parasympathetic dominates during _____.
   a. sleep; wakefulness
   b. an emergency; relaxation
   c. work; play
   d. work; anger

2. According to recent evidence, which part of your brain is probably *not* directly involved in emotion?
   a. thalamus
   b. hypothalamus
   c. limbic system
   d. amygdala

3. According to the text, which of the following beliefs about crisis reactions is probably true?
   a. There are universal reactions to crisis.
   b. People go through stages as they respond to crisis.
   c. Response to crises vary widely from person to person.
   d. Crises are ultimately resolved.

4. Suppose you were measuring the physiological response of psychopaths. According to research in the text you might expect their ratio of norepinephrine to epinephrine to be:
   a. higher than normal
   b. lower than normal
   c. about the same as normal
   d. widely varying from one person to another

5. Suppose you are shown a series of twenty erotic pictures and are given false feedback regarding your physiological arousal level. According to Valins, which pictures would you like best?
   a. those accompanied by fake arousal feedback
   b. those not accompanied by fake arousal feedback
   c. those accompanied by real arousal
   d. no clear preference

6. Mary was just divorced. John just got fired. Bob just borrowed some money. Judy started working the night shift. According to the SRRS, who is under the most stress?
   a. Mary
   b. John
   c. Bob
   d. Judy

7. Freud categorized human instincts into two basic groups:
   a. primary drives and secondary drives
   b. drives and incentives
   c. emotion and motivation
   d. life and death

8. Schachter believes that the major reason people are overweight is:
   a. they have more fat cells

b. they have slower metabolism
c. they are more responsive to external cues
d. they constantly feel hungry

9. The most controversial findings of Kinsey's studies included all of the following *except:*
a. homosexuality was more common than expected
b. sexual dysfunction was more common than expected
c. premarital sex was more common than expected
d. extramarital sex was more common than expected

10. According to Eysenck, as compared to introverts, extroverts have _____ levels of internal stimulation and seek _____ levels of external stimulation.
a. higher; the same
b. lower; the same
c. higher; lower
d. lower; higher

11. Which of the following is an example of a secondary drive rather than a primary drive?
a. food
b. warmth
c. creativity
d. water

12. In order to replicate Masters and Johnson's studies, you would have to:
a. lesion the brains of experimental animals
b. observe human couples during intercourse
c. prepare and give questionnaires
d. work with hormone balances and imbalances

13. Suppose you have been on a bland diet for several weeks. According to optimal level theory, when you are taken off the bland diet, the food you would probably first prefer is:
a. bland food, since that is what you've been used to
b. food just a little more interesting than the bland
c. the same kind as you usually ate before being on the bland diet
d. exotic foods

14. "A qualitative alteration in overall mental functioning" is the definition of:
a. consciousness
b. hypnosis
c. altered state of consciousness
d. meditation

15. According to role enactment theory, hypnotism is most similar to:
a. being awake
b. stage 1 sleep
c. stage 4 sleep
d. REM sleep

16. The major difference between stimulants and alcohol is that stimulants are:
a. stronger
b. more dangerous
c. pleasant to use
d. produce central nervous system arousal

17. You observe a sleeper's eyes move up and down repetitively. You wake the sleeper up and find that she has been dreaming about watching cliff divers. This experience would support:
a. neodissociation theory
b. the scanning hypothesis
c. role-enactment theory
d. none of the above

18. A recent television program showed a yogi fit his large body into a very small box, which was then submerged in water. A normal person would have suffocated, but the yogi emerged unharmed. How does this feat differ from dreaming or hypnosis?
    a. One is a true change in state of consciousness; the others are fictional changes.
    b. The yogi's state of consciousness was self-regulated.
    c. The yogi's consciousness was not limited.
    d. It did not differ.

19. Suppose you drink fifteen ounces of alcohol per week. According to research presented in the text, to stay the healthiest:
    a. you should drink about two ounces per day
    b. you should drink only on weekdays, not weekends
    c. you should drink it all in one day
    d. your drinking pattern doesn't matter; only the total amount you drink affects health

20. For Freud, which of the following was the major motivating force in personality?
    a. unconscious
    b. conscious
    c. ego
    d. conscience

21. Which of the following defense mechanisms underlies all of the others?
    a. projection
    b. fixation
    c. regression
    d. repression

22. Most of the psychoanalytic theorists who broke away from Freud came to place more emphasis than Freud on the:
    a. ego
    b. id
    c. unconscious
    d. conscience

23. Eysenck concluded that personality structure varies on two dimensions, neuroticism versus emotional stability and introversion versus extroversion. Underlying these traits are differences in:
    a. drive
    b. genetic composition
    c. brain stimulation
    d. early experiences in the environment

24. Jack finds any mention of male femininity offensive: His therapist suggests that, in actuality, this may be Jack's method of reducing anxiety from his true fear of being a homosexual. If so, Jack is using the defense mechanism of:
    a. reaction formation
    b. displacement
    c. projection
    d. regression

25. Which of the following is an example of an approach-avoidance conflict?
    a. Mary cannot decide which of two dresses to buy.
    b. If Mary goes out with Bill (her current heartthrob) she will flunk the math test tomorrow.
    c. Mary does not want to go to the dentist, but she also does not want to get cavities.
    d. none of the above

26. As presented in this chapter, Mischel's research on the consistency of personality would be most threatening to which of the following theoretical positions?
    a. psychoanalytic theory
    b. phenomenological theory

  c. trait theory

  d. behavioral theory

27. A group of scores against which an individual's test score is compared is called a:

  a. norm

  b. reference group

  c. positive reference group

  d. construct

28. According to the text, intelligence tests measure:

  a. genetic influence

  b. environmental influences

  c. both a and b

  d. neither a nor b

29. Selecting test items that are answered differently by "normal" and mentally ill people and using them to test for possible mental illness is the rationale behind which of the following tests?

  a. Rorschach Inkblot Test

  b. MMPI

  c. free-association tests

  d. TAT

30. Suppose you have three trained observers recording aggressive behaviors exhibited by a particular child. You would be most interested in:

  a. alternate forms reliability

  b. interjudge reliability

  c. split-half reliability

  d. test-retest reliability

31. Suppose you determine that genes are responsible for 90 percent of the individual variation of a particular trait—for instance, eye color. You are considering eye color's:

  a. reaction range

  b. heritability

  c. normative distribution

  d. Jensen factor

32. You take the MMPI and are given several assertions such as "I never think bad thoughts about other people." You answer all these statements with the "applies to me" response. You would probably score unusually high on:

  a. the L scale

  b. the depression scale

  c. the hypochondria scale

  d. all the clinical scales

33. Applying the term "abnormal" to some behaviors that are statistically frequent but not considered a subject for concern is *not* a problem with which criterion for abnormality?

  a. statistical criterion

  b. absolute criterion

  c. social norms criterion

  d. all of the above

34. The therapist most likely to treat the symptoms rather than an underlying problem is the:

  a. psychoanalytic therapist

  b. family, or systems, therapist

  c. learning theory therapist

  d. medical model therapist

35. Which of the following statements about the classification manual used for diagnosing mental illness is *false*?

  a. Its usefulness probably outweighs its hazards.

  b. It currently views homosexuality as a category of abnormal behavior.

    c. Its categories change with changing times and attitudes.

    d. Its new edition tries to be more specific in describing the various disorders.

36. "Learned helplessness" is a possible explanation for:
   a. depression
   b. schizophrenia
   c. affective disorders
   d. dissociative disorders

37. The theoretical perspective that would most agree that normal and abnormal behavior are caused by the same variables would be the:
   a. psychoanalytic perspective
   b. learning theory perspective
   c. psychoanalytic perspective
   d. family, or systems, approach

38. Julia is so afraid of riding in an elevator that she will shop only in stores on the ground level. She would be classified as:
   a. obsessive-compulsive
   b. paranoid
   c. phobic
   d. schizophrenic

39. Bill is arrested for murdering his mother, wife, and two children and for trying to kill himself. He reports that he feels no sadness or guilt over his actions. You would diagnose Bill as a:
   a. manic depressive
   b. schizophrenic
   c. suicidal depressive
   d. sociopathic personality

40. Psychotherapy refers to:
   a. Freudian analysis
   b. behavioral therapy
   c. group therapy
   d. all of the above

41. One therapy consists of helping clients recognize the irrational nature of long-held negative beliefs about themselves. This therapy is called:
   a. rational-emotive therapy
   b. psychoanalysis
   c. transactional analysis
   d. participant modeling

42. From a study conducted in 1952, Hans Eysenck concluded that psychotherapy was about:
   a. as effective as drug therapy
   b. twice as effective as no therapy
   c. three times more effective than no therapy
   d. equally effective as no therapy

43. John believes that abnormal behaviors are governed by the same principles as normal behaviors and that the environment plays a crucial role in determining behavior. His theory would be most similar to that of:
   a. Sigmund Freud
   b. transactional analysis
   c. an environmentalist
   d. behavioral therapists

44. Martha says "I'm not going to work today because I'm tired and I just want to have some fun." A transactional analyst would conclude that her behavior is being controlled by:
   a. reinforcement
   b. her Child

    c. her Adult

    d. anxiety

45. You walk into a mental hospital and see a person who is making grotesque facial movements. You conclude that this has resulted from prolonged use of:

    a. Valium

    b. electroconvulsive therapy

    c. Thorazine

    d. antidepressants

46. Which of the following would probably lead to the *least* amount of attitude change in an educated audience?

    a. an expert speaker

    b. a trustworthy speaker

    c. a one-sided message

    d. a two-sided message

47. Bem's self-perception theory has the advantage over cognitive dissonance theory in that Bem's theory is able to explain:

    a. why more attitude change takes place for one dollar than twenty dollars

    b. why more attitude change takes place for twenty dollars than one dollar

    c. cognitive factors in attitude change

    d. the greater decrease in a positive attitude for twenty dollars than one dollar

48. The "fundamental attribution error" involves:

    a. inferring causation from correlational evidence

    b. overestimating the role of situational factors

    c. overestimating the role of dispositional factors

    d. making attributions that are totally inappropriate

49. Which of the following is *not* predictive of whether a love relationship will last?

    a. similarity of age of partners

    b. equal involvement by both partners in the relationship

    c. living together before marriage

    d. similarity of physical attractiveness

50. Suppose you convince your roommate to call your professor and tell her that you are too sick to take the exam. According to cognitive dissonance theory, your roommate is most likely to believe you are really sick if you pay her which of the following sums for making the call?

    a. ten cents

    b. one dollar

    c. ten dollars

    d. fifty dollars

51. John has heard that Mary is shy. When he meets her, he treats her as if she were shy, and she responds as if she were shy, even though she is not. This is an example of:

    a. psychological reactance

    b. the "Romeo and Juliet" effect

    c. cognitive dissonance

    d. a self-fulfilling prophecy

52. Mary believes that women have always been discriminated against and that, even in the United States, women are still the victims of discrimination. After reading the text, you would:

    a. disagree; women have not historically been victims of discrimination

    b. disagree; women in the United States are not now the victims of discrimination

    c. disagree, for the reasons in both a and b

    d. agree with Mary

53. The text cites the My Lai incident as an example of:

    a. conformity

    b. prejudice

c. the frustration–aggression hypothesis

d. the autokinetic effect

54. In Milgram's obedience experiment, subjects believed that Milgram was studying:

a. obedience

b. learning

c. aggression

d. all of the above

55. Zajonc's resolution of the social facilitation contradiction described in the text was to suggest that the presence of others serves to:

a. increase drive

b. provide reinforcement

c. encourage obedience

d. eliminate distraction

56. Who are the most frequent victims of burnout?

a. minority group members

b. people who do not really care about their job

c. dedicated professionals in help-related careers

d. people who entered the work force at too early an age

57. Lisa goes to college and joins a sorority. Now she dresses like the other girls dress, dates the same kind of boys the other girls date, and takes the same classes the other girls take. These "other girls" are serving as her:

a. compliance group

b. positive reference group

c. negative reference group

d. brainwashers

58. Suppose your decision-making committee was accused of groupthink. To get rid of the group-think effect, you would be best advised to:

a. call another secret meeting of the group

b. reexamine the group's decisions with additional observers present to challenge the decision

c. use compliance to prevent the group members from further discussing the decisions

d. act on the decision immediately

59. According to research conducted by Darley and Latané, if you were the victim in an emergency, you would want how many observers present?

a. none

b. one

c. five

d. twenty-five

60. Karen, who works as a public health nurse, has been feeling apathetic about her job and has not been very effective with her patients. You suspect she is suffering from:

a. burnout

b. depression

c. bystander apathy

d. groupthink

1. By recording a person's heart rate, blood pressure, and breathing rate, you are measuring which component of emotion?
   a. overt behavior
   b. subjective feeling
   c. physiological change
   d. all of the above

2. According to research presented in the text, depression may be associated with a lack of:
   a. suproxin
   b. norepinephrine
   c. epinephrine
   d. adrenalin

3. According to the Cannon-Bard theory, which of the following parts of the nervous system is activated in an emotional response?
   a. thalamus
   b. sympathetic nervous system
   c. cerebral cortex
   d. all of the above

4. Selye's research was based on work done with:
   a. terminally ill cancer patients
   b. blue-collar workers
   c. men (not women)
   d. animals

5. Bob believes that different situations produce different physiological response patterns. These, in turn, arouse their corresponding emotions. Bob's theory most closely corresponds to:
   a. Schachter's two-factor theory
   b. Cannon-Bard theory
   c. Selye's general adaptation syndrome
   d. James-Lange theory

6. You just find out you are going to be called on in class to give a twenty-minute lecture on material you hardly understand. You are in which stage of Selye's general adaptation syndrome?
   a. panic
   b. alarm
   c. resistance
   d. exhaustion

7. John believes that happiness is only achieved when you are too involved to be aware of it. He would probably subscribe to which theory?
   a. comparison theory
   b. adaptation theory
   c. trait theory
   d. "stepping off the hedonistic treadmill"

8. Eating behavior and hunger have been found to be related to:
   a. distension of the stomach
   b. changes in the sensation of taste
   c. glucose levels in the blood
   d. all of the above

9. A female rat is sexually responsive:
   a. whenever an interested male is present
   b. only during ovulation
   c. when her testosterone levels are high
   d. when her estrogen levels are low

10. Masters and Johnson believe that most cases of sexual dysfunction are caused by:
    a. hormone imbalances
    b. psychological factors
    c. improper exercise
    d. damage to sensitive genital tissue

11. In playing a ring-toss game, people with a high need for achievement generally:
    a. stand close to the target
    b. stand an intermediate distance from the target
    c. stand far from the target
    d. refuse to play

12. Kelly maintains a normal body weight by her near-constant dieting. In an experiment she is forced to eat a large piece of chocolate cream pie, after which she can eat as many pieces of other kinds of pie as she wishes. According to research presented in the text, you would expect her to:
    a. eat no more pie
    b. eat a little more pie
    c. eat about as much more pie as a normal eater
    d. eat much more pie than normal eaters

13. Which of the following behaviors is most easily explained by a drive-reduction theory of motivation?
    a. A hungry person gets food from a refrigerator.
    b. A religious person fasts for weeks before eating.
    c. Students stay up all night watching old movies on cable television.
    d. None of the above behavior can be explained by a drive-reduction model.

14. Suppose you are asked by a psychologist to look at some pictures and write a story about each one. Chances are that the test you are taking is the:
    a. Rorschach Inkblot Test
    b. Thematic Apperception Test (TAT)
    c. Minnesota Multiphasic Personality Inventory (MMPI)
    d. Schachter Scale of Motivational Responses

15. The average person goes through about how many sleep cycles in a typical night's sleep?
    a. one
    b. five
    c. eight
    d. hundreds

16. Which of the following is *not* a technique or tool used to help a meditator center his or her attention?
    a. mantra
    b. zazen
    c. mandala
    d. bodily sensations

17. According to the text, the most widely used mind-altering drug in the United States is:
    a. cocaine
    b. marijuana
    c. Thorazine (chlorpromazine)
    d. alcohol

18. According to the text, what is the relationship between taking drugs and creativity?
    a. Drugs usually produce creativity.
    b. Drugs almost never produce creativity.
    c. Drugs can lay the groundwork for creativity.
    d. Drugs are a deterrent to creativity.

19. Generalizing from an experiment described in the text, if you hypnotized a person and suggested to him that he was blind in his left eye, you would expect him to:
    a. be truly blind in that eye
    b. be able to see with that eye only when his right eye was closed
    c. be able to see with that eye but deny the sight
    d. admit to being able to see if confronted with evidence that the eye was working

20. Pamela goes to her doctor complaining of headaches. Her doctor attaches electrodes to her head and instructs her to do anything she wants that will produce a green light on the far wall. Her doctor is using:
    a. hypnotism
    b. Zen
    c. biofeedback
    d. transcendental meditation

21. Every time you get drunk, you remember past sexual conquests that you do not remember when you are sober. This is an example of:
    a. transfer of memory
    b. consolidation of memory
    c. state-dependent memory
    d. proactive interference

22. According to the discussion of Freud's theory in the text, the id, ego, and superego are:
    a. physical divisions in the brain
    b. different ways of processing information
    c. various biochemical processes in the brain
    d. strong motivation forces

23. Horney's major objection to Freud's theory was Freud's:
    a. notion of unconscious desires
    b. emphasis on the ego
    c. bias about female inferiority
    d. emphasis on childhood sexuality

24. According to Skinner the causes of behavior are:
    a. drives
    b. outside the organism
    c. basic anxieties
    d. unconscious conflicts

25. Social learning theorists believe that reinforcement is very important in:
    a. learning a behavior
    b. maintaining a behavior
    c. both a and b
    d. none of the above

26. James believes that the major motivation in a person's life is to strive for perfection. In this respect, his views are most like those of:
    a. Sigmund Freud
    b. Alfred Adler
    c. Carl Jung
    d. Karen Horney

27. Suzanne has recently acquired a taste for spicy foods. According to Allport, this preference would best be considered a:
    a. secondary trait
    b. cardinal trait
    c. central trait
    d. source trait

28. Joe's wife always treats him with respect and is warm, accepting, and sympathetic. She encourages Joe to speak his mind on whatever is troubling him. According to Rogers, she is offering Joe:
    a. unconditional positive regard
    b. conditional positive regard
    c. self-actualization
    d. phenomenological worth

29. Bob is outgoing, sociable, excitement seeking, and loves a good time. He also has a good job and a stable family life. According to Eysenck, he would be especially high on which of the following dimensions?
    a. neuroticism
    b. introversion
    c. psychoticism
    d. extroversion

30. According to the text, which of the following is the best predictor of success in college?
    a. high-school grades
    b. SAT scores
    c. a combination of a and b
    d. student self-reports of motivation

31. According to the text, what is the relationship between intelligence and creativity?
    a. They are very strongly correlated.
    b. They are unrelated.
    c. Intelligence is necessary but not sufficient for creativity.
    d. Creativity is necessary but not sufficient for intelligence.

32. The federal law PL 94–142 that deals with rights of retarded and disabled children specifies that:
    a. children cannot be assigned to special-education classes solely on the basis of an IQ score
    b. colleges cannot discriminate in student selections on the basis of IQ scores
    c. intelligence tests can no longer be used in placing children in special-education classes
    d. different intelligence tests must be used with retarded or disabled children

33. Suppose you want to know whether a test you have developed to place students in an advanced math class is consistently measuring the same characteristic. You would want to assess your test's:
    a. norms
    b. validity
    c. standardization
    d. reliability

34. Janet is ten years old and her IQ is 120. According to Binet's original IQ formula, what is Janet's mental age?
    a. six
    b. eight
    c. ten
    d. twelve

35. You are walking outside with your friend when he says, "What does that cloud look like to you?" You know that this situation is very much like which of the following tests?
    a. MMPI (Minnesota Multiphasic Personality Inventory)
    b. TAT (Thematic Apperception Test)
    c. Rorschach Inkblot Test
    d. a free-association test

36. The theory of mental illness proposing that abnormal behavior has an organic cause that produces a specific set of symptoms is the:
    a. psychoanalytic perspective
    b. learning theory perspective
    c. medical model
    d. humanistic-existential perspective

37. The therapy most likely to consider the patient's entire network of relationships is the:
    a. family, or systems, therapy
    b. learning therapy
    c. medical model therapy
    d. psychoanalytic therapy

38. A senseless but recurring irrational thought that a patient tries to suppress is a(n):
    a. phobia
    b. compulsion
    c. obsession
    d. panic attack

39. Disordered thought, delusions, hallucinations, nonsensical speech, and inappropriate expressions of emotions are symptoms associated with:
    a. schizophrenia
    b. paranoia
    c. affective disorders
    d. anxiety disorders

40. Jennifer is treated by a therapist who believes that her abnormal behavior consists of a series of symptoms caused by an underlying physical problem. This therapist probably subscribes to which tradition?
    a. humanistic-existential perspective
    b. family, or systems, perspective
    c. medical model
    d. sociocultural perspective

41. Matt's therapist believes that her job is to help Matt recognize his potential for positive growth. This therapist probably subscribes to the:
    a. psychoanalytic approach
    b. humanistic-existential approach
    c. sociocultural approach
    d. learning theory approach

42. Mark believes that his wife's depression exists because she gets reinforcement and pleasure from being depressed. His theoretical position is similar to the:
    a. psychoanalytic perspective
    b. learning theory perspective
    c. biological perspective
    d. family, or systems, approach

43. Freud's followers who later broke away (such as Jung, Adler, Horney, Sullivan, Fromm, and Erikson) placed much more emphasis than Freud on the concept of the:
    a. unconscious
    b. superego
    c. ego
    d. id

44. Family, or systems, therapy would be especially useful in treating which kind of problems?
    a. those arising from a generation gap
    b. those based on fear of objects
    c. those based on fear of people
    d. those involving generalized anxiety

45. According to the Temple study, which of the following forms of therapy is generally the most effective?
    a. behavioral therapy
    b. psychoanalytic therapy
    c. group therapy
    d. participant modeling

46. The Supreme Court has ruled that mental patients have certain rights that cannot be violated. Which of the following is *not* one of their guaranteed rights?
    a. the right to adequate meals
    b. the right to be outdoors regularly
    c. the right to have visitors
    d. the right to refuse treatment

47. Julie notices that on her therapist's wall, there is a diploma from a medical college which grants her therapist an M.D. degree. She concludes her therapist must be:
    a. a clinical psychologist
    b. a psychiatrist
    c. a psychoanalyst
    d. none of the above

48. Mack is afraid of snakes. His therapist leads him through a series of gradual steps in which he approaches snakes more and more closely. This technique is called:
    a. participant modeling
    b. covert sensitization
    c. aversive conditioning
    d. symbolic modeling

49. Genie is having trouble sleeping at night and feels anxious most of the time. If a drug is prescribed for her condition, it will probably be:
    a. an antianxiety drug
    b. an antipsychotic drug
    c. an antidepressant
    d. a major tranquilizer

50. According to the "computer dance" study described in the text, which of the following variables predicted how much each person liked his or her date?
    a. intelligence
    b. physical attractiveness
    c. personality
    d. all of the above

51. According to the text, the most important factor in friendship formation is:
    a. similarity of attitudes
    b. similarity of attractiveness
    c. similarity of values
    d. close physical proximity

52. Prejudice against a group of people generally results in all of the following *except:*
    a. increased self-esteem for group members
    b. low incomes
    c. high mortality rates
    d. poor nutrition

53. Martha decides to determine John's attitude about television viewing by recording how many hours of TV he watches per week. What component of attitudes is she measuring?
    a. affective
    b. behavioral
    c. cognitive
    d. message

54. As you are about to mark your ballot in an election, someone tells you that you *must* vote for candidate A. According to the principle of psychological reactance you probably:
    a. vote for candidate A
    b. vote for candidate B
    c. vote for your original choice
    d. do not vote at all

55. If Schachter's theory of love is correct, you would be most likely to fall in love with someone:
    a. with whom you had just been stuck in an elevator in a burning building
    b. who had been your pen-pal when you were children
    c. your parents chose for you to marry
    d. you find overwhelmingly physically attractive

56. Which of the following increased the conformity revealed in Asch's line-judging experiment?
    a. unanimity of the other group members
    b. previous coaching of the subject
    c. six of the confederates
    d. the amount of frustration the subject felt

57. For a social psychologist, which of the following is *not* a necessary condition in defining a group?
    a. regular interactions among the members
    b. orientation toward a specific goal
    c. a feeling of group identity and solidarity
    d. lack of disagreement among group members

58. Berkowitz argues that frustration and aggression are connected by a third factor. It is:
    a. altruism
    b. hostility
    c. withdrawal
    d. anger

59. Your performance on an assembly line is described as under the control of social facilitation. This means that you will work harder when:
    a. you are rewarded for hard work
    b. you are punished for insufficient effort
    c. you are alone
    d. other people are working with you

60. Which of the following theorists or groups of theorists would argue most strongly to remove violence from television programming?
    a. Konrad Lorenz (ethologists)
    b. Sigmund Freud
    c. frustration–aggression theorists
    d. social learning theorists

COMPREHENSIVE FINAL I
Chapters 1–18

1. According to research cited in the text, normally affectionate female monkeys can be made to throw their babies violently against the wall of their cage by:
   a. stimulating a region of their brain with a mild electric current
   b. giving them drugs
   c. using conditioning to change their behavior
   d. depriving them of social contact with other monkeys

2. Sir Francis Galton emphasized the importance of heredity in his intensive study of:
   a. eye color
   b. genius
   c. learning
   d. development

3. The *methods* of study used in psychology are most closely related to those used in:
   a. sociology
   b. religion
   c. physics
   d. philosophy

4. Research conducted by watching the behavior of older people as they go about their normal routine is called:
   a. naturalistic observation
   b. participant observation
   c. survey
   d. case study

5. Suppose you are tossing a fair coin and it comes up heads, heads, heads, heads, and heads on the first five tosses. The probability of its coming up heads again on the sixth toss is:
   a. one in two
   b. one in six
   c. one in thirty-two
   d. one in a hundred

6. Given the following set of scores—3, 4, 4, 4, 5, 7, 7, 8, 9—4 is the:
   a. mean
   b. median
   c. mode
   d. range

7. When the interior of a neuron is positive and the exterior negative, it produces a state known as:
   a. polarization
   b. resting potential
   c. action potential
   d. none of the above

8. The study of people or animals who have suffered brain damage is called:
   a. lesioning
   b. clinical observation

    c. electrical stimulation

    d. evoked potential

9. A tumor growing in John's brain has stopped his growth at a height of only four feet, nine inches. This tumor is probably located near his:

    a. thyroid

    b. limbic system

    c. pituitary gland

    d. reticular formation

10. Blaine is suffering from a head injury that is causing him a great deal of difficulty in regulating his breathing and blood flow. Also, his face is contorting, and he is salivating heavily and making chewing movements. You conclude the accident caused injury to his:

    a. amygdala

    b. cerebellum

    c. medulla

    d. hypothalamus

11. Which of the following is a function of the quality of a stimulus?

    a. pitch

    b. loudness

    c. brightness

    d. saltiness

12. The actual organ of transduction in the ear is the:

    a. Organ of Corti

    b. cochlea

    c. hair cells

    d. basilar membrane

13. Which of the following is technically *not* a transducer?

    a. Meissner's corpuscles

    b. taste buds

    c. nasal passage

    d. rods and cones

14. As a psychologist, Edward Thorndike had the most in common with:

    a. Ivan Pavlov

    b. Edward Tolman

    c. John B. Watson

    d. B. F. Skinner

15. New operant behavior is usually best established by using which of the following reinforcement schedules?

    a. fixed interval

    b. various interval

    c. continuous

    d. variable ratio

16. Marty is terrified of spiders. He goes to a therapist who teaches him relaxation techniques and gradually introduces mildly arousing "spider" situations. Marty's therapist is using the technique of:

    a. classical conditioning

    b. operant conditioning

    c. behavior modification

    d. systematic desensitization

17. One way to interfere with information held in short-term memory is to:

    a. engage in elaborative rehearsal

    b. engage in maintenance rehearsal

    c. count backwards from one hundred by threes

    d. none of the above

18. Which of the following supports a depth of processing view?
    a. anterograde amnesia
    b. serial position curve
    c. the greater effectiveness of semantic rehearsal as opposed to visual or auditory rehearsal
    d. all of the above

19. Which of the following groups of letters most likely exceeds the limits of short-term memory?
    a. I-O-U
    b. P-B-G-Q-X-R
    c. Q-X-L-T-M-A-R-C-F-P
    d. D-O-G-C-A-T-C-O-W-H-O-R-S-E

20. Marlene is raped as a child but has no memory of this traumatic event. The theory that best accounts for this memory loss is:
    a. motivated forgetting
    b. interference
    c. consolidation
    d. decay

21. According to the text, the building blocks of thought are:
    a. heuristics
    b. insights
    c. algorithms
    d. concepts

22. The first step in solving a problem is:
    a. interpreting the problem
    b. deciding when a satisfactory answer has been found
    c. searching for solutions
    d. establishing a mental set

23. Suppose you are receiving some help in making a difficult decision. Your consultant first has you specify all possible outcomes and, second, asks you to evaluate how desirable each outcome would be. This second step is called establishing:
    a. probability
    b. a rationalization
    c. utility
    d. a means–end analysis

24. According to an experiment reported in the text, if you tied a string from a baby's arm to a mobile hanging above her crib, what outcome could you expect?
    a. She would cry and be frightened.
    b. She would go to sleep.
    c. She would exhibit pleasure when she learned she could control the mobile.
    d. She would not learn the relationship between her movement and that of the mobile.

25. Generally, studies of attachment deprivation have not been conducted with humans because:
    a. humans are extremely resistant to attachment deprivation
    b. humans do not form strong attachments
    c. such research is unethical
    d. the consequences of such research on humans are not particularly interesting

26. John refuses to jaywalk because he is afraid he will get stopped by a policeman and ticketed. According to Kohlberg's theory of moral development, John is functioning at which of the following levels?
    a. conventional
    b. agreed
    c. preconventional
    d. authority

27. According to the text, probably the major distinction between the human and chimpanzee brains as they are adapted for language learning is that the human brain is:
    a. larger

b. heavier
c. lateralized
d. more convoluted

28. The linguistic relativity hypothesis holds that:
    a. language determines thought
    b. thought determines language
    c. intelligence determines thought
    d. culture determines language

29. You analyze *anticommunism* into *anti* plus *commun* plus *ism*. You are analyzing this word according to its:
    a. syntax
    b. grammar
    c. morphology
    d. phonology

30. Jack believes that if a child has not learned to talk by age six, the child will never acquire normal language. Jack's notion is that of a(n):
    a. aphasia
    b. imprinting
    c. syntactic approach
    d. critical period

31. When various emotions are activated, there appear to be physiological differences in which of the following processes?
    a. digestion
    b. breathing
    c. blood pressure
    d. all of the above

32. Which of the following is *not* a criticism of Schachter and Singer's research?
    a. Epinephrine does not produce arousal.
    b. They may have failed to use the double-blind technique.
    c. Subjects may have responded according to demand characteristics.
    d. Subjects may have assumed their arousal resulted from the injection.

33. Suppose you are coping with a crisis but are not following the stages thought by health care professionals to be beneficial. According to the text, you are likely to be labeled:
    a. normal
    b. retarded
    c. deviant
    d. needing help

34. A lesion in which part of the brain will suppress (stop) eating behavior?
    a. ventromedial hypothalamus
    b. reticular formation
    c. lateral hypothalamus
    d. all of the above

35. The concept of optimal level of arousal is based on the finding that all of the following parts of the brain are stimulated in arousal *except* the:
    a. hypothalamus
    b. thalamus
    c. cerebral cortex
    d. reticular formation

36. Jean has just become sexually active, and she finds that her first partner is unable to have a second erection and orgasm for quite some time after his first. She accurately concludes her partner is:
    a. suffering from premature ejaculation
    b. suffering from nonemissive erection

    c. suffering from impotence
    d. normal

37. The "position effect" in consumer behavior refers to the finding that:
    a. people will buy more when their financial position is strong
    b. people will buy more when their financial position is weak
    c. people buy most items from an intermediate price range, neither cheap nor expensive
    d. people are influenced in buying by the placement of the product

38. Biofeedback has been found to be effective in controlling all of the following *except:*
    a. tension headaches
    b. alpha wave output
    c. heart arrhythmias
    d. constriction of blood vessels in the hands and feet

39. You are working in a lab, and you analyze a blood sample that contains .6 percent alcohol. You conclude that the person it was drawn from probably:
    a. had a drink before a routine physical
    b. got picked up for drunk driving
    c. passed out from drinking too much
    d. died from drinking too much alcohol

40. Sublimation is a special kind of:
    a. repression
    b. regression
    c. displacement
    d. projection

41. According to the text, a major problem with Freudian theory is that it cannot:
    a. describe behavior
    b. predict behavior
    c. explain behavior
    d. all of the above

42. Which of the following problems is sometimes erroneously diagnosed as mental illness?
    a. coming from a non-English-speaking home
    b. emotional disturbance
    c. physical or perceptual difficulties
    d. all of the above

43. According to the text, the reaction range for intelligence as measured by an intelligence test is about:
    a. three to five points
    b. ten to fifteen points
    c. twenty to twenty-five points
    d. forty to fifty points

44. You are taking a personality test and are asked to respond to the words the tester says by saying the first word that comes into your mind. You are probably taking:
    a. the MMPI
    b. an intelligence test
    c. a projective test
    d. an interest test

45. According to learning theorists, which factors most directly account for abnormal behaviors?
    a. modeling and conditioning
    b. id, ego, and superego
    c. poor family structure
    d. a stressful society

46. The dissociation of a healthy personality into two or more complete and distinct behavior organizations is called:
    a. multiple personality

    b. depression

    c. schizophrenia

    d. an affective disorder

47. A person who is seven feet, eight inches tall would be considered abnormal according to which of the following criteria?

    a. statistical criterion

    b. absolute criterion

    c. neurotic criterion

    d. deviation from social norms criterion

48. Little Janie's mother sometimes treats her lovingly and sometimes treats her hatefully. Janie develops the symptoms of schizophrenia. This condition is an example of:

    a. learned helplessness

    b. a fugue state

    c. a double-bind situation

    d. a manic-depressive environment

49. In psychoanalysis, transference refers to:

    a. repression

    b. projection of feelings about others onto the therapist

    c. psychoanalysis

    d. free association

50. Group therapies are almost exclusively based on the principles of:

    a. behaviorism

    b. psychoanalysis

    c. family, or systems, analysis

    d. none of the above

51. John has been diagnosed as suffering from manic-depressive psychosis. The drug most likely to be prescribed for him would be:

    a. Thorazine

    b. an antidepressant

    c. lithium

    d. Valium

52. Bem, in his self-perception theory, believes we arrive at our attitudes by:

    a. a dissonance reduction

    b. trying to explain our behavior

    c. being reinforced for them

    d. learning them from our parents

53. Jones and Nisbett argue that we tend to attribute our own behavior to environmental causes, whereas we attribute others' behavior to some enduring personality trait. This is called:

    a. the actor–observer bias

    b. the fundamental attribution error

    c. causation-correlation confounding

    d. the salience effect

54. Suppose you are in charge of a sixth-grade class that is prejudiced against two Vietnamese children in the class. According to the text, the best way to reduce the prejudice is to:

    a. move the two Vietnamese students out of the classroom

    b. lecture the class about the evils of prejudice, especially racism

    c. create a positive situation in which all students are forced to cooperate

    d. ask the students individually to be nice to the Vietnamese students

55. In his prison study, Zimbardo demonstrated the importance of _____ on conformity.

    a. groups

    b. brainwashing

    c. obedience

    d. roles

56. Which of the following is *not* characteristic of the field called environmental psychology?
    a. It studies relationships between people and their surroundings.
    b. It is becoming increasingly popular and important.
    c. It focuses on basic rather than applied research questions.
    d. It is an interdisciplinary field.

57. Suppose you are discussing your choice of candidates in an upcoming political election. All of the others in your group strongly endorse candidate A. You wish to vote for candidate B. Generalizing from Asch's experiment studying line judging, if your friends ask you whom you're going to vote for, you would say:
    a. candidate A
    b. candidate B
    c. "I have not decided."
    d. "It is none of your business."

58. Rudy has undergone a training program in which he was socially isolated, his values were attacked, and he was forced to participate in the training group's activities. You suspect this situation is similar to:
    a. the Asch experiment
    b. the Zimbardo prison study
    c. brainwashing
    d. being exposed to a positive reference group

59. Matt believes that jogging every night after work helps him reduce his aggressive tendencies. According to the text, such a theory would suggest that aggression stems from:
    a. biological influences
    b. psychological influences
    c. social learning influences
    d. frustration

60. In choosing between moving into a dorm with long hallways and one with short hallways, you consider research that suggests that students in dorms with long hallways:
    a. have more friends
    b. are better decision makers
    c. were less motivated
    d. all of the above

COMPREHENSIVE FINAL II
Chapters 1–18

1. Approximately how many professional psychologists are there in the United States?
   a. 10,000
   b. 50,000
   c. 80,000
   d. 125,000

2. Psychologists involved in the field of health and health care are probably particularly interested in:
   a. what causes accidents
   b. the effect of stress on disease
   c. adjustment to a terminal illness
   d. all of the above

3. The major difference between a Ph.D. in psychology and a Psy.D. is:
   a. a Ph.D. requires more education
   b. a Ph.D. emphasizes basic research; a Psy.D. emphasizes applied skills
   c. a Ph.D. prepares you for academic work; a Psy.D. prepares you for a job as a psychiatrist
   d. nonexistent; they are two degrees awarded for the same training

4. Behaviorists view learning as the development of:
   a. memory traces in the brain
   b. consciousness
   c. an association between events
   d. reflexes

5. A Ph.D. who works with fairly common social problems such as drug addiction, marriage and divorce therapy, and family life therapy would typically be trained as a:
   a. psychoanalyst
   b. counseling psychologist
   c. psychiatrist
   d. clinical psychologist

6. The study in which a group is divided into subgroups according to certain criteria and then the subgroups are compared is a(n):
   a. experiment
   b. random sample
   c. longitudinal study
   d. cross-sectional study

7. The variable that the experimenter intentionally manipulates in an experiment is called the:
   a. placebo
   b. dependent variable
   c. experimental condition
   d. independent variable

8. Most experimental subjects try to help the researcher by doing very well at the experimental task, probably behaving differently than they normally would. This problem is called:
   a. the self-fulfilling prophecy
   b. demand characteristics

c. the placebo effect
d. measurement bias

9. A group of four-year-olds are given an IQ test, then are retested at ages eight, twelve, sixteen, twenty, thirty, and fifty. This is an example of:
   a. an experiment
   b. a longitudinal study
   c. a cross-sectional study
   d. a replication

10. Jack's parents have always expected him to be a lawyer and now that he is twenty-one, he is applying to law school. This may be an example of:
    a. demand characteristics
    b. the self-fulfilling prophecy
    c. experimenter bias
    d. a double-bind situation

11. Cells specialized for receiving various types of stimulation are:
    a. neurons
    b. receptors
    c. effectors
    d. afferent neurons

12. In which of the following situations will your pupils dilate?
    a. you see something you want to buy
    b. you are looking at a pleasantly erotic picture
    c. you are in dim light
    d. all of the above

13. The major function of the hypothalamus is to:
    a. control attention
    b. coordinate body movements
    c. maintain a steady internal environment for the body
    d. transfer information from one part of the brain to another

14. You are walking home at night from the library and a person jumps out of the bush in front of you and acts as if he is going to hurt you. Your body mobilizes for action and, in so doing, calls into play the:
    a. sympathetic division
    b. parasympathetic division
    c. hypothalamus
    d. somatic system

15. You are a subject in an experiment in which electrodes are attached to your scalp and you are asked to think about certain memories. This researcher is probably using the technique of:
    a. evoked potential
    b. lesioning
    c. brain stimulation
    d. clinical observation

16. After passing through the optic chiasma, which fibers go to the right hemisphere of the brain?
    a. left half of the right eye and right half of the left eye
    b. right half of the right eye and left half of the left eye
    c. left half of both eyes
    d. right half of both eyes

17. Which of the following is *not* one of the basic categories of taste?
    a. sour
    b. salty
    c. bland
    d. bitter

18. The finding that identical twins tend to see illusions the same way more frequently than best friends indicates the importance of _____ on perception.
    a. heredity
    b. experience
    c. motivation
    d. age of the subject

19. You suspect that you have a hearing loss and go to a specialist, who fits you with earphones and tells you to raise your right hand whenever you hear a tone. She is testing your:
    a. just noticeable difference
    b. absolute threshold
    c. Weber's ratio
    d. adaptation

20. Suppose I believe that vision is best described by a series of on-off switches and that the pattern of ons and offs determines the colors I see. I would subscribe to:
    a. place theory
    b. trichromatic theory
    c. volley theory
    d. opponent-process theory

21. In most cases of classical conditioning, the:
    a. CS occurs just before the UCS
    b. CS occurs just after the UCS
    c. CR occurs before the CS
    d. CS and UCS occur randomly

22. A light flashes, a bell sounds, then a dog is given food. If the dog begins salivating as soon as the light flashes, this is called:
    a. primary reinforcement
    b. secondary reinforcement
    c. first-order conditioning
    d. second-order conditioning

23. Modeling refers to a process of learning through:
    a. reinforcement
    b. observation
    c. operant conditioning
    d. classical conditioning

24. Teaching a tiger to jump through a flaming hoop (something it would never do on its own) almost certainly involves the process of:
    a. shaping
    b. systematic desensitization
    c. discrimination training
    d. classical conditioning

25. You have conditioned your dog to bark every time you say the word *Friday*. You then stop reinforcing the dog for barking. This second circumstance should produce:
    a. spontaneous recovery
    b. extinction
    c. the Garcia effect
    d. a phobia

26. In his research on sensory memory, Sperling flashed a twelve-item pattern on a screen. He found that subjects could report:
    a. only the top row of four items
    b. only the bottom row of four items
    c. any one of the rows
    d. all three rows

27. Techniques we can use to improve our memories are called:
    a. eidetic techniques

    b. confabulation techniques

    c. consolidation techniques

    d. mnemonic devices

28. Which of the following pieces of experimental evidence indicates that memories are *not* permanent and unchangeable?

    a. Penfield's brain stimulation studies

    b. improved recall under hypnosis

    c. improved recall in psychoanalysis

    d. Loftus's studies of eyewitness testimony

29. You are in an experiment in which each eye sees a different slide projected for a fraction of a second. This experiment is similar to experiments in:

    a. dichotic listening

    b. selective attention

    c. sensory gating

    d. retroactive interference

30. Retrograde amnesia is supportive of the existence of:

    a. confabulation

    b. consolidation

    c. elaborative rehearsal

    d. genetic influences in human memory

31. The person most likely to use a scanning strategy for problem solving is:

    a. an adult male

    b. an adult female

    c. a child

    d. a psychologist

32. Another name for a rule-of-thumb problem-solving strategy is:

    a. algorithm

    b. heuristic

    c. mental set

    d. subgoal analysis

33. Frequent events are generally better recalled than infrequent events. This is the assumption underlying:

    a. means–end analysis

    b. subgoal analysis

    c. the availability heuristic

    d. the representativeness heuristic

34. Seeing a birch tree, you declare that the defining characteristics of all trees are: white bark; drops leaves in fall; seeds are catkins. The concept formation strategy you are using is:

    a. global hypothesis

    b. scanning strategy

    c. focusing strategy

    d. win-stay, lose-shift

35. You have been working hard at solving a problem with no success. Your professor tells you to go for a walk and relax. She is prescribing:

    a. an algorithm

    b. a period of incubation

    c. a period of insight

    d. a mental set

36. Developmental psychologists believe that human development progresses:

    a. sequentially

    b. unpredictably

    c. with little individual variation

    d. all of the above

37. At least some decline in old age is typically associated with which of the following memory systems?
    a. short-term memory
    b. long-term memory
    c. both a and b
    d. none of the above

38. Research has shown that there appear to be differences between the sexes in their:
    a. aggressiveness
    b. intelligence
    c. creativity
    d. dominance

39. Suppose you believe that human development is sequential, with each new aspect of development stemming directly from past abilities. Your theory would qualify as:
    a. quantitative
    b. qualitative
    c. both a and b
    d. none of the above

40. Jack approaches an experiment he is conducting by first specifying all possible solutions and then systematically testing each until he arrives at the correct answer. He is probably in which of Piaget's stages?
    a. preoperational
    b. concrete operations
    c. hypothetical
    d. formal operations

41. Why was the chimpanzee Vicki unable to learn more than four words?
    a. She was retarded.
    b. She did not have the necessary vocal apparatus.
    c. She was culturally deprived.
    d. English is too difficult for a chimpanzee.

42. Which of the following pieces of evidence does *not* support the notion of a critical period in language learning?
    a. Deaf people have greater difficulty learning language after puberty.
    b. Once you have learned two languages, others are much easier to learn.
    c. A second language is more easily learned before puberty.
    d. Children are more likely to recover speech lost due to brain injury than are adults.

43. If you want to measure how sensitive a group of subjects is to nonverbal cues, you could administer the:
    a. PONS
    b. ITBS
    c. IQ test
    d. Rorschach Inkblot Test

44. Which of the following sentences has surface structure but no underlying representation?
    a. I must go.
    b. Ran stop go.
    c. Monkeys borrow justice.
    d. I can't go.

45. Which of the following people would typically be the most receptive to nonverbal cues?
    a. a girl, age four
    b. a boy, age four
    c. a male truckdriver
    d. a female housewife

46. In an emergency, which of the following would *not* typically occur?
    a. Blood moves from the stomach to the skeletal muscles.

b. Sugar is released into the bloodstream.

c. Pupils of the eyes dilate.

d. Breathing becomes shallower and slower as attention is concentrated on the emergency.

47. Research has demonstrated that type A persons are more likely to:

a. have heart disease

b. be intelligent

c. score higher on the SRRS

d. have large families

48. Which of the following traits is most typically associated with happiness?

a. youth

b. high quality sex

c. money

d. being single

49. Extrapolating from evidence presented in the text, if your best friend suddenly developed violent outbursts of temper, you might suspect the presence of a tumor in his:

a. sympathetic nervous system

b. parasympathetic nervous system

c. amygdala

d. thalamus

50. Mathilde has just been raped. Her recovery will probably be most enhanced if:

a. she does not report the rape

b. she lies about the rape

c. she has a supportive group of friends to talk to about the rape

d. she never gets married

51. According to the text, the most effective long-term weight loss technique is:

a. psychotherapy

b. behavior modification

c. hypnotism

d. fad diets, especially Stillman's diet

52. As compared to animals, the human sexual response is more controlled by:

a. hormones

b. the preoptic region of the hypothalamus

c. the reticular formation

d. the cerebral cortex

53. According to Solomon and Corbin's opponent-process model, the activation of a strong emotion is accomplished by:

a. fear

b. desire to reduce the emotion to a normal level

c. the opposite response

d. increased levels of arousal

54. Bob always seems to be on a diet, and he constantly feels hungry when he diets. He fits the pattern of:

a. an unrestrained eater

b. a restrained eater

c. a grossly obese person

d. a person with a tumor in the ventromedial hypothalamus

55. A fire begins in your classroom, and everyone stands paralyzed, looking at it grow. This situation is _____ optimal level theory.

a. supportive of

b. contradictory to

c. unrelated to

d. both supportive of and contradictory to

56. According to Hilgard's neodissociation view, hypnosis is:
    a. an illusion
    b. an altered state of consciousness
    c. a hoax
    d. an extreme form of persuasion

57. Formication is a hallucination that would cause a person to say:
    a. "I am dead."
    b. "There are bugs crawling under my skin."
    c. "I see wonderful shapes and colors."
    d. "I can't control myself."

58. In its effect on memory loss, marijuana in low doses acts much like:
    a. alcohol
    b. cocaine
    c. LSD
    d. amphetamines

59. A person whose EEG shows a very high level of alpha waves would be:
    a. relaxed but not asleep
    b. in stage 2 sleep
    c. in stage 4 sleep
    d. dreaming

60. Bob recalls that the last person named Tommie he met was a girl, but he cannot recall how he knows that. This is an example of:
    a. neodissociation
    b. role enactment
    c. free association
    d. source amnesia

61. Which of the following is present at birth?
    a. superego
    b. id
    c. ego
    d. all of the above

62. The intense desire to take the place of the same-sex parent in the affections of the parent of the opposite sex is called:
    a. the oedipal conflict
    b. reaction formation
    c. sublimation
    d. the pleasure principle

63. Which of the following theorists has worked primarily with normally functioning adult humans?
    a. Rogers
    b. Skinner
    c. Freud
    d. Maslow

64. Maria is continually worrying about whether her actions are going to be socially acceptable. You might say her personality was being controlled by her:
    a. ego
    b. id
    c. superego
    d. defense mechanisms

65. Marty believes that humans have an inborn potential for growth, creativity, and spontaneity. He would best be classified as advocating which of the following approaches?
    a. psychoanalytic
    b. trait
    c. social learning
    d. phenomenological

66. About 95 percent of the American population scores between _____ and _____ on a standardized intelligence test.
    a. 85 and 115
    b. 70 and 130
    c. 55 and 145
    d. 30 and 170

67. According to the text, one problem gifted children face is:
    a. being bored in school
    b. being unpopular
    c. being physically unhealthy
    d. all of the above

68. The authors of the text believe that the use of tests:
    a. is generally good
    b. is generally bad
    c. can be either good or bad
    d. is neither good nor bad

69. You are taking a test in which you arrange the following letters into as many words as possible: A G B D F C E G D F. You conclude that this test is probably measuring:
    a. creativity
    b. intelligence
    c. personality
    d. interest

70. You are taking a test that asks you whether you like, dislike, or are indifferent to activities such as playing with children or working with your hands. You conclude you are taking the:
    a. Strong-Campbell Interest Inventory
    b. Wechsler Adult Intelligence Scale
    c. Thematic Apperception Test
    d. System of Multicultural Pluralistic Assessment

71. According to the psychoanalytic perspective, neurosis and psychosis are produced by:
    a. brain injury
    b. biochemical imbalances in the brain
    c. the isolation produced by modern society
    d. fixations in childhood

72. The standard guide for diagnosing mental illness is:
    a. *The Mental Measurements Yearbook*
    b. *The Diagnostic and Statistical Manual of Mental Disorders*
    c. *The Guide to Psychiatric Illness*
    d. *The Etiology, Diagnosis and Prognosis of Mental Disease*

73. Sociological theorists have found that schizophrenia is most common among which socioeconomic class?
    a. upper class
    b. lower class
    c. middle class
    d. none of the above; it is equally represented in all three classes

74. Jack believes that the causes of most mental illness are poverty, poor nutrition and education, and overcrowding. He would probably prefer the:
    a. learning theory perspective
    b. humanistic-existential perspective
    c. family, or systems, approach
    d. sociocultural perspective

75. Judy sees her mother raped and killed by a violent man. She then develops a psychically induced blindness. This disorder is called:
    a. a conversion disorder
    b. depression

c. obsession

d. glove anesthesia

76. In a token economy system, behavior is maintained by giving the patient:
    a. electric shocks
    b. praise
    c. drugs
    d. conditioned reinforcers

77. The major side effect of electroconvulsive therapy is:
    a. speech problems
    b. respiratory difficulty
    c. uncontrollable facial movements
    d. memory loss

78. Community mental health centers have arisen mainly to:
    a. provide better facilities for electroconvulsive therapy
    b. provide a place to train young psychiatrists
    c. provide an alternative to sending people away to large institutions
    d. make it easier for relatives to visit inpatients

79. Jack dreams that he is eaten by a snake. He insists that this dream signifies his homosexual preferences. The latent content of this dream involves:
    a. the snake
    b. being eaten
    c. the homosexual interpretation
    d. finding out what he ate before he went to sleep

80. John attends a group therapy session in which the participants are encouraged to touch each other, tell others what they think of them, and be honest about themselves. This type of therapy is most similar to:
    a. Gestalt therapy
    b. self-help groups
    c. transactional analysis
    d. encounter groups

81. Zimbardo's prison study was terminated because:
    a. he ran out of funding
    b. it was considered to be unethical
    c. subjects became too involved with the roles they were playing
    d. it was obvious it wasn't going to work

82. The factor that makes Kelley's theory of attribution broader than Jones and Davis's is his inclusion of:
    a. personality variables
    b. original expectations
    c. an analysis of the situation
    d. comparisons made over a long period of time

83. According to the research presented in the text, an abundance of phenylethylamine in the brain may be associated with:
    a. frequent attitude change
    b. reduced resistance to persuasion
    c. the tendency to commit the fundamental attribution error
    d. being in love

84. According to the text, if a doctor is about to give a patient a highly frightening report about his or her health, the doctor could best reduce the patient's fear by:
    a. giving the patient directions to alleviate the feared condition
    b. presenting himself as an expert
    c. trying to be highly trustworthy
    d. giving the patient a one-sided presentation

85. You see four of Dustin Hoffman's movies. In the first he plays a kind father, in the second an outlaw, in the third a psychopathic murderer, and in the fourth a drug pusher. According to the primacy effect you probably think of him most as:
    a. a psychopath
    b. an outlaw
    c. a drug pusher
    d. none of the above

86. The predominant criticisms of Milgram's obedience experiment involve:
    a. his choice of subjects
    b. the ethical implications of the procedure
    c. the lack of an appropriate control group
    d. the possibility that his results were unreliable

87. According to Darley and Latané, one reason that bystanders may fail to help the victim in an emergency is:
    a. diffusions of responsibility
    b. they do not want to get involved
    c. the autokinetic effect
    d. emergencies are so obvious they cannot be mistaken for nonserious events

88. Calhoun's studies of crowded rats indicated that crowding caused:
    a. increased aggression
    b. inappropriate sexual behavior
    c. failure to build satisfactory nests
    d. all of the above

89. According to Zajonc, social facilitation would probably occur in which of the following situations?
    a. making a difficult shot during an important basketball game
    b. sight-reading a piece of music in a symphony audition
    c. demonstrating for the thousandth time how to operate a computer terminal
    d. all of the above

90. According to research presented in the text, if you worked in a noisy environment, the characteristic that would most substantially interfere with your performance would be if the noise were:
    a. loud
    b. so soft you can barely hear it
    c. uncontrollable
    d. frequent

Answer Key

□ **Chapter 1**

A. Matching Questions

1. d, *15* 2. a, *15* 3. b, *17–18* 4. e, *13* 5. c, *14* 6. f, *27* 7. e, *27* 8. k, *21* 9. c, *23* 10. j, *25*

B. Multiple Choice Questions

1. d, *5* 2. d, *6* 3. c, *9* 4. a, *8* 5. c, *10* 6. b, *10* 7. d, *14* 8. d, *21*
9. d, *28* 10. a, *13* 11. b, *16* 12. a, *15* 13. b, *16* 14. a, *18* 15. d, *18* 16. c, *18*
17. b, *16–17* 18. c, *26* 19. b, *27* 20. b, *29–30* 21. a, *5* 22. c, *6* 23. a, *10–11* 24. c, *20*
25. b, *13* 26. c, *14* 27. d, *14–16* 28. d, *18* 29. c, *24* 30. d, *26* 31. b, *23; 27* 32. b, *27*

□ **Chapter 2**

A. Matching Questions

1. d, *38–39* 2. e, *49* 3. b, *42* 4. h, *45* 5. c, *45–46* 6. f, *50*
7. d, *50* 8. h, *54* 9. c, *50* 10. i, *56* 11. j, *51* 12. a, *50*

B. Multiple Choice Questions

1. b, *37* 2. c, *40* 3. b, *42* 4. d, *43* 5. a, *44–45* 6. c, *45–46* 7. d, *36* 8. d, *49*
9. a, *47* 10. a, *38–39* 11. d, *40* 12. c, *55* 13. b, *51–52* 14. a, *53* 15. a, *56* 16. d, *62*
17. c, *58* 18. b, *58* 19. c, *58–60* 20. c, *64–65* 21. d, *37* 22. a, *45* 23. b, *49* 24. c, *46–47*
25. d, *39* 26. a, *40* 27. c, *50* 28. d, *50* 29. a, *54–55* 30. b, *54–55* 31. b, *57* 32. b, *61*

□ **Chapter 3**

A. Matching Questions

1. f, *81* 2. b, *82* 3. h, *84* 4. d, *85* 5. g, *85* 6. i, *85*
7. f, *88* 8. h, *88–89* 9. b, *89* 10. g, *90* 11. d, *89*

B. Multiple Choice Questions

1. b, *73* 2. d, *74* 3. b, *74* 4. c, *75–76* 5. d, *76* 6. d, *77–78* 7. c, *78* 8. a, *79*
9. a, *79* 10. c, *79–80* 11. a, *80–81* 12. b, *83–84* 13. c, *84–85* 14. c, *85–86* 15. a, *87* 16. b, *88*
17. c, *90* 18. d, *91* 19. b, *95* 20. a, *88; 96* 21. d, *71–72* 22. a, *74* 23. a, *75–76* 24. c, *81*
25. b, *82* 26. c, *84* 27. b, *85* 28. b, *86–87* 29. d, *88* 30. a, *98–99* 31. c, *100–101* 32. d, *100*

□ Chapter 4

A. Matching Questions

1. a, *105–106* 2. c, *108* 3. h, *107* 4. e, *108* 5. d, *109* 6. j, *110* 7. g, *112* 8. b, *111* 9. a, *113* 10. e, *113* 11. h, *112* 12. d, *113* 13. i, *121* 14. b, *121* 15. f, *122* 16. d, *122* 17. a, *122–123* 18. f, *124* 19. b, *124* 20. h, *125* 21. c, *125–126* 22. g, *127–128* 23. e, *134*

B. Multiple Choice Questions

1. c, *106* 2. a, *106* 3. d, *109* 4. b, *110* 5. b, *107–108* 6. c, *109* 7. a, *111–112* 8. d, *113* 9. b, *113–115* 10. a, *116* 11. d, *117–120* 12. a, *120* 13. c, *122* 14. d, *110* 15. b, *123* 16. c, *125* 17. c, *126–127* 18. d, *134–137* 19. a, *133* 20. b, *135* 21. b, *107* 22. b, *108–109* 23. c, *111* 24. a, *113* 25. d, *115–116* 26. a, *115–117* 27. c, *121* 28. d, *121–122* 29. c, *124* 30. d, *122–123* 31. b, *129* 32. a, *128*

□ Chapter 5

A. Matching Questions

1. e, *145* 2. h, *145* 3. a, *146* 4. g, *147* 5. f, *150* 6. b, *152* 7. e, *153* 8. g, *154* 9. c, *155* 10. f, *156–157* 11. g, *158* 12. c, *159* 13. b, *163* 14. h, *163–164* 15. a, *171*

B. Multiple Choice Questions

1. c, *144–145* 2. b, *146* 3. d, *147* 4. a, *150* 5. a, *150* 6. c, *151–152* 7. d, *154* 8. d, *156* 9. d, *167* 10. b, *154* 11. a, *155* 12. c, *158–159* 13. d, *165–166* 14. b, *167–169* 15. a, *164–165* 16. b, *160* 17. a, *160–161* 18. c, *161* 19. c, *169* 20. b, *171* 21. a, *145* 22. c, *143–145* 23. d, *154* 24. a, *157–158* 25. d, *158–159* 26. b, *155* 27. c, *162–163* 28. d, *153* 29. b, *163–164* 30. b, *160–161* 31. c, *169* 32. a, *170*

□ Chapter 6

A. Matching Questions

1. c, *180* 2. e, *180* 3. h, *181* 4. b, *182* 5. d, *183–184* 6. i, *184* 7. f, *186* 8. b, *188* 9. a, *195–196* 10. g, *198* 11. e, *202*

B. Multiple Choice Questions

1. a, *178* 2. d, *179* 3. c, *182* 4. b, *180* 5. c, *178–179* 6. c, *182* 7. b, *183* 8. a, *184* 9. a, *184* 10. d, *186* 11. d, *188* 12. d, *189–191* 13. b, *191–195* 14. b, *195–196* 15. c, *195* 16. c, *197* 17. d, *198* 18. a, *198* 19. b, *202* 20. d, *204–205* 21. c, *182* 22. c, *195–196* 23. d, *179–180* 24. b, *180* 25. a, *180* 26. b, *186* 27. c, *197* 28. a, *196* 29. b, *198* 30. d, *202* 31. a, *203* 32. d, *198*

□ Chapter 7

A. Matching Questions

1. e, *209–210* 2. h, *209* 3. b, *212* 4. d, *212* 5. f, *214* 6. a, *215* 7. d, *217* 8. c, *218–219* 9. e, *221* 10. b, *228* 11. j, *222*

B. Multiple Choice Questions

1. b, *209–210* 2. a, *211* 3. d, *211* 4. d, *213* 5. c, *212* 6. c, *212* 7. b, *212* 8. c, *213*
9. a, *222* 10. d, *222* 11. c, *223–224* 12. a, *215* 13. d, *215–216* 14. a, *221* 15. b, *218* 16. b, *225*
17. a, *226* 18. b, *227* 19. d, *227* 20. c, *230* 21. c, *209–210* 22. a, *212* 23. d, *212* 24. d, *213*
25. b, *214* 26. b, *215* 27. a, *218–219* 28. b, *221* 29. c, *217–218* 30. c, *225* 31. a, *227* 32. d, *228*

□ Chapter 8

A. Matching Questions

1. h, *240* 2. b, *242* 3. i, *243* 4. d, *245* 5. g, *247* 6. f, *249* 7. c, *253* 8. a, *254*
9. g, *258* 10. e, *258* 11. e, *261* 12. a, *262* 13. f, *264* 14. i, *266* 15. g, *268*

B. Multiple Choice Questions

1. a, *240* 2. d, *240–241* 3. b, *241–242* 4. c, *242* 5. a, *243* 6. d, *245* 7. c, *246* 8. a, *246–247*
9. d, *247* 10. b, *253* 11. a, *255* 12. b, *256* 13. c, *258–259* 14. c, *260* 15. d, *260* 16. a, *260*
17. a, *262* 18. b, *268* 19. a, *270* 20. c, *270* 21. c, *241–242* 22. a, *245* 23. a, *246–248* 24. b, *249–250*
25. b, *251–252* 26. d, *254–255* 27. b, *255* 28. a, *258–260* 29. d, *262–263* 30. c, *261* 31. d, *263–264*
32. c, *266*

□ Chapter 9

A. Matching Questions

1. a, *276* 2. h, *277* 3. d, *278* 4. b, *279* 5. f, *279* 6. e, *280* 7. b, *282* 8. g, *285* 9. f, *290* 10. c, *292*

B. Multiple Choice Questions

1. b, *276* 2. c, *277* 3. d, *279* 4. a, *279* 5. c, *280* 6. d, *280–281* 7. b, *283* 8. a, *283–284*
9. d, *283–285* 10. c, *285* 11. b, *286* 12. d, *286* 13. b, *287–288* 14. a, *289* 15. a, *292* 16. c, *293–294*
17. b, *295* 18. a, *295* 19. c, *296* 20. a, *299* 21. d, *277–278* 22. a, *277* 23. c, *278–279* 24. b, *278*
25. c, *279* 26. a, *282* 27. d, *287* 28. c, *290* 29. b, *292* 30. b, *295–296* 31. d, *300* 32. d, *300–301*

□ Chapter 10

A. Matching Questions

1. c, *311* 2. h, *313* 3. b, *313* 4. f, *314–315* 5. e, *318*
6. e, *324* 7. g, *326* 8. h, *327* 9. d, *327* 10. f, *333*

B. Multiple Choice Questions

1. c, *310* 2. b, *311* 3. d, *311–312* 4. d, *311* 5. b, *312* 6. b, *317* 7. c, *317* 8. a, *313*
9. a, *313* 10. d, *315–316* 11. d, *316* 12. b, *319* 13. a, *321–323* 14. c, *323* 15. a, *326* 16. d, *326*
17. a, *327* 18. c, *327* 19. c, *332* 20. b, *334* 21. a, *311–312* 22. b, *317* 23. c, *313* 24. d, *315*
25. d, *319* 26. a, *320* 27. c, *324* 28. b, *326* 29. b, *327* 30. a, *327–328* 31. c, *330* 32. d, *333–334*

☐ Chapter 11

A. Matching Questions

1. h, *339* 2. b, *340* 3. f, *340* 4. c, *341* 5. g, *342* 6. d, *345* 7. g, *352* 8. b, *353*
9. c, *355* 10. f, *359* 11. c, *356* 12. e, *361* 13. a, *362* 14. d, *365* 15. f, *367*

B. Multiple Choice Questions

1. b, *340* 2. d, *340* 3. a, *342* 4. d, *343–345* 5. c, *345* 6. c, *346* 7. c, *347* 8. b, *351*
9. b, *352* 10. d, *352–354* 11. d, *354* 12. b, *354* 13. c, *356* 14. b, *356* 15. a, *358* 16. c, *360*
17. d, *361* 18. c, *362* 19. b, *365* 20. b, *366–367* 21. a, *340* 22. c, *341* 23. b, *348* 24. d, *350*
25. c, *354* 26. b, *355* 27. d, *356* 28. a, *341* 29. c, *360* 30. d, *359–360* 31. a, *360* 32. b, *364*

☐ Chapter 12

A. Matching Questions

1. b, *373* 2. c, *377–378* 3. h, *376* 4. e, *378* 5. g, *381*
6. g, *385* 7. a, *387* 8. e, *389* 9. c, *392* 10. i, *392*

B. Multiple Choice Questions

1. a, *374* 2. d, *374* 3. c, *375* 4. a, *378* 5. b, *377* 6. d, *379* 7. c, *383* 8. b, *385*
9. a, *386* 10. b, *387* 11. d, *388* 12. c, *390* 13. b, *390* 14. d, *391* 15. d, *392* 16. b, *397*
17. c, *397–398* 18. c, *392* 19. a, *396* 20. c, *399* 21. a, *376* 22. b, *378* 23. d, *381* 24. c, *384–385*
25. d, *385* 26. b, *389* 27. c, *390* 28. a, *391* 29. d, *392* 30. a, *393* 31. b, *394* 32. c, *392*

☐ Chapter 13

A. Matching Questions

1. d, *405* 2. g, *407* 3. a, *408* 4. h, *409* 5. c, *409* 6. h, *410* 7. e, *411* 8. b, *412*
9. i, *415* 10. f, *417* 11. b, *422* 12. d, *422* 13. h, *423* 14. g, *428* 15. e, *429*

B. Multiple Choice Questions

1. b, *407* 2. a, *408* 3. c, *408* 4. d, *409* 5. b, *409* 6. d, *410* 7. c, *411* 8. a, *412*
9. d, *413–414* 10. c, *414* 11. a, *414* 12. b, *416–417* 13. a, *416* 14. c, *417* 15. d, *417* 16. b, *418*
17. b, *420* 18. a, *423* 19. c, *424* 20. d, *430* 21. c, *409* 22. a, *411* 23. c, *412* 24. b, *415*
25. b, *415* 26. b, *417* 27. d, *421* 28. a, *422* 29. d, *424* 30. c, *425* 31. d, *428* 32. a, *429*

☐ Chapter 14

A. Matching Questions

1. h, *439* 2. c, *439* 3. e, *439* 4. d, *440* 5. j, *441* 6. b, *441*
7. c, *443* 8. f, *444* 9. a, *445* 10. h, *455* 11. d, *460* 12. e, *465*

B. Multiple Choice Questions

1. a, *442* 2. b, *442* 3. c, *444* 4. c, *446* 5. b, *446* 6. c, *446* 7. d, *447* 8. c, *448*
9. a, *149* 10. c, *449* 11. c, *450* 12. c, *451* 13. d, *451* 14. d, *454* 15. a, *455* 16. a, *456*
17. b, *461* 18. d, *465* 19. d, *466* 20. c, *466* 21. d, *439* 22. c, *439* 23. b, *440* 24. a, *441*
25. d, *443* 26. a, *450* 27. b, *451* 28. c, *458* 29. c, *458* 30. b, *460–461* 31. a, *463* 32. a, *465*

☐ Chapter 15

A. Matching Questions

1. f, *476* 2. c, *476* 3. a, *477* 4. e, *478–479* 5. d, *481* 6. b, *483* 7. f, *486* 8. h, *487*
9. d, *488* 10. g, *489* 11. f, *490* 12. b, *491* 13. g, *499* 14. d, *501* 15. e, *504*

B. Multiple Choice Questions

1. b, *475* 2. d, *475* 3. c, *476* 4. b, *477* 5. d, *477* 6. a, *478* 7. c, *479* 8. a, *480*
9. d, *482* 10. b, *482–483* 11. d, *483* 12. b, *485* 13. c, *488* 14. a, *490* 15. c, *491* 16. d, *492*
17. a, *494* 18. a, *497* 19. c, *497* 20. b, *500* 21. a, *474* 22. c, *476* 23. d, *477* 24. b, *478*
25. d, *480* 26. b, *481* 27. a, *486* 28. c, *487* 29. a, *489* 30. b, *493* 31. c, *501* 32. d, *504*

☐ Chapter 16

A. Matching Questions

1. e, *510* 2. a, *510* 3. f, *511* 4. c, *511* 5. i, *515* 6. g, *516* 7. h, *518* 8. b, *519* 9. d, *520*
10. c, *522* 11. f, *523* 12. b, *531* 13. h, *532–533* 14. d, *534* 15. g, *534–535* 16. c, *537* 17. e, *537*

B. Multiple Choice Questions

1. d, *509* 2. a, *511* 3. b, *511* 4. c, *514* 5. b, *516* 6. d, *518* 7. a, *520* 8. c, *522*
9. a, *523* 10. a, *524* 11. d, *525–526* 12. c, *527* 13. d, *528* 14. a, *530* 15. b, *531* 16. c, *532*
17. d, *534* 18. c, *535* 19. b, *536* 20. d, *539* 21. b, *510* 22. c, *511* 23. d, *514–515* 24. a, *515–516*
25. a, *519* 26. b, *523–524* 27. b, *526* 28. d, *527* 29. a, *531* 30. c, *534* 31. c, *532–533* 32. a, *537*

☐ Chapter 17

A. Matching Questions

1. h, *546* 2. c, *551* 3. a, *553* 4. d, *554* 5. g, *556* 6. e, *558* 7. g, *559* 8. b, *562* 9. a, *562* 10. h, *569*

B. Multiple Choice Questions

1. c, *545* 2. d, *546* 3. c, *548* 4. c, *548* 5. a, *551* 6. b, *553* 7. a, *553* 8. d, *554*
9. b, *555* 10. b, *557* 11. a, *560* 12. d, *561* 13. c, *561* 14. a, *562* 15. d, *564* 16. b, *565*
17. d, *567* 18. c, *568* 19. b, *569* 20. a, *573* 21. b, *546* 22. a, *550* 23. a, *552* 24. c, *552*
25. b, *554* 26. d, *556* 27. d, *558* 28. c, *559–560* 29. a, *567–568* 30. d, *570* 31. a, *571* 32. c, *574–575*

☐ Chapter 18

A. Matching Questions

1. b, *580* 2. f, *582* 3. h, *584* 4. g, *589* 5. e, *589* 6. g, *593*
7. e, *594* 8. a, *600* 9. d, *599* 10. f, *602* 11. c, *605*

B. Multiple Choice Questions

1. a, *580* 2. b, *580* 3. a, *581* 4. d, *582* 5. b, *584* 6. c, *585* 7. b, *586* 8. d, *588–589*
9. b, *590* 10. d, *592* 11. a, *593–594* 12. c, *595* 13. b, *597* 14. d, *600* 15. a, *602* 16. b, *604*
17. c, *605* 18. c, *606* 19. d, *608* 20. d, *608* 21. a, *581* 22. b, *589* 23. c, *591* 24. d, *593*
25. c, *594* 26. b, *595* 27. a, *596* 28. d, *598* 29. b, *602–603* 30. a, *605* 31. c, *607* 32. c, *609*

☐ MIDTERM I, *Chapters 1–9*

1. d, *6* 2. d, *21* 3. a, *18* 4. a, *5* 5. c, *20* 6. c, *24*
7. c, *40* 8. d, *36* 9. c, *55* 10. d, *62* 11. a, *45* 12. a, *40*
13. b, *54–55* 14. b, *74* 15. a, *79* 16. d, *84–85* 17. d, *91* 18. d, *71–72*
19. b, *82* 20. d, *88* 21. d, *109* 22. b, *113–115* 23. b, *123* 24. b, *108–109*
25. a, *115–117* 26. d, *122–123* 27. c, *144–145* 28. c, *151–152* 29. a, *155* 30. a, *160–161*
31. d, *154* 32. c, *162–163* 33. c, *169* 34. d, *179* 35. b, *183* 36. d, *189–191*
37. d, *198* 38. b, *180* 39. a, *196* 40. d, *198* 41. b, *209–210* 42. b, *212*
43. d, *215–216* 44. d, *212* 45. a, *218–219* 46. d, *228* 47. b, *241–242* 48. a, *246–247*
49. c, *258–259* 50. b, *268* 51. a, *246–248* 52. b, *255* 53. d, *263–264*
54. b, *276* 55. c, *280* 56. d, *286* 57. c, *293–294* 58. a, *277* 59. a, *282* 60. b, *295–296*

☐ MIDTERM II, *Chapters 1–9*

1. d, *5* 2. b, *10* 3. b, *16* 4. b, *16–17* 5. a, *10–11* 6. d, *14–16*
7. d, *43* 8. a, *47* 9. a, *53* 10. c, *64–65* 11. c, *46–47* 12. d, *50*
13. b, *61* 14. d, *76* 15. a. *80–81* 16. a, *88; 96* 17. a, *75–76* 18. b, *91*
19. c, *100–101* 20. b, *107–108* 21. a, *116* 22. d, *110* 23. b, *135* 24. a, *113*
25. d, *121–122* 26. a, *128* 27. a, *150* 28. b, *154* 29. b, *160* 30. a, *145*
31. d, *158–159* 32. b, *163–164* 33. c, *182* 34. a, *184* 35. b, *191–195* 36. a, *198*
37. c, *195–196* 38. b, *186* 39. d, *202* 40. d, *213* 41. a, *222* 42. a, *221*
43. d, *227* 44. c, *209–210* 45. b, *214* 46. c, *217–218* 47. a, *243* 48. b, *253*
49. d, *260* 50. c, *270* 51. c, *241–242* 52. b, *251–252* 53. d, *262–263*
54. c, *277* 55. a, *283–284* 56. a, *289* 57. b, *278* 58. c, *290* 59. b, *292* 60. d, *300–301*

☐ FINAL I, *Chapters 10–18*

1. b, *311* 2. a, *313* 3. c, *323* 4. b, *317* 5. a, *320* 6. a, *327–328*
7. d, *340* 8. c, *347* 9. b, *354* 10. d, *361* 11. c, *341* 12. b, *355*
13. d, *359–360* 14. c, *375* 15. a, *386* 16. d, *392* 17. b, *378* 18. b, *389*
19. a, *393* 20. a, *408* 21. d, *410* 22. a, *414* 23. c, *424* 24. a, *411*
25. b, *416* 26. c, *425* 27. a, *442* 28. c, *450* 29. b, *461* 30. b, *440*
31. b, *451* 32. a, *463* 33. b, *475* 34. c, *479* 35. b, *485* 36. a, *494*
37. b, *478* 38. c, *487* 39. d, *504* 40. d, *509* 41. a, *520* 42. d, *528*
43. d, *514–515* 44. b, *526* 45. c, *532–533* 46. c, *548* 47. d, *554* 48. c, *561*
49. c, *568* 50. a, *552* 51. d, *558* 52. d, *570* 53. a, *580*
54. b, *584* 55. a, *593–594* 56. c, *605* 57. b, *589* 58. b, *595* 59. b, *602–603* 60. a, *605*

☐ FINAL II, *Chapters 10–18*

1. c, *310* 2. b, *317* 3. d, *316* 4. d, *326* 5. d, *315* 6. b, *326*
7. d, *333–334* 8. d, *343–345* 9. b, *352* 10. b, *356* 11. b, *365* 12. d, *350*
13. a, *341* 14. b, *364* 15. b, *377* 16. b, *387* 17. d, *391* 18. c, *399*
19. c, *384–385* 20. c, *390* 21. c, *392* 22. d, *409* 23. c, *414* 24. b, *418*
25. b, *420* 26. b, *415* 27. a, *422* 28. a, *429* 29. d, *424* 30. c, *446*
31. c, *449* 32. a, *456* 33. d, *439* 34. d, *443* 35. c, *458* 36. c, *476*
37. a, *480* 38. c, *488* 39. a, *497* 40. c, *476* 41. b, *481* 42. b, *493*
43. c, *514* 44. a, *523* 45. a, *530* 46. d, *539* 47. b, *510* 48. a, *519*
49. a, *531* 50. b, *557* 51. d, *564* 52. a, *573* 53. b, *546*
54. b, *554* 55. a, *567–568* 56. a, *581* 57. d, *588–589* 58. d, *600* 59. d, *593* 60. d, *598*

☐ COMPREHENSIVE FINAL I, *Chapters 1–18*

1. a, *8* 2. b, *16* 3. c, *6* 4. a, *44–45* 5. a, *56* 6. c, *50*
7. c, *78* 8. b, *95* 9. c, *81* 10. c, *84* 11. a, *106* 12. c, *122*
13. c, *124* 14. d, *154* 15. c, *158–159* 16. d, *153* 17. c, *182* 18. c, *197*
19. c, *182* 20. a, *203* 21. d, *211* 22. a, *215* 23. c, *225* 24. c, *246*
25. c, *260* 26. c, *266* 27. c, *285* 28. a, *295* 29. c, *278–279* 30. d, *287*
31. d, *311* 32. a, *321–323* 33. c, *324* 34. c, *345* 35. a, *358* 36. d, *356*
37. d, *374* 38. b, *390* 39. d, *392* 40. c, *411* 41. b, *416–417* 42. d, *447*
43. c, *451* 44. c, *458* 45. a, *478* 46. a, *490* 47. a, *474* 48. c, *501*
49. b, *511* 50. d, *525–526* 51. c, *534* 52. b, *553* 53. a, *562*
54. c, *574–575* 55. d, *592* 56. c, *606* 57. a, *581* 58. c, *591* 59. a, *596* 60. c, *609*

☐ COMPREHENSIVE FINAL II, *Chapters 1–18*

1. c, *9* 2. d, *28* 3. b, *29–30* 4. c, *14* 5. b, *27* 6. d, *49*
7. d, *40* 8. b, *58* 9. b, *49* 10. b, *57* 11. b, *73* 12. d, *77–78*
13. c, *85–86* 14. a, *74* 15. a, *98–99* 16. d, *113* 17. c, *125* 18. a, *133*
19. b, *107* 20. d, *115–116* 21. a, *150* 22. d, *167* 23. b, *171* 24. a, *157–158*
25. b, *160–161* 26. c, *178–179* 27. d, *186* 28. d, *204–205* 29. a, *180* 30. b, *198*
31. c, *212* 32. b, *218* 33. c, *230* 34. a, *212* 35. b, *221* 36. a, *240*
37. b, *256* 38. a, *262* 39. a, *245* 40. d, *254–255* 41. b, *283* 42. b, *287–288*
43. a, *299* 44. c, *279* 45. d, *300* 46. d, *311–312* 47. a, *327* 48. b, *334*
49. c, *313* 50. c, *330* 51. b, *351* 52. d, *354* 53. c, *362*
54. b, *348* 55. a, *360* 56. b, *385* 57. b, *397* 58. a, *396* 59. a, *376*
60. d, *385* 61. b, *409* 62. a, *412* 63. d, *430* 64. c, *409* 65. d, *428*
66. b, *446* 67. a, *449* 68. c, *466* 69. a, *450* 70. a, *465* 71. d, *477*
72. b, *482–483* 73. b, *500* 74. d, *480* 75. a, *489* 76. d, *518* 77. d, *534*
78. c, *535* 79. c, *511* 80. d, *527* 81. c, *545* 82. d, *561* 83. d, *567*
84. a, *550* 85. d, *556* 86. b, *586* 87. a, *602* 88. d, *608* 89. c, *594* 90. c, *607*